Also by Margaret Storrie

Arran 1980–81: 2,021?

*Continuity and Change: The Islay, Jura and Colonsay Agricultural Association
1981–1988*

Canada: a geographical perspective

Islay

BIOGRAPHY OF AN ISLAND

Margaret Storrie

The Press

First Edition 1981
Second Edition 1997

ISBN 0-907651-03-8

Printed by Henry Ling Ltd

Cover design by Buffey and Buffey

The Oa Press
Isle of Islay
PA42 7AL

Islay

BIOGRAPHY OF AN ISLAND

Cover: Islay's renowned cattle on the saltings, across Loch Indaal to Bowmore (Lorne Gill, Scottish Natural Heritage) vi

List of illustrations and tables

Illustrations

Short titles for frequent citations

Anderson, *Account:* J. Anderson, *An Account of the Present State of the Hebrides and Western Coasts of Scotland . . . being the Substance of a Report to the Lords of the Treasury together with the evidence before the Committee of Fisheries,* (Edinburgh, 1785).

Brown, *Report to the Creditors:* J. Brown, Report to the Creditors and General View of the Funds Realised, Campbell of Jura Papers SRO, GD64.

Devine, *Clanship:* T. M. Devine, *Clanship to Crofters' War,* (Manchester, 1994).

Innes, *Thanes of Cawdor:* C. Innes, *The Book of the Thanes of Cawdor, A Series of Papers selected from the Charter Room at Cawdor, 1236–1742,* (Edinburgh, 1859).

Lamont, *Early History:* W. D. Lamont, *The Early History of Islay,* (Glasgow, 1966).

Lamont, *Sculptured Stones:* W. D. Lamont, *Ancient and Mediaeval Sculptured Stones of Islay,* (Edinburgh, 1972).

Lumsden, *Steam-Boat Companion:* J. Lumsden and Son, *The Steam-Boat Companion and Stranger's Guide to the Western Islands and Highlands of Scotland,* (Glasgow, 1825).

MacDonald, *General View:* J. Macdonald, *General View of the Agriculture of the Hebrides or Western Isles of Scotland: with Observations on the Means of their Improvement together with a Separate Account of the Principal Islands,* (Edinburgh, 1811).

Munro and Munro, *Acts of the Lords:* J. Munro and R. W. Munro, *Acts of the Lords of the Isles 1336–1493,* (Edinburgh, 1986).

NSA, The Statistical Account of Scotland by the Ministers of the Respective Parishes, (Edinburgh, 1843–6) 33 vols., (1845), *Argyleshire.* Kilchoman, Rev. A. Cameron, (1844), pp. 644–59; Kildalton, Rev. A. MacTavish, (184 4), pp. 659–67; Killarow and Kilmeny, Rev. A. Stewart, (184 3), pp. 668–71.

Pennant, *Tour:* T. Pennant, *A Tour in Scotland and Voyage to the Hebrides, 1772,* (Chester, 1774).

Ramsay, *Stent Book:* L. Ramsay (ed.), *The Stent Book and Acts of the Balliary of Islay 1718–1843,* (Kildalton, 1890).

RCAHMS, *Argyll Inventory:* Royal Commission on the Ancient and Historical Monuments of Scotland, *Argyll: An Inventory of the Monuments, V. Islay, Jura, Colonsay and Oronsay,* (Edinburgh, 1984).

Shore, *Sketches:* C. J. Shore, Baron Teignmouth, *Sketches of the Coasts and Islands of Scotland, and the Isle of Man,* (London, 1836), 2 vols.

Sinclair, *OSA:* Sir J. Sinclair (ed.), *The Statistical Account of Scotland drawn up from the communications of the ministers of the different Parishes,* (Edinburgh, 1794), XI. Kilchoman, Rev. J. McLeish, pp. 276–85; Kildalton, Rev. A. Robertson, pp. 286–97; Killarow and Kilmeny, Rev. J. Murdoch, pp. 298–302.

Smith, *Book of Islay:* G. G. Smith (ed)., *The Book of Islay,* (Edinburgh, 1895).

Abbreviations

Periodicals and official publications

AHR	Agricultural History Review
Adv Sci	Advancement of Science
BSBI	Botanical Society of the British Isles
BPP	British Parliamentary Papers
CC	Coleraine Chronicle
CP	Cawdor Ppaers, Cawdor Castle, Nairn
EA	Edinburgh Advertiser
EUL	Edinburgh University Library
IEP	Islay Estate Papers, Estate Office, Bridgend, Islay
GH	Glasgow Herald
GR	Geographical Review
GUL	Glasgow University Library
KP	Ramsay of Kildalton Papers, on loan to City of Glasgow Archives
NLS	National Library of Scotland
OT	Oban Times
PRSE	Proceedings of the Royal Society of Edinburgh
PSAS	Proceedings of the Society of Antiquaries of Scotland
RCAHMS	Royal Commission on the Ancient and Historical Monuments of Scotland
SAF	Scottish Archaeological Forum
SAS	Scottish Abstract of Statistics
SCHS	Scottish Church History Society
SF	Scottish Field
SHR	Scottish Historical Review
SM	Scotland's Magazine
SRO	Scottish Record Office, Edinburgh
SS	Scottish Studies
Sc J Geol	Scottish Journal of Geology
TGAS	Transactions of the Glasgow Archaeological Society
TGI	Transactions of the Gaelic Society of Inverness
TIBG	Transactions of the Institute of British Geographers
THAS	Transactions of the Highland and Agricultural Society
TRHAS	Transactions of the Royal Highland and Agricultural Society

To the islanders

Preface to first edition

Organist and composer Healey Willan (1880–1960) is reputed to have claimed that he was English by birth, Canadian by adoption and Scotch by absorption. Recently a sale of work in Islay was declared open by a gracious lady introduced as 'not coming from Islay, but she has lived here for over fifty years'. 1981 is the silver jubilee of my first visit to Islay, arriving on a wet Saturday on the *Lochiel*, with pushbike. As a geography undergraduate in the University of Glasgow, I had literally stuck a pin in the map of Scotland to choose a dissertation area; there was no thought of a lifetime's study ahead. Since then, Islay has not only contributed to my doctorate, but has also been the venue for family holidays and undergraduate field classes, as well as a home from which the lights of Kintyre and Antrim can be seen.

Throughout this quarter-century, many colleagues and friends on the island and elsewhere have enriched my enjoyment and knowledge of the island's life, past and present. To the Margadale family and their factors, David B. Boyd and the late John H. Cranston, their wives and secretaries, I owe enormous gratitude for unstinted hospitality and access to estate papers and personnel. Catherine Crawford and the late Tom M. Crawford always extended open house and encouragement. Gordon Booth's drive in helping to establish the thriving Museum of Islay Life and his enthusiasm for sharing knowledge have been a much-prized bonus in recent years. The Keeper of the Museum, Mairi McArthur and her assistant, Katie Ferguson, have gone far beyond their duties in helping with queries and illustrations. Bobby Hodkinson's turn of phrase and views of events have been exhilarating. There is, however, insufficient space here to name all other islanders who have contributed in so many ways over the years, not forgetting the delicious baking of Margaret McLellan of Kilchiaran and the late Miss McGibbon of Cattadale, amongst others.

University and government researchers, archivists and librarians in Britain and beyond are also too numerous to name individually, but their invaluable contributions are gratefully acknowledged. So too are those of my secretarial and technical colleagues in the Geography Department of Queen Mary College in the University of London. The sketches, from photographs, were drawn by one of my former students, David Phillips. I have been particularly fortunate in being allowed to reproduce some of Eric Thorburn's recent photographs of Islay. Others are individually acknowledged, and where no source is given, the illustration is from the author's collection. Tom McCulloch of Gordon Watt Lithographics Ltd.

was adept at juggling with text and illustrations. All members of my immediate family have been closely and laboriously involved, particularly in the final stages of publishing this book, and I am greatly in their debt. Without the interest of Bruno Schroder of Dunlossit this would not have been a jubilee book.

The internal knowledge of the island's past and present is today much more extensive than even a decade ago, and I shall be glad to hear from Ilich and others on the views and facts experienced in this book. After Froude, I may perhaps plead that 'facts by selection and arrangement can be made to spell anything; and nothing can be arranged so easily as facts'.

Griobhagach, Islay, 1981   Margaret Storrie

Preface to second edition

The gratifying response to the earlier edition of this book enables me to acknowledge even more gratefully all those who have helped to extend my island life and enjoyment. In the intervening decade since the book went out of print, many people have requested a reprint. The tenor of much that was written in the first edition remains little changed; even in the last chapter on the prospect for Islay, the tone remains the same. Nevertheless, changes there have been, and this second edition contains several new chapters, with others substantially revised to take into account the findings of intervening research and other events.

Perhaps the biggest change, however, has been the islanders' own awareness and increasing knowledge of their island. Although 'the mainland's been cut off' is a phrase still heard during storms, there now appears to be a greater understanding and realisation of Islay's role in the United Kingdom, Europe and beyond. The research of individuals and groups has added considerably to the knowledge of the island's society, economy and environment. Debate on the island's future is thus becoming more focused and more vigilant, boding well for the island community.

Having chronicled the 150 years of the Islay, Jura and Colonsay Agricultural Association in 1988, I subsequently embarked on compiling a very large relational database of islanders in the eighteenth and nineteenth centuries. It includes their exiled ancestors on the mainland and overseas. I have visited pioneer cemeteries and graveyards in Islay, Ontario and Islay, Alberta, and elsewhere, matching computer print-outs with the many Islay names carved on the granite headstones. Such complex links will form the basis for future writings.

The topographical focus in this book is on the people and processes that have made their imprint on the visible landscape of the island at different periods, eventually resulting in Islay becoming a Hebridean exception.[1] What we see today is a palimpsest; there is more evidence in the landscape for some periods than for others. The imprints are particularly accessible to the alert eye in low angles of the sun or when there is a light covering of snow. Lines of former cultivation ridges, lazybeds, turf dykes and ruined buildings of all kinds can be clearly seen before they are smothered later in the season by the ubiquitous bracken, itself a speedy coloniser of abandoned tilled soils.

For this edition I once again gratefully acknowledge the hospitable access and help encountered in the many archives, particularly those of Islay Estate, Argyll and Bute Council, the City of Glasgow and national repositories in Edinburgh. Again, I am greatly in debt to those who gave permission to reproduce illustrations. As ever, it has been a pleasure to collaborate with the enthusiastic and vigilant reader, Fred Dodd. Invaluable are the continued encouragement and critical interest of Clare Jackson. The varied skills of Edward Oliver, the staff of Henry Ling Ltd. and Richard and Susan Buffey all contributed to the final production of this book. Lastly, the island and islanders still absorb me, in all seasons and moods, and both continue to provide me with a challenging and invigorating research base.

Griobhagach, Islay, May, 1997.   Margaret Storrie

[1] M. C. Storrie, 'Islay: A Hebridean Exception', *GR*, 1961, 51, pp. 87–108.

'Leaving West Loch-Tarbert, a most extensive prospect of the Atlantic Ocean opens up to view, in which is seen a multitude of islands . . . and the extensive peninsula of Cantyre, stretching many a rugged point far into the sea . . . and behind the lofty Goatfell in Arran . . . through Islay the roads are excellent, and the natives are proverbial for their hospitality' (Lumsden, *Steam-Boat Companion*).

CHAPTER 1

Perspective

Almost the first requirement of a prospective visitor to Islay is some help in pronouncing its name. Probably the most definite thing that can be said is that it is not pronounced the way it is spelled, except perhaps by airline or travel agents in London. Gaelic speakers on Islay usually call it *eel-uh*, and other Scots say *eye-la* as in island, with a pause between syllables and an upward lilt at the end. Others, including BBC Shipping forecasters, may say *eye-lay*, but it should never be pronounced as in 'mislay'. For those who are inclined to trust the written rather than the spoken word, the latter appears to have remained fairly consistent over the centuries, whereas it is the present spelling that is the source of confusion. Since Adomnàn recorded it as Ilea at the end of the seventh century AD the written name has had various forms, but to begin with these were usually phonetically faithful to the Gaelic Ìle.[1] The anglicised spelling appeared by the seventeenth century and still seems almost perversely different; in addition, the meanings offered for the name are almost as diverse as the spellings.[2]

Anomalous and varied Hebridean isle
The person sailing or flying to Islay finds an island less Highland in its physical grandeur than neighbouring Jura, or than Mull. At the same time it is not typically Hebridean either, in the sense of the crofting and grazing islands of Skye or the Outer Hebrides. It is one presenting rapid contrasts and constantly changing scenes, both on large and small scales. An Atlantic-washed wildscape in the west; the farmscapes along the tidy coasts and in the central valleys; plantations of hardwoods and conifers; the rugged eastern hills and the cliffs of the Oa promontory; monotonous peat bogs over much of the lowland; the indented south-east coast; the planned villages and the industrial distillery villages; a large Georgian mansion and traditional cottages, all amid a kaleidoscope of magnificent beaches, moors and lochs. From the extensive sand dunes on several of the coasts, across the peat moors to the settled areas of the foothills and valleys, there are many details to catch the inquisitive eye. The splendid

On one of the earliest printed maps of Scotland in 1573, Ortelius described Islay as 'the greatest of all . . . and the most renowned' of the Hebrides, 'fertile in grain and rich in minerals'. Neighbouring Jura is mis-identified as Iona.

Raised beach deposits between Lochs Indaal and Gruinart link the two parts of Islay together. Former shorelines stand out near Blackrock (foreground) and Uisgeantsuidhe.

tradition of whitewashing enhances the attractiveness of the villages and the scattered rural buildings. Based originally on locally-quarried Dalradian limestone, it is now largely maintained by imported paint. The rapid weathering of the local product required a fresh coat of whitewash to be an annual part of Islay's life in late spring and early summer; then the whole appearance of the island was at its best. Nowadays, less regular treatment adds further diversity to the scene.

As the southernmost of the Inner Hebrides, south even of the latitude of Glasgow, it is not surprising that Islay shows characteristics of both Highland and Lowland Scotland. The geographical situation of the island has affected the development of its economy, society and landscape from archaeological to present times. Relative accessibility to, as well as isolation from, political and cultural centres elsewhere in Highland, Hebridean or Lowland Scotland and beyond, has affected the ways in which people have influenced and left their imprint on Islay. For example, during the late-medieval Lordship of the Isles, Islay was a focus of political power and cultural influence along and beyond the western seaboard of Highland Scotland; in the eighteenth century, innovations in agriculture, industry and village planning, adapted from the Lowlands, were amongst the earliest attempted in the Highlands and Hebrides. Until then, most of the population lived in amorphous clusters of buildings similar to those to be found at the time over much of the Highlands and Lowlands of Scotland. These clusters of turf or stone buildings housed up to a score of families and their beasts. The remains of many of the stone buildings are still to be seen in the remoter parts of the island where it has not been considered worthwhile to clear away their traces.

The present features of the island and its life have mainly developed since the early-eighteenth century, when Daniel Campbell of Shawfield, by Glasgow, became the owner of the greater part of the island. Islay's distinctiveness was recognised much earlier; the island had for long been known to the Hebrideans as 'Bann-righ', 'Queen of the Isles', as a 'green island', and so on. As early as 1573 Abraham Ortelius had eulogised on the reverse of his map of Scotland, 'Maxima omnium & nominatissima Ila est, frumenti ferax, & metalli dives', ['Of all (the Hebrides) the greatest and most renowned is Ila, fertile for grain, and rich in minerals'].[3] But at the beginning of the eighteenth century, the island's resources were still relatively undeveloped. Scotland herself was on the threshold of change, after parliamentary union with England in 1707. In Islay, as over the rest of Scotland, however, the eighteenth century had some way to go before economic, social and landscape changes were achieved. They were part of the more general Scottish period of renaissance and enlightenment that

eventually flowered half a century after the Union. The creation of the
village of Bowmore in Islay in 1768 and of Edinburgh New Town, were
simultaneous events, albeit different in scale.

One of the most notable and characteristic features of the Islay landscape
consists of the villages around the shores of Loch Indaal and the south-
east of the island. The number, size and importance of the Islay villages
are features inherited from the changes of the late-eighteenth century and
after. Here Islay differs from most other areas in the Highlands and
Islands of Scotland, which possess few villages. Bowmore was one of
several early villages, deliberately planned to absorb population in Highland
and Lowland Scotland, like the weavers' village of Eaglesham in
Renfrewshire, founded by the tenth earl of Eglinton, also in 1768. Other
villages in Islay such as Port Wemyss were established later, in the 1830s,
as fishermen's settlements. However, in a closer view of many of the
island's villages, the distinctive features included a tall chimney and pagoda-
like malt-drying kilns typical of a whisky distillery. Some of these distilleries
were founded before the nineteenth century, while others date from then.
It is the presence of all these different villages in Islay that provides the
most obvious contrast between the island and all other Highland and
Hebridean areas.

Evidence of change
Since Islay's distinctiveness rests to a large extent in its somewhat unusual
historical evolution, it is fortunate that a wide variety of evidence about
this evolution has survived. For example, Islay is rich in sites and examples
of archaeological interest, with relics of Mesolithic, Neolithic, Bronze and
Iron Ages; and of Early Christian, Norse and medieval times. Apart from
such visible evidence on the island's surface, whether archaeological,
historical or modern, there are other sources that illuminate the interaction
between the island and its peoples.

Published sources of information for a Hebridean island are inevitably
incomplete; but Islay is generally well-documented. Early topographers
and agriculturalists left worthwhile accounts of changing times on Islay
from the eighteenth century: they include Thomas Pennant, James
Anderson, John Walker and James Macdonald.[4] Proto-social scientists
such as Alexander Webster, Sir John Sinclair and their successors also
provided invaluable accounts for our use today.[5] The most detailed
published material relating to Islay's earlier story appeared after the middle
of the nineteenth century. In the *Book of The Thanes of Cawdor*, published
by the Spalding Club of Aberdeen in 1859, Cosmo Innes, a noted
antiquarian, included many documents relating to the Cawdor Campbells

and seventeenth-century Islay; this remains the most readily accessible source for this period.[6]

In the 1890s three important volumes appeared. Two were sponsored by Mrs Lucy Ramsay, wife of one of the then island landowners. Each tome was printed privately in editions limited to 250 copies. In her preface to The *Stent Book*, Mrs Ramsay explained that the passing of the Local Government (Scotland) Act of 1889 had prompted her to publish the minutes taken at meetings of what was known as 'The Local Parliament' in Islay, from 1718 until 1843 when the 'annual meeting came to an abrupt termination'.[7] *The Stent Book* contains much information on the type of business now dealt with by local government, including responsibilities for roads, education, housing and public utilities. Rather different to it is the *The Book of Islay*, which Gregory Smith subsequently edited for Mrs Ramsay.[8] This is a collection of items from different sources that refer to the island mainly since Norse times; it concludes with a considerable amount of material on the early decades of the eighteenth century, selected from archives in Cawdor, Islay, Edinburgh and elsewhere. Also in 1895 the antiquarian R. C. Graham, then laird of Skipness in Kintyre, compiled The *Carved Stones of Islay*.[9] Twentieth-century landmarks were the publication in 1984 of the *Argyll Inventory* of the monuments of Islay, Jura, Colonsay and Oronsay produced by the Royal Commission on the Ancient and Historic Monuments of Scotland and *The Acts of the Lords of the Isles* collated and edited by J. and R. W. Munro in 1986.[10]

Much of the material incorporated in the present book comes from the original sources themselves, in the archives of the earl of Cawdor, lord Margadale of Islay Estate and of the Ramsay family, formerly of the Kildalton Estate.[11] In addition, documents in many Scottish, British and overseas archives, governmental and other agencies have been scrutinised. Many islanders have also contributed to the author's knowledge of, and happy experiences in, the island. While much of the island's heritage and present life still remains unstudied and unpublished, an important focus and repository for the island's social heritage was established in 1977 with the opening in Port Charlotte of the award-winning Museum of Islay Life.[12] The Finlaggan Trust and the National Museums of Scotland have also unearthed and displayed artefacts, commemorative stones and interpretative material from the islands in Loch Finlaggan which were at the centre of the medieval Lordship of the Isles. The Islay Natural History Trust displays its collections and runs a fieldwork centre in a converted whisky warehouse in Port Charlotte, while the Royal Society for the Protection of Birds has developed ornithological fieldwork, research and displays in and around their visitor centre at Loch Gruinart. In the 1990s, Scottish Natural Heritage extended its research and activities in the island. An active Islay Land Use Forum was set up to promote the development of an integrated approach to the use of land in Islay in order to sustain the outstanding quality of the island's natural resources. Other organisations have periodically organised conferences covering themes from the more academic to those of topical interest.

Island names

The variety of place-names in the island is only one result of the interaction of differing cultures that the inquiring visitor can absorb. Many of the traces of the different peoples who have lived in Islay are not so clearly seen in the landscape as are, for instance, the Neolithic chambered cairns, the later hill forts or the many deserted villages. But there are fascinating areas of study still to be further explored, in place-names, language, folklore and in the contribution of Islaymen beyond the island. One of the earlier writers on Islay's place-names was Captain Thomas in the 1880s.[13] It is a little difficult for us to appreciate that perhaps the most recent map available to him then was well over a hundred years old. Probably unaware of the existence of the estate maps of the early-nineteenth century, Thomas's research started with a list of farms compiled from the current valuation roll. He concluded that Gaelic farm names were nearly twice as common as Norse ones in Islay and he also claimed that the Scandinavian element, compared to the Gaelic element in Islay names, was only one-eighth as strong as, for example, in Lewis in the Outer Hebrides. His explanation was in terms of Islay's distance from Scandinavia on the one hand and greater proximity to and contact with Gaelic Ireland on the other, perhaps ignoring differences in environment. Since then, other writers on place-names have made brief reference to the island in their wider scope.[14] So far only a small proportion of all the scales of Islay names has been seriously studied.

The evolution of Islay's place-names is of course not unique nor even unusual. Scotland as a whole has had a chequered linguistic history; many names have passed from one language to another and perhaps even into a third. At first sight, the modern Ordnance Survey 1:50,000 map of Islay reflects the situation in the island about a century and a half ago, when Gaelic was the predominant language. The place-names on the map today have early Gaelic, Norse, later Gaelic and English origins. Gaelic names do still predominate, although often, as with Norse names, in an anglicised form. Many of the Gaelic names relating to fields, coastal features and other smaller topographical features on the larger-scale Ordnance Survey maps and plans of the late-nineteenth century and in the original Name Books of the Ordnance Survey, are now no longer in use, nor even remembered.[15] More recent names of houses and roads reflect the increasing use of English, but Gaelic street names were put up during the 1960s in Port Charlotte, followed by others elsewhere in the 1990s, some even translated from their English originals – Port Charlotte is Port Sgioba, Port Wemyss is Port Bun Othan and in Port Ellen the street sign, Sràid Theàrlaig, has been erected beside the stone tablet on which the original name of Charlotte Street is incised.

It is possible to link a tentative chronology of settlement with the changing place-names of the island. Predominantly Gaelic names describe topographical features such as hills (e.g. Beinn Tart a'Mhill, Sliabh Mòr, Coire Sgiathach, Mullach Dubh), or rivers (Uisge an t-Suidh). Names such as those with the prefix cill-, anglicised to kil-, commemorating the Irish Celtic saints and missionaries who came to Islay, are found in parish, church and settlement names including Kilchoman, Kilchiaran, Kiells and Kilcolumkill. Other Gaelic settlement names include Tighandrom and Ballygrant. In some instances Gaelic topographic names have been transferred to adjacent settlements, as at Coul or Machrie. The Norse contribution to place names in the island is especially obvious in the names of some of the most important hydrographic features such as Lochs Indaal and Gruinart, Leodamus Bay and the Sorn River, as well as of several of the larger islands around Islay's coasts. During the Scandinavian period, both Gaelic and Norse speakers and dialects presumably existed side by side, as suggested in the name Ballinaby, just as Gaelic and English have done more recently. Norse place-names include Persabus, Scarabus, Margadale and Smaull. Hybrid names, like Octomore Hill, were a later feature. For many of the smaller topographic features, such as streams or burns, small islands and hillocks, and for expanded settlements and shielings, Gaelic names are more common than Norse ones. By the sixteenth century, some anglicisation was taking place. With the progress of the agrarian revolution this process became more common and English place names were given to the new planned villages and their streets in the early-nineteenth century (Port Ellen, Frederick Crescent). Former Gaelic names were transcribed so that Bunnahabhain became Bonahaven.

From the romantic, if rather ghoulish, study of kirkyard headstones through the manuscripts to the more prosaic electoral registers of the present day, similar influences have changed the composition and sources of islanders' surnames; as also of forenames, although the latter are more susceptible to changes in fashion. From about the twelfth century, surnames developed from Clan Donald and its branches. By the time of the

seventeenth-century Campbells of Cawdor and after Daniel Campbell of
Shawfield became laird of Islay in 1726, the surname of many of the
larger tenants or tacksmen was Campbell, while many of the islanders
were still Macdonalds or from related clans. At the end of the eighteenth
century there was already more variety and the first complete list of every
person in the island to which we have access, the copies of the census
schedules for 1841, carried this process further.[16] By then there were
more extraneous names, although they still formed only a small proportion
of the total. Since that time, however, the wholly Hebridean and Highland
names have been further eroded and present electoral registers show
much less dominance of one name or group than ever before. In earlier
days the use of nicknames to distinguish different people with the same
forename and surname was common. The habit still persists today, but
the use of more varied forenames from different sources and societies
provides less justification.

Islay Gaelic and lore

As in place-names, similar difficulties exist when trying to analyse the
changing spoken language of Islay folk. The language today includes
elements from the Irish Gaelic-speaking colonisation of the island, possibly
superimposed on Pictish-speaking tongues, through the period of
Scandinavian influences, to the later Scots Gaelic and English-speaking
times. Just as the decline of Gaelic usage and the concomitant rise of
English can be seen from the island's place and personal names, a similar
change can be traced in the spoken language, in the published volumes of
the Census of Scotland. The first census in which questions on Gaelic
usage were asked was that of 1891, when over 70 per cent were recorded
as speaking Gaelic and English, while sixteen per cent only spoke Gaelic.[17]
By 1961, almost two-thirds of the islanders were still recorded as speaking
Gaelic, a high proportion for an island which was the most southerly of
the Hebrides and which had some of the earliest connections with the
mainland.[18] But by 1991 the percentage had fallen to about one-third,
with only eleven per cent able to speak, read and write Gaelic.[19] While
Gaelic is spoken by some of the older adults at home, in shops and in
occasional church services, less is heard in the school playgrounds, except
in Bowmore, where there has been a Gaelic immersion unit in the primary
school since 1989.

   As in much of Gaeldom today, the balance between vitality and decline
in Islay's culture is precarious. But there are many encouraging signs.
Strenuous efforts are being made to encourage many and varied Gaelic
activities. There is an annual festival or feis and An Commun Gaidhealach

and other organisations in the Islay, Jura and Colonsay Gaelic Partnership are involved in running events and workshops throughout the year. Individuals and choirs have for long had major successes at local, provincial and national Gaelic Mods. In 1995 the Port Ellen children's Gaelic choir successfully competed in the Canadian Mod held in Vancouver. The annual Islay gathering of the Glasgow Islay Association begun in 1862 is one of the largest meetings of Highland exiles on the Scottish mainland. Highland dancing and piping have revived, with dancers and the Islay Pipe Band competing at the Cowal Gathering and elsewhere. In summertime there are almost nightly ceilidhs in village halls, hotels and homes with traditional and more modern music performed by islanders and visitors. Satellite television has reached Islay, but there is still little sign that it will eradicate local oral individuality and traditions.

A century ago some of the differences between Islay and other Gaelic were noted: 'peasants come from Connaught to Islay, and in a very short time converse freely, though their accent betrays them; an Islay man is detected in Mull, and a native of one parish in Islay is detected when he speaks in another'.[20] Today Islay Gaelic is still regarded as idiosyncratic by speakers of surrounding dialects. Moving from Jura to Islay, a first impression is that Islay Gaelic is more staccato than Jura Gaelic, but it is also rather slower in sound and delivery. The most striking illustration of this difference in dialect is the insertion of the glottal stop before certain consonants in the middle of words, or a hiatus instead of an aspirated consonant. Particularly in the Rinns, words beginning with a broad l in Gaelic, sound as if they were a *d* in some of the older words, though not in recent borrowings from English. So *doch* is said for loch, but lamp remains *lamp*. Archaic forms of words and vocal peculiarities also exist. Older people in particular pronounce common words like uisge (water) differently, with greater emphasis on the 'sh' sound.

Some words common in Islay usage are rare or unique. A renowned Ileach, Neil McAlpine, compiled one of the few Scots Gaelic dictionaries, in which he included many of these Islay words in it such as caile (girl), gealbhan (domestic hearth), gearraidh (hare), fail-moine (peat spade) and sgeir-moine (peat bank), measured by the peirsa (perch).[21] As well as these differences in words, there are also some idiosyncratic grammatical habits, as well as Islay sayings and proverbs, with some hints of connections with Irish Gaelic. With the decline in the use of the Gaelic language, there has also been a decline in the standard and size of vocabulary and grammar. Noun and adjective declensions are obsolescent today, for example; nevertheless there are stronger traditional or idiosyncratic forms of spoken Gaelic than one might expect in an area with many external contacts over

John Francis Campbell of Islay was a man of many parts; here in a public house in Paisley, as folklorist, he listens to an Ileach shoemaker, Lachlan MacNeill. Campbell's former tutor, Hector MacLean of Ballygrant, writes down part of the week-long tale of 'Kane's leg', which filled 260 pages of foolscap, despite Campbell's remark that both of his companions were 'rather screwed, Hector the worse' (Trustees of the National Library of Scotland).

JOHN FRANCIS CAMPBELL,
OF ISLAY
AN EMINENT CELTIC SCHOLAR LINGUIST SCIENTIST & TRAVELLER
A TRUE AND PATRIOTIC HIGHLANDER,
LOVED ALIKE BY PEER AND PEASANT.
BY HIS
"POPULAR TALES OF THE WEST HIGHLANDS",
"LEABHAR NA FEINNE"
AND OTHER LITERARY WORKS,
HE PRESERVED AND RENDERED CLASSIC THE
FOLK-LORE OF THE SCOTTISH HIGHLANDS

HE LIES BURIED AT CANNES IN FRANCE;
HIS MEMORY LIVES IN THE HEARTS OF HIS COUNTRYMEN

BORN 1821. —— DIED 1885.

The inscription on the obelisk at Bridgend, erected by the Glasgow Islay Association, commemorates one of the most famous of Ilich.

the past two centuries. Tales and anecdotes are still to be heard on the island today but, as informants pass away, less remain.

Just outside Bridgend, on a prominent hillock, stands an obelisk erected in 1887 by the Glasgow Islay Association with a fulsome inscription in Gaelic and English to John Francis Campbell or Iain og Ìle. One of the island's most renowned figures, he has been described as the 'world-famous father of Celtic Folklore Studies'.[22] Born in 1822 as heir to the Islay estate, a world-wide traveller, barrister, secretary to various government commissions, a courtier to Queen Victoria, fluent speaker of several languages including Norwegian, Danish, Lapp and Swedish, with some knowledge of others, and an inventor, he nevertheless found time for the folklore of Scottish west and it is for this work that he is perhaps most remembered. His still-unpublished manuscripts, diaries and travel sketches are in the National Library of Scotland in Edinburgh.

In the Easter period and summer of 1857 John Francis Campbell did some fieldwork when he visited Islay, his family by then no longer owning Islay House. He used the Gaelic he had acquired in his youth from his island tutor, Hector MacLean. Collection continued for several years and his network of story-tellers and collectors grew. In his introduction to the first volume of these tales, published in 1860, he outlined his working method in considerable detail, including his return to the sources of the stories, with proofs in hand, to check the accuracy of transcriptions and translations.[23] With the help of his various research assistants, two further volumes of tales and a final volume of various Celtic matters including the Ossian controversy, were subsequently published in English, with some Gaelic examples. A second edition was run in 1890, five years after John Francis's death in Cannes. A century later the Scottish composer, Judith Weir, used three of the tales in her opera *The Vanishing Bridegroom*; each story remains distinct in the libretto, but some characters are shared in the general theme of loss and deliverance.[24]

Notes and references

1   These include, in alphabetical order, Ela, Eylla, Eyllay, Eyley, Hyle, Il, Ila, Ilaa, Ilae, Illagh, Ilay, Ile, Ilea, Iley, Ili, Ilia, Illa, Illay, Illaye, Isla, Iyla, Yla, Ylay, Yle, Yley, Ylla, Yllaye, Ylse and Ysle. For discussion of spelling evolution see K. H. Steer and J. W. M. Bannerman, *Late Medieval Monumental Sculpture in the West Highlands*, (Edinburgh, 1977), pp. 126–7.

2   For meaning of name, see A. B. Taylor, 'Skio and Il', Pridiji Vikingafundur, Third Viking Congress, Reykjavik 1956, *Arbók hins islenzka Fornleifafélags Fylgirit*, 1957, pp. 52–60.

3   A. Ortelius, *Scotiae Tabula in Theatrum Orbis Terrarum*, (Antwerp, 1573).

4   T. Pennant, *A Tour in Scotland and Voyage to the Hebrides, 1772*, (Chester, 1774); J.

Anderson, *An Account of the Present State of the Hebrides and Western Coasts of Scotland . . . being the Substance of a Report to the Lords of the Treasury together with the evidence before the Committee of Fisheries*, (Edinburgh, 1785); J. Walker, *An Economical History of the Hebrides and Highlands of Scotland*, (Edinburgh, 1808), 2 vols., and J. Macdonald, *General View of the Agriculture of the Hebrides or Western Isles of Scotland: with Observations on the Means of their Improvement together with a Separate Account of the Principal Islands*, (Edinburgh, 1811).

[5]   J. G. Kyd, *Scottish Population Statistics*, (Edinburgh, 1952), p. 33; Sir John Sinclair (ed.), *The Statistical Account of Scotland, drawn up from the communications of the ministers of the different Parishes*, (Edinburgh, 1791-1799), 21 vols., (1794), XI, pp. 298-302.

[6]   C. Innes, *The Book of the Thanes of Cawdor, A Series of Papers selected from the Charter Room at Cawdor, 1236-1742*, (Edinburgh, 1859).

[7]   L. Ramsay (ed.), *The Stent Book and Acts of the Balliary of Islay 1718–1843,* (Kildalton, 1890).

[8]   G. G. Smith (ed.), *The Book of Islay*, (Edinburgh, 1895).

[9]   R. C. Graham, *The Carved Stones of Islay*, (Glasgow, 1895); see also A. Graham, *Skipness: Memories of a Highland Estate*, (Edinburgh, 1993).

[10] Royal Commission on the Ancient and Historical Monuments of Scotland (RCAHMS), *Argyll: An Inventory of the Monuments, V. Islay, Jura, Colonsay and Oronsay*, (Edinburgh, 1984); J. Munro and R. W. Munro, *Acts of the Lords of the Isles 1336–1493*, (Edinburgh, 1986).

[11] The Cawdor Papers (CP) in Cawdor Castle, Nairn, are listed in the National Register of Archives (NRA) (Scotland) Survey 1400.

   The Islay Estate Papers (IEP) in the Islay Estate Office, Bridgend, Isle of Islay, are listed in the NRA (Scotland) Survey 0123. Certain of the Papers are deposited on loan in the City of Glasgow Archives. Photocopies of Islay Estate Plans are held in West Register House, Scottish Record Office (SRO), Edinburgh.

   The Ramsay of Kildalton Papers (KP) are deposited on loan in the City of Glasgow Archives, listed under TD1284. See F. Ramsay (ed.), *John Ramsay of Kildalton, Being an Account of his life in Islay and including the Diary of his Trip to Canada in 1870,* (Toronto, 1970) and *The Day Book of Daniel Campbell of Shawfield 1767, with relevant papers concerning the Estate of Islay*, (Aberdeen, 1991).

[12] The Museum of Islay Life was given First Prize in the Museum of the Year Award for Scotland in 1980, by the Scottish Group of National Heritage, sponsored by Scottish and Newcastle Breweries. The Scottish Group of National Heritage presented a special award in the Museum of the Year Awards for 1985 to the Museum.

[13] F. W. L. Thomas, 'On Islay Place Names', *PSAS*, New Series IV, 1881–2, pp. 241–96.

[14] L. Alcock and E. Alcock, 'Scandinavian Settlement in the Inner Hebrides: Recent research on place-names and in the Field', *SAF*, 1980, 10, pp. 61–73; H. C. Gillies, *The Place Names of Argyll*, (London, 1906); A. Gray, *The History of Islay Place Names*, (Glasgow, 1940); A. MacBain, *Place Names, the Highlands and Islands of Scotland*, (Stirling, 1922); D. Maceacharna, *The Lands of the Lordship*, (Islay, 1976); W. F. H. Nicolaisen, *Scottish Place Names*, (London, 1976) and W. J. Watson, *The History of Celtic Place-names of Scotland*, (Edinburgh, 1926).

[15] The Name Books of the Ordnance Survey, Edinburgh.

[16] Copies of the Census of Scotland enumerators' schedules are in New Register House, Edinburgh.

[17]   *Census of Scotland, 1891,* Table I.

[18]   *Census 1961, Supplementary Leaflet 27: Gaelic,* 1966.

[19]   *Census 1991, Small Area Statistics.*

[20]   J. F. Campbell, *Popular Tales of the West Highlands,* (Edinburgh, 1860-2), 4 vols., I, cxxi.

[21]   N. MacAlpine, *The Argyleshire Pronouncing Gaelic Dictionary,* (Edinburgh, 1832) and *A Pronouncing Gaelic Dictionary,* (Edinburgh, 1847).

[22]   K. H. Jackson, *Campbell of Islay,* Celtica Catalogue 6, National Library of Scotland (NLS), (Edinburgh, 1967), p. 32; R. M. Dorson, *The British Folklorists; A History,* (London, 1968), chapter 11.

[23]   Campbell, *Popular Tales*; J. G. Mackay (ed.), *More West Highland Tales* I, (Edinburgh, 1940), II, (Edinburgh, 1960); J. Mackechnie, (ed.), *The Dewar Manuscripts,* (Glasgow, 1964), I; J. H. Delargy, 'Three Men of Islay', *SS,* 1960, 4, pp. 126–33; A. Duncan, 'Hector MacLean of Islay, 1818–1893', *An Gaidheal,* 1964, January, pp. 9–11; and National Library of Scotland, *Lamplighter and Story-teller, John Francis Campbell of Islay, 1821–1885,* (Edinburgh, 1985).

  J. F. Campbell in 1853 designed a 'self-registering sundial', which, modified, has become the Campbell-Stokes sunshine recorder still in use today. See W. E. K. Middleton, *Invention of the Meteorological Instruments,* (Baltimore, 1969), pp. 238–43.

[24]   S. Sadie, *The New Grove Dictionary of Opera,* (London, 1992), 4 vols., 4, p. 1131.

The shores along the Sound of Islay, as depicted by marine watercolourist Schetky in the mid-nineteenth century, apparently contradict Sir Walter Scott's allusion in *The Lord of the Isles* to 'green Islay's fertile shore'. Yet signs of former homes and cultivation even in these glens and along the shores can still be seen from the ferry. Such remote glens and caves were also useful for illegal distilling and smuggling.

CHAPTER 2

Island frame

The physical landscape on which the human history has taken place is rather atypical of the Hebridean islands and of the West Highlands. Apart from the east coast on the Sound of Islay the island's relief is not on so grand a scale as Harris, Skye, Mull, Jura or Arran. Islay is almost divided into two by the indentations of Lochs Indaal and Gruinart; although it is approximately 40 kilometres from Rubha a'Mhail in the north-east to the Mull of Oa in the south and about 25 kilometres from Coul Point in the west to McArthur's Head on the Sound of Islay, the total area is only just over 600 square kilometres.

Sailing to Islay on a fine day, one is impressed by neighbouring Jura's glistening Paps or Bens, which reach almost 800 metres. From many viewpoints on Islay these conical mountains notably enhance the scenery. On Islay similar quartzitic rocks do not have quite the same visual impact; instead of distinct peaks they form two dissected upland areas, one in the in the south-east, culminating in Beinn Bheigir (491m) and the other reaching 364m in Sgarbh Breac. The dissected upland in the south-east forms the largest area of high ground in Islay and includes several summits between 450 and 500m. On the east coast of the island a steep face is presented to the Sound of Islay, broken only by a few hanging glens such as Glen Logan. At McArthur's Head the lighthouse is perched somewhat precariously on cliffs that rise over a hundred metres above the Sound. Other quartzitic outcrops also form high ground along the north-western coast of the Oa promontory and between Bowmore and Beinn Bhàn. These rocks have been quarried for building, especially for decorative purposes, as in the lodges of the former Kildalton estate in the south-east. The north-eastern upland is lower and is bounded by magnificently-developed Quaternary cliffs, marine platforms and a 'classic' series of interglacial and postglacial raised beaches that impress the layman as much as they do the geomorphologist.[1] To the west of this upland, kilometres of sand dunes and raised beaches border Loch Gruinart, south of which an extensive area of bog developed.

Between these two quartzitic uplands, the central lowlands are underlain

N

Rhubha a'Mhail

Nave Island

Sgarbh Breac
364

Bunnahabhain

Caol Ila
Port
Askaig

Ballygrant

Loch Gruinart

Loch Gorm

KILCHOMAN

Machir
Bay

KILLAROW and KILMENY

Bruichladdich

Bridgend

Bowmore

Beinn Bheigeir
491

Port-Charlotte

Beinn Bhan 471

THE   Beinn Tart
         a'Mhill 232

RINNS

Ardtalla

Loch Indaal

Portnahaven

Laggan
Bay

Port Wemyss

KILDALTON

Kildalton

Ardbeg
Lagavulin
Laphroaig

THE OA

Port
Ellen

	Raised Beach
	Blown Sand
	Limestone
	Quartzite and Conglomerates
	Slates and Phyllites
	Grits and Slates

	Intrusive Epidiorites and Hornblende Schist
	Lewisian Gneiss

10 km

Islay's varied lithology and superficial deposits have produced a varied environment and scene for man's use and enjoyment. Most important have been the limestone, minerals, peat, and beach, river and other deposits (Based on Geological Survey of Scotland, *Quarter Inch Geology*, sheet 13 and *One Inch Solid and Drift* sheets 19 and 27).

by strongly-metamorphosed Precambrian slates and phyllites, with some calcareous quartzose schists, and igneous intrusions. These give rise to a more varied topography quite different in character to the relatively bare areas of the hills. The topography of the central belt, from the Mull of Oa in the south through to Bunnahabhain in the north-east, is generally of lower altitude, although relative relief is sometimes considerable. In the northern part of the Oa promontory, outcrops of black slates and grey phyllites form spectacular cliffs, especially along the southern edge of Laggan Bay and near the Mull of Oa. From Dùn Mòr Ghil to Port nan Gallon east of the Mull, the cliffs fall almost sheer to the sea. Near the monument which commemorates the loss of the SS *Tuscania* in 1917, they are 200 metres high.

Further north, in other Precambrian areas of the central belt, these rocks have been more eroded and underlie 'The Glen' (the upper drainage basin of the Laggan) and much of the Sorn basin. They include the Esknish slates, similar to the more renowned Easdale slates and formerly quarried in Islay at Emeraconart between Bridgend and Ballygrant. More remarkable is the extensive occurrence of fairly pure and little-metamorphosed Dalradian limestone. Islay has an unusual amount of limestone, whereas neighbouring Jura has scarcely any. Its outcrop in Islay is easily visible, as in the very green area around Tallant farm and in many parts of the Sorn valley. The limestone has been used as a building material, as decorative whitewash and as road metal, but its most important use until recently has been agricultural. The Islay limestone is almost pure calcium carbonate, which makes it useful for agricultural purposes. Five major quarries have been worked in the Islay limestone; these are visible today, as are some of the kilns, where the limestone was burned to form quicklime, then dissolved in water and applied to the ground. The older quarries can be seen at Lower Cragabus, Leorin, Persabus and Bridgend; the fifth, opened in the late 1940s at Ballygrant, is the only one still in use, producing road metal and ground limestone. Veins of minerals intruded into the limestone have also been worked at various times, the most important being lead, copper and silver; evidence of these former workings is still visible near Ballygrant at Mulreesh, Robolls and elsewhere. Subsequently, there has only been spasmodic interest in these minerals. The early 1990s saw the possibility of a superquarry being opened up to produce aggregate at Baleachdrach on the Sound of Islay, but the controversial project did not then go ahead.

South-east of the main Beinn Bheigir upland is another, narrower, zone of more highly-metamorphosed and contorted slates and phyllites extending from Port Ellen to Ardtalla, but there is no limestone outcrop.

Dalradian limestone was burned in peat-fired kilns, dissolved in water and then used to counteract soil acidity.

There are additional quartzitic and calcareous schists outcropping along the coast from Laphroaig to Kildalton and north from Claggain to Carraig Mhòr. Texa, one of the larger of Islay's many offshore islands, is also built of these rocks. In this south-eastern area of Kildalton the slates and phyllites have been much more extensively intruded by igneous sills of epidioritic material than in the central belt. In an area almost free of superficial deposits, differential erosion of the harder intrusive rocks and the relatively softer country rocks has created a sequence of minor ridges and valleys. Trending south-west to north-east, the ridges continue seawards in the form of many small islets and skerries. The scenery is further complicated here, as in the central belt, by the intrusion of many Tertiary doleritic dykes traversing all rocks in a north-west to south-east direction. The distinctive hill of Cnoc Rhaonastil and its extension jutting out into Ardelistry Bay, is the largest of these doleritic intrusions. The igneous and metamorphic rocks have all been used as building materials, mainly in the south-east of the island; easily identifiable are the dolerite from a quarry near Kildalton House used for houses and farm buildings, the chlorite schists of the ancient and medieval crosses and roofing slates from a large quarry near Port Ellen lighthouse, now disused.

The two main upland masses and the areas adjacent to them, show considerable evidence of the movement of ice sheets from east-south-east to west-north-west during the Quaternary period. Examples of striae notched deeply into the quartzite can been seen for instance on Glas Beinn (471m) to the north of Loch Allallaidh and in many other areas that require less energetic searching such as at Kilchiaran. In the glens much glacial drift has accumulated, on which some of the largest peat bogs in Islay have developed. These bogs also cover parts of the raised beaches and are bordered by the windblown sands along Laggan Bay in

Loch Indaal. Much of Islay's glacial drift is of reddish colour and it can be seen capping the cliffs at McArthur's Head or flanking the sides of Glen Ghaireasdail and Glen Logan along the Sound of Islay. The drift is also well developed in other glens of the south-eastern hills and along the valleys of the Laggan and its tributaries, where river action has exposed depths of over 13m of drift. The tiny valley glaciers which remained towards the end of the Ice Age have also left their own moraines in the glens, as can be noticed east of the road between Port Ellen and Bridgend: the farmhouse of Leorin stands on one of these. Sands and gravels in the form of kames and eskers can be seen near Torra Farm and some of the large rivers have fluvoglacial and deltaic deposits of considerable extent, such as the delta of the Laggan river.

Raised beaches around the head of Loch Indaal join the eastern part of Islay to the western portion comprising the Rinns of Islay. Except for numerous intrusive igneous dykes, the western peninsula is entirely made up of rocks of Precambrian age. The northern and larger portion of the region consists of Torridonian grits, slates and conglomerates, while the acid and basic gneisses of the Lewisian complex occupy the area of the Rinns south of Kilchiaran Bay and Bruichladdich. The rolling landscape of much of the northern Rinns is covered with glacial drift on which extensive peat bogs, marshes and the largest inland loch in Islay, Loch Gorm, have developed. Where the rocks are exposed there is some fine coastal and cliff scenery. The highly individual appearance of the Sanaig cliffs, developed on Torridonian grits, the numerous basalt dykes intruded into the slates and phyllites further east and the many caves, offer fascinating explorations, as does Nave Island. The eastern shores of the northern Rinns along Loch Gruinart and of the southern Rinns along Loch Indaal have well-developed raised beaches and windblown sands, providing yet further contrasts.

Almost all of the western coastline, from Ardnave Point south to Portnahaven, shows fairly spectacular cliff development, interrupted occasionally by stretches of sands and dunes, as in Machir Bay and Saligo Bay. Intrusive dykes and differential erosion along the coasts of the Rinns south of Port Charlotte have given rise to a highly-accidented topography. Orsay Island, on which the earliest Islay lighthouse was constructed, is separated from the rest of the Rinns by a narrow strait through which strong tidal currents flow. The highest point in the Rinns, Beinn Tart a'Mhill (232m) is in fact not composed of Precambrian rocks, but owes its characteristic bulky shape to intrusive epidiorite.

The geological and lithological base of Islay is thus varied and gives rise to very varied scenery, even if the grandeur of scale found in certain of the more 'Highland' Hebrides is lacking. Islay, however, has been particularly fortunate in superficial deposits. Much of the area from Port Askaig to Bridgend and Bowmore is overlain by glacial, postglacial, fluvoglacial and fluvial materials. Especially where these have been derived from underlying limestone, they provide a soil and land with a reasonable agricultural quality and capability rarely encountered in the Highland zone of Britain. For centuries it has been because of its farming that Islay has been regarded as favoured and even exceptional in the Hebrides, valued by its earliest settlers, then the Norse, and the focus for the Lordship of the Isles in the fourteenth and fifteenth centuries. The varied soils facilitated the agricultural changes of the eighteenth and nineteenth centuries, when the island's owners and farmers were extolled by many agriculturalists and other observers. As subsequent chapters show, the island's population increased to a maximum in 1831 of almost 15,000, the limits of cultivation being extended by reclaiming hill and peat lands. Today there are many signs of these times visible in the central and northern Rinns, the Glen and the Oa. The island's other land-based resources of minerals and peat and its many beaches, have likewise contributed to the island's varied economy.

The vagaries of island weather

Islay's varied landscapes are further enhanced by constant changes in weather and colours on the island, on the large indentations of Lochs Indaal and Gruinart and on the many lochs and streams. The weather may make its first and most memorable impact while the visitor is *en route* to the island. The early-nineteenth century lack of lighthouses, the small vessels and the chances of being wrecked, as four craft were in a single night in September 1870, and four more in November 1881, have all changed.[2] But winds of storm or gale force can still disrupt communications by sea, while the ability to enjoy scenery, as well as the number of days when aircraft can bring in mail and other commodities, are controlled by the height of the cloud base.

Weather observations for different parts of the island are relatively few. In the relatively sheltered garden at Eallabus at the head of Loch Indaal, daily precipitation has been recorded almost continuously since 1866.[3] Temperature and precipitation records have also been kept for varying lengths of time at some of the lighthouses: at Port Charlotte and Rhuvaal from 1900 and at McArthur's Head from 1900. Rainfall records were also kept for brief periods during the Second World War at the airfield at Glenegedale, near Port Ellen, and at the seaplane base at Bowmore. Islay airport recorded daily maximum and minimum temperatures and daily rainfall, but no cloud cover or wind readings were published and systematic readings ceased in the 1990s.

As in the other Hebridean islands, the most noticeable weather features are expressed better as frequencies than as absolutes or averages. The average number of days with winds of gale force on nearby Tiree is 35 per year and Islay's experience is likely to be similar.[4] Fog occurs, on average, less than five times a year on Islay, but the number of days with low cloud base is much higher. The amount of precipitation in the Islay lowlands averages over 130cm (50 ins) per year; very little of this normally falls as snow. Rainfall is distributed unevenly throughout the year, with more in the winter half of the year from October to March, while between one-half and two-thirds of the days are likely to have some rain.[5] Cloud cover and the related number of sunshine hours are also highly variable. There is usually more sunshine than in mountainous Jura, but less than in flatter Tiree. The average duration of sunshine is four hours per day, varying from an hour or two on average in winter to over six in summer. Temperatures are rarely excessively high or low and frosts are likewise rare. The growing season has been suggested as 216 days, fairly long in British terms, but winds can often deter growth.[6]

There are, of course, exceptional periods. Grim winters, with blocking high pressure over much of Britain, can, in Islay, be ones with relatively little cloud cover and precipitation and a high total of sunshine hours. Similarly, wet and grey early summers over much of England may contrast with the near-drought conditions in Islay, causing concern to farmers, fishermen and whisky distillers, but providing weeks of continuous sunshine for the other islanders and visitors. Then, even the sphagnum moss crackles underfoot on the moors and fire is a constant island hazard, especially if heather-burning gets out of control on the moors. The weather often varies from one part of the island to another. In particular, it is almost always possible to find some beach or favoured spot, sheltered from the day's prevailing wind.

Islay's peaty habitat

The island provides a considerable range of habitat and even although the highest hill, Beinn Bheigir, rising only to just under 500m, excludes subalpine plants, a 'rich native flora' has been claimed; almost 800 taxa have been recorded, including introduced species.[7] One of Islay's Hebridean anomalies is the amount of long-established woodland and plantations of hard and soft woods, including exotics. Extensive sand dunes, salt marshes, limestone and slate outcrops and the many lochs each have their own distinctive flora and fauna.

Peat-banks are an important feature of the Islay scene. They are cut annually for both domestic and distillery needs.

But it is perhaps in the wide expanses of peat bogs that the combined effects of topography, soils, climate and flora have had the most noticeable impact on Islay's economy and landscape. Vegetation on the bogs at present consists mainly of heather and purple moor grass, with lesser proportions of cotton grass, cross-leaved heather and sphagnum moss. The bulk of the peat itself has been formed through the centuries from the remains of sphagnum species, the resistant leaf sheaths of cotton grass, small twigs of heather and in the lower layers, reeds and some sedges; a few pieces of birch were found in the two bogs sampled by the Scottish Peat Survey of the 1950s and 1960s.[8] Peat has traditionally been cut by foot for domestic fuel from rented pieces or banks of moor and it is still an important part of the domestic economy. At the cost of a few pounds' rent, some hard work and a mass of midge bites, the fuel supply for heating many island homes is assured. Peat has also long been used in the distilleries as an integral part of the whisky-making process and formerly also as a fuel. Extensive new cuttings were opened up in 1980 for cutting by machine and a new access road was subsequently constructed along the Laggan river west of the 'High Road' between Port Ellen and Bridgend and east to Castlehill.

Islay's main peat bogs cover around ten per cent of the surface. There are others that are smaller in extent, shallower in depth or higher in altitude. Since much of the peat overlies raised beach and river-borne materials, reclamation for other uses is not difficult. In the 1960s the Forestry Commission began to plant conifers, predominantly Sitka spruce, on peatlands in the valley of the Laggan and some of its tributaries, on land purchased from the Dunlossit estate and subsequently from the Laggan estate. Felling began in the middle of the 1990s, with timber being exported by barge and ship. The cleared land was left as open ground, allowed to regenerate naturally into woodland, or planted with indigenous species. In 1980 the Commission drained part of the Rinns near Ballimony prior to planting and for much of the 1980s fiscal forestry resulted in further plantings in north-east Islay and in the Oa.

Tourists, naturalists and sportsmen

By the nineteenth century, writings about Islay by topographers and early agricultural scientists and by survey-conscious ministers, were being supplemented by early guidebooks for visitors to the island. The renowned *Steam-Boat Companion* of James Lumsden, in its various editions of the 1820s and later, and various topographical dictionaries made the island better-known to the public.[9] The Victorian expansion of leisure activities for the upper classes encouraged this new interest in Islay. A later guidebook explained that the variety of Islay's shootings was due to the 'remarkable diversity of natural features, to the combination of moor and pasture, of rich cornfields and desolate hillside . . . the bag includes red fallow and roe deer, grouse, partridges, pheasants, blackgame, snipe, rock pigeons, wild duck, golden plover, teal, wild geese, hares and rabbits'.[10] Today, shootings still form part of the island's seasonal activities and economy on several of the estates. Another sport attracted attention to Islay from the late-nineteenth century. Salmon and trout and fishing often warranted praise in the appropriate journals and guides. When in spate, the major salmon rivers are the Sorn, Laggan and Duich and trout lochs are numerous. Surveys, stocking and poaching have been a main concern of the lairds and their agents. Sea-angling is also popular with islanders and visitors alike. Crabs, clams or scallops and lobsters are fished commercially for export.

Even before the Forestry Commission plantings began in the later 1960s, the map of Islay showed much more evidence of natural woodlands and plantations than has been characteristic of most of the other Hebrides since the eighteenth century. The woodlands are a sheltered haven in winter and early spring, with their succession of snowdrops, wild daffodils and bluebells. The hedgerows too were planted mostly during the agrarian reforms of the late-eighteenth and early-nineteenth centuries; fewer stone dykes were necessary in the less stony, lower parts of the island. The

The Atlantic breaks over the Big Strand beside the links golf course at Machrie, opened in 1891 (Eric Thorburn).

hedges provide shelter for a profusion of wildflowers in spring and early summer, when the island is ablaze with gorse and they also provide sanctuary for birds and game.

The extremely varied habitat of Islay with its varied flora and fauna on land and in water has led to the designation of several Sites of Special Scientific Interest, RAMSAR sites, and of the Argyll Islands Environmentally Sensitive Area. It is particularly for its bird life that the island is renowned. Many ornithologists have testified to the large range of birds inhabiting or visiting the island on migration. Due to an amazing variety of bird habitat, woodland, moor, hill, seacliff, machair and sand dunes, agricultural land, hedgerows, rivers, marshes, freshwater lochs and shallow sea lochs, over 250 bird species have been recorded, almost half of which breed on Islay.[11] In a week's visit it is often possible to see over a hundred different birds, including fairly uncommon ones such as the barn owl, chough, corncrake and golden eagle. In winter and early spring, Islay is host to tens of thousands of the barnacle geese and several thousand Greenland white-fronted geese, grazing the fields near the tidal flats and lochs, or wheeling overhead at dusk in their great V-shaped chevrons. Smaller numbers of other visitors include Brent and Canada geese and there are many rafts of waders including wigeon and scaup.

As well as providing for those visitors interested in shooting, fishing and watching seals, otters and birds, the island attracted golfers after 1891 when Mrs Lucy Ramsay opened the Machrie course beside the Big Strand of Laggan Bay. By the end of the decade the Rev J. G. MacNeill was commenting in his guidebook that 'this splendid course of eighteen holes is second to none in Scotland . . . many of our foremost statesmen, titled and untitled, are here frequently seen on the golfing links'.[12] Competitions were instituted, the main one being the Kildalton Cross Championship held annually in the first week of August. Shorter courses at Gartmain and Uisgeantsuidhe were also played earlier this century and 'an excellent nine-hole golf course' has even been claimed for Port Askaig.[13] The nine-hole pitch-and-putt course behind the White Hart Hotel has been superseded by the one at the Port Ellen Playing Fields, established in 1953.

The sands of Islay have not all been laid down to golf links; the sandy beaches include the sometimes wild and dangerous ones of the western Rinns at Lossit, Kilchiaran, Machir, Saligo and around Sanaig. There are extensive beaches on both sides of Loch Gruinart and around Loch Indaal, while there are many smaller, sometimes sheltered ones along the south-eastern coasts of Kildalton and the Oa. Only the eastern shore of the island along the Sound of Islay is without accessible beaches.[14]

An island of considerable character and contrasts, one of the few Hebridean islands with woodlands, one with a wild and bare west, a tidy central heartland and a fragmented south-east, Islay's distinctiveness is in part a reflection of its physical setting and structure. To a much greater extent it is the result of a history very different from that of the remainder of the Hebrides and the Highlands. More particularly it reflects the perception and initiative of relatively few individuals during a century or more after about 1750. To appreciate their vision, it is necessary to go back in time to see what Islay was like before the early-eighteenth century.

Notes and references

[1]   Ordnance Survey, *1:50,000 Second Series*, *60*, 1987; *1: 25,000*; *Pathfinder Series*, 1987–8; *1: 10,000. Second Edition*, 1899, revised 1981.

Geological Survey of Scotland *Quarter Inch Geology*, *Sheet 13*, 1921; *One Inch Solid and Drift*, *Sheet 98*, 1918 and *Sheet 27*, 1900; British Geological Survey *1:50,000 South Islay Sheet 19 (Scotland) Solid and Drift Geology Provisional Series* 1996; and *North Islay Sheet 27*, 1995; and S. B. Wilkinson, *The Geology of Islay*, including Oronsay and portions of Colonsay and Jura, (Glasgow, 1907).

A. G. Dawson, 'Lateglacial sea-level changes and ice-limits in Islay, Jura and Scarba, Scottish Inner Hebrides', *Sc J Geol*, 1982, 18, pp. 253–65; J. M. Gray, 'Glacio-isostatic shoreline development in Scotland: an overview', *Queen Mary College Occasional Papers*, (London, 1985), 24; S. B. McCann 'The Raised Beaches of North-East Islay and Western Jura', *TIBG*, 1964, 35, pp. 1–15; and F. M. Synge and N. Stephens, 'Late and Post-glacial Shorelines and Ice Limits in Argyll and North-East Ulster', ibid., 1966, 39, pp. 101–25.

2   Register of Examinations . . . concerning Wrecks and Casualties, SRO, CE60/4/24.

3   Meteorological Office communication, 1972. Gales are winds of 34 knots or over (8 on Beaufort scale) blowing for at least ten minutes.

4   Meteorological Office communication, 1981.

5   *The Monthly Weather Report*, 1976, Table 3.

6   M. L. Anderson and W. A. Fairbairn, 'Division of Scotland into Climatic Sub-regions as an Aid to Silviculture', *Bulletin of the Forestry Department, University of Edinburgh*, 1955, 1, p. 8.

7   J. K. Morton, 'The Flora of Islay and Jura (V.C. 102)', *Proceedings of the BSBI, Supplement*, 1958–60, part 3, pp. 1–59.

8   Department of Agriculture and Fisheries for Scotland, *Scottish Peat Surveys: Western Highlands and Islands*, (Edinburgh, 1966), 5 vols. Islay is in vol. 2.

9   J. Lumsden and Son, *The Steam-Boat Companion and Stranger's Guide to the Western Islands and Highlands of Scotland*, (Glasgow, 1825); S. Lewis, A *Topographical Dictionary of Scotland*, (London, 1846), 2 vols. and *Atlas*.

10 L. MacN. Weir, *Guide to Islay*, (1924 edition, revised, Glasgow, 1936), pp. 48–51.

11 C. G. Booth, *Birds in Islay*, (Islay, 1981), p. 11; R. E. Elliott, *Birds of Islay*, (London, 1989); M. A. Ogilvie, *Wild Geese*, (Islay, 1978) and 'Wildfowl of Islay', *PRSE*, 1983, 83B, pp. 473–89.

12 J. G. MacNeill, *The New Guide to Islay*, (Glasgow, 1900), p. 23. See also J. Cubbage, *The Chronicle of Islay Golf Club and Machrie Links*, (Glasgow, 1996).

13 J. W. Robertson, *Islay Official Guide*, 2nd edition, (n.d), p. 27.

14 W. G. Ritchie and R. Crofts, *The Beaches of Islay, Jura and Colonsay*, (Aberdeen, 1974).

CHAPTER 3

Earlier islanders

In what has been termed the Atlantic Ends of Europe, from the Lofoten Islands to the mouth of the Douro in Portugal, the seas around the Highlands and Islands have always been important for transport and as a source of food.[1] The south-west to north-east geological trend of Islay provides a long coastline with shelter around the compass. It was probably from south-western Europe in Mesolithic times that the first of the visitors came by sea to Islay, an island still uninhabited after the retreat of the last ice sheet around 10,000 years ago. Islay abounds in visible sites of archaeological interest.

The *Statistical Account* authors of the late-eighteenth century and subsequent topographers noted some of Islay's antiquities, but the estate maps of the early-nineteenth century, made for innovative purposes, did not show many. It was not until the first edition of the Six-Inch Ordnance Survey maps of the later-nineteenth century and in several publications around that time, that the evidence of rich archaeological heritage of the island was hinted at in publications. Various workers, including Childe in the 1930s and Piggott in the 1940s, were followed in the later 1950s by Lacaille who was the instigator of a branch of the Thames Basin Archaeological Observers' Group being formed, called the Islay Archaeological Survey Group.[2] It attempted to produce an exhaustive survey of all the antiquities of Islay. *The Preliminary Handbook of the Archaeology of Islay*, published in 1960, recorded much archaeological and historical material, but the IASG became defunct in 1971. At about the same time as it had begun its work, the Natural History and Antiquarian Society of Islay had been formed and with the activities of this, of the Museum of Islay Life and, especially, of the Royal Commission on the Ancient and Historical Monuments of Scotland, and of the National Museums of Scotland, more of Islay's archaeological and later story has been unravelled.[3]

Prehistoric islanders' relics
When the Mesolithic hunters and fishers approached Islay from the adjacent mainland about 7000BC, sea-level was higher than it is today, with less

The Neolithic chambered cairn at Cragabus is a reminder that this settlement has probably been occupied for several thousand years.

The compact, multivallate fort at Nosebridge defended the upper Laggan valley during the Iron Age or later. It contrasts with the scattered buildings occupied when Islay's population reached its maximum around 1830 (John D. H. Radford).

land, for instance, between Lochs Indaal and Gruinart, or around Ardnave Point or Machir Bay.[4] The climate was milder than at present, with warmer summers and consequently Islay may have been more wooded. Shell middens such as that found at Ardnave resulted from the use of limpet hammers and bone fish hooks belonging to the Mesolithic fisher folk. Deer supplied meat, bones for implements and skins for shelter and clothing. Other flint implements and weapons have been found on the valleyside near Bolsay in the Rinns.

The search for food was changing to one of permanent settlement based on farming and the evidence for Neolithic times in Islay from about 3500BC to about 2500BC shows that woods were cleared with stone axes for pasture and pottery was used for the first time. Greater numbers of immigrant farmers and their progeny led in time to the multi-chambered burial tombs with cairns, such as at Cragabus or Port Charlotte. Sea-level fell its present limits. To the later-Neolithic and earlier-Bronze Age times the many standing stones and the Cultoon stone circle belong. Islay is well endowed with standing stones, single, or aligned in pairs or trios. At Cultoon only three stones stand upright, with a dozen prone. While the sockets were excavated in an oval arrangement, Cultoon was probably never completed, despite its astronomical possibilities. Bronze Age cultivation and settlement to about 600BC have been confirmed at Ardnave and Kilellan, by the beakers, food vessels and tools uncovered in the sandhills. Burial in chambered tombs was replaced by the use of round cairns as at Carnduncan and in individual cists. Hut-circle settlements in isolated, dispersed or nucleated groups and associated field systems on the low-lying moorlands also belong to this time. Some are isolated houses, others are in dispersed groups and still others in nucleated settlements. The field systems provided plots for paddocks or fields for cattle and grain, as at An Sithean, near Carnduncan, where grains of pollen have been recovered.

Following this somewhat benign period, there was gradual climatic deterioration, resulting in moorland and more peaty lands during the wetter period that continued through the Iron Age to around AD400. In Islay this seems to have been a time of conflict, with 80 fortified sites of varied sizes. There were small stone hill forts like Dùn Chroisprig, with many others in the hills, ridges, promonotories and offshore islets. The peoples of the early Iron Age have left us with timber-framed hill forts and Trudernish vitrified hill fort. The only drystone defended settlement or broch on Islay is that of Dùn Bhoraraic, characteristically circular and galleried. Towards the end of the Iron Age or later, two large forts were constructed that are unique in the west of Scotland: the two multivallate,

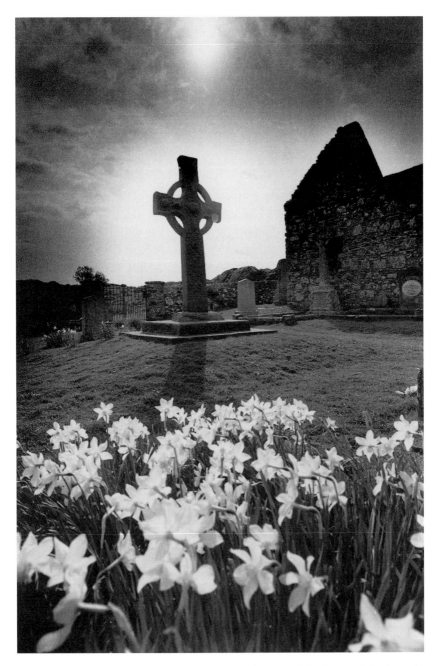

The Celtic High Ring Cross in Kildalton churchyard is one of the few surviving intact in Scotland. It was carved from local stone about AD800, probably by a sculptor from Iona. Pictish, Irish, Northumbrian and Celtic motifs include the virgin and the child, David and the Lion on the front, and animals and carved bosses on the back (Eric Thorburn).

earthwork fortifications of Dùn Nosebridge, near Neriby, in a commanding site in the upper Laggan valley, and Dùn Guaidhre, near Kilmeny, in the upper Sorn valley. Neither of these has been excavated and little about them is agreed among archaeologists, but both command strategic positions overlooking fertile valleys and were probably subsequently reoccupied.

Early Christian missions

Islay had probably been occupied by peoples from both western and eastern directions before Gaelic-speaking Scots built coracles towards the end of the fifth century AD, to cross what is now known as the North Channel, establishing the Dàl Riàta kingdom in Earra-ghaidheal or Argyll on the western seaboard.[5] The earliest written references to Islay are perhaps those of the Irish chroniclers of the fifth century and subsequently of Columba's biographer, Adomnàn.[6] In the early-sixth century, Angus MacErc claimed Islay where his descendants formed Clan Donald and later became the lords of the Isles. Columban missionaries were responsible for the establishment of many of the Early Christian sites marked 'chapel' on the maps and in place-names beginning with the gaelic prefix *cill* anglicised as *kil*. At first these missionaries probably lived as hermit monks or priests in tiny buildings, ministering to islanders and answering to an abbot. Those subsequently canonised included not only Columba who founded Iona monastery, but others whose names live on in the parish names and place-names of Islay such as St Maelrubha (Kilarrow) and St Kiaran (Kilchiaran). The chapel at Kilslevan has a doorway at the west end that might indicate an early dating and the almost circular enclosure there may also be early Celtic. At other places the shape is more rectangular and greater Norse influences seem to have appeared later on. These tiny churches probably continued in use with Norse colonists adopting the Christian religion, each district building its own small chapel and burial ground.[7] While Celtic churches and burial grounds have traditionally been associated with several sites and islets of Islay, the preservation of at least fifteen of these drystone and turf ecclesiastical buildings on Islay has been deemed 'quite exceptional'.[8]

It gradually became the practice to set up commemorative crosses in the burial grounds to dedicate places and people to the Lord. The Islay carved stones were first illustrated by Graham in 1895 and more recent surveys have been made by Lamont, by Steer and Bannerman and by the Royal Commission on the Ancient and Historical Monuments of Scotland.[9] There are many types and ages of carved stones on Islay, some hewn from local rocks, others carved locally from imported stones and others imported already-carved. Many are still to be seen in the island, though some are now in the National Museums of Scotland in Edinburgh. Most of the earliest of stones stood upright and were simple incised-outline cross slabs, then, about the eighth century, carving in relief began. At first this was also simple, but later the carving became more elaborate in the Celtic Ring Crosses, erected to the glory of God. Visually the most outstanding are the High Crosses at Kilnave and Kildalton which Lamont has described as being 'in astonishing contrast' to the simple cross slabs. He has suggested that the 2.5m-high Kilnave Cross dates from around AD 759, and may be ascribed to the Irish and Iona traditions. It is carved on a thin slab of local flagstone, with only one face carved. The remarkably preserved spiral motif of the top arm recalls the illustrations in the Book of Kells.[10] The 2.7m-high Kildalton Ring Cross, the last one of its kind, one of the few remaining intact in Scotland, can probably be dated to around AD800; both of its faces are carved with the artistic sophistication of the Iona tradition, with Pictish, Irish, Northumbrian and Celtic motifs. The grey-green epidiorite, with numerous granules of felspar was quarried over a kilometre away at Port na Cille. Lamont's assessment of these crosses is that 'artistically as well as physically the crosses of Kilnave and Kildalton tower above everything else in the ancient sculpture of Islay'.[11]

The Norse and the Gael-Gall
The Norse or Viking longships or galleys which plied the seas off western Europe from about AD600 to 1000, pulled from 50 to 80 oars. They carried a mast which was always lowered aft when using oars. A single square sail was hoisted on a yard for working to windward and for running. There was no deck or keel and so they were fairly unstable vessels and gave no protection to crews. They experienced difficulty operating in rougher winter seas, even in the climatic optimum of the time, yet still managed some remarkable voyages. From about AD800 the Scandinavians raided, traded and settled in Islay as well as in many parts of the Atlantic fringe of Europe. They spread from the Nordreys or Northern Isles southwards into what became the Sudreys, or Inner Hebrides, and beyond as far south as the Isle of Man and Ireland. Their active association with these areas lasted for almost five centuries, but 'the Argyll islands were never completely Norsised'.[12] These islands were always recognised as essentially Gaelic islands in which Gaels lived, in contrast to the Outer Hebrides which were called the 'Innsegall' or islands of the strangers or foreigners. The Norse arrived as pagans, but intermarriage with the local Celtic or Gaelic-speaking population produced the Gael-Gall, Gaelic foreigners, and most were probably converted to Christianity. There are several burial grounds in sandhill areas of Islay associated with Viking

The twelfth-century parish boundaries followed an earlier tripartite division of Islay. With the increased population of the nineteenth century, each was further divided into *quoad sacra* parishes of Portnahaven, Kilmeny and the Oa.

settlers, such as those at Cruach Mhòr and Ballinaby, which have yielded some personal brooches. Equal numbers of men's and women's graves give some indication of permanent settlers.[13] Most of the funerary slabs continued in the older Celtic tradition, but the Dòid Mhàiri slab, now in Edinburgh, was completely alien to any other stone found on the island. With both Celtic and Norse symbols, it probably marked the grave of an important Gael-Gall chief.[14] Many place-names survive that are associated with the Norse peoples, but no Viking settlement site has yet been authenticated on Islay.

When Kenneth MacAlpine united Picts and Scots north of the Forth as king of Alba in 843, the Highlands and Islands were virtually left in Norse hands and these areas subsequently developed differently from the rest of Scotland. The Sudreys and Man formed almost an independent kingdom and acknowledged Norwegian sovereignty. An outstanding 'King' of Man and the Isles in the last quarter of the eleventh century was Godred Crovan who ruled in Man with a Council which included many local lords from Man and the other isles. Towards the end of the century, King Magnus Barelegs of Norway sailed to claim sovereignty and in the

resulting Treaty of Tarbert in 1098 between Magnus and Edgar, king of
the Scots, Magnus gave up all claim to the mainland but was confirmed in
his control of the islands. Allegiances in Man and the islands continued in
both directions, to the Norse and Scottish kings, apparently with very
little interference from either.

In the twelfth century Godred Crovan's son, Olaf, endowed the
bishopric of the Isles under the See of the Sudreys (Sodor) and parishes
were established.[15] An older tripartite division of Islay was perpetuated.
Southward became Kildalton and Oa, Midward, Killarow and Kilmeny,
and the Rinns, Kilchoman. The eastern ends of the churches at Kilnaughton
and Kilchiaran may belong to this period. Kilbride, Kilchoman and Kilnave
can probably be dated to the end of the twelfth century, Kildalton parish
church to the early-thirteenth century and Killarow parish church to the
late-thirteenth century.

Somerled and Clan Donald

Towards the end of the reign of David I of Scotland in the middle of the
twelfth century, Godred's Celtic-Norse grandson, Somerled, married
Ragnhild, daughter of Olaf of Man and emerged as the key political figure
of the Hebrides in mid-century.[16] Early Celtic society was kin-based,
ruled by a rí or king; tanistry decided succession. Somerled was Rí Airir
Goídel – ruler of the coastland of the Gael (Lorn, Mull, Tiree and Coll).[17]
Olaf's unpopular son, Godfred, was deposed by some of the island chiefs,
led by his brother-in-law, Somerled. After a sea battle off Islay in 1156, in
his fleet of small and manoeuvrable galleys or birlinns, equipped with the
newly-introduced rudder (as opposed to the Viking steering oar), Somerled
defeated the Godfred forces and forced a division of the Norse Kingdom
of Man and the Isles, which stretched from the Isle of Man to Lewis. He
became Rì Innse Gall – king or ruler of the Isles of the Strangers[18] as well
as Rì Airir Goídel,[19] and ruled over a wide-ranging lordship of islands and
the mountainous western seaboard. The relationship between David I
and Somerled was based on the Celtic system of 'a rì rendering tribute to
a rì ruirech, not on any kind of feudal system . . . the importance of
Somerled's title needs to be stressed in this context'.[20] David being much
preoccupied with English affairs, Somerled became a kind of regional
governor for the Scots king, overseeing a seaboard province. The site at
Dunyvaig probably invited occupation and fortification from at least the
Early Historic period.[21] A stronghold could be created on the coastal
promontory on the east side of Lagavulin Bay, guarding the entrance to
the anchorage there and commanding a prospect of the coasts of Kintyre
and Antrim. Somerled's alliances suggest a very real and very close-knit

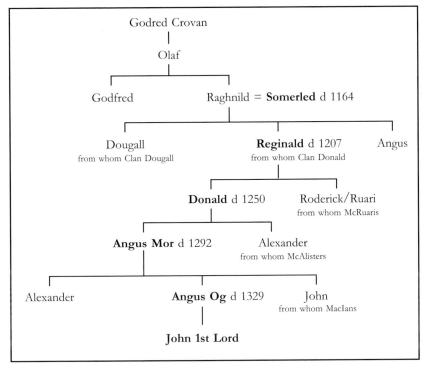

Outline genealogy of Somerled and Clan Donald (Various sources).

community within the western isles, an Atlantic sea-faring community encompassing Man, Ireland, the Hebrides, Orkney, Zetland and Norway.

While Somerled had ruled his lands in semi-independence in David I's reign, the young Malcolm IV, acting under the influence of the Anglo-French barons, was determined to extend his power westward. Fluid clan organisation was at odds with the formal, universal feudalism imposed by the Crown. Land grants were given by the Crown to 'foreign' settlers, bringing them into closer proximity to Somerled's territory and to the Atlantic community in general. Tensions in twelfth-century Scotland often ran high between natives and incomers and the feudalisation of Scotland was anything but peaceful.[22] Somerled was not alone in being concerned that the expansionist policies of the Crown were threatening to encroach on his traditional territory and undermine his powers. By 1153 his relations with the kings of Scots reached a low ebb over the feudal, primogeniture succession of David's grandson, Malcolm, as king, instead of a Gaelic collateral choice from among several branches of the ruling house. In 1164, Somerled invaded the mainland and sailed up the Clyde with 160 galleys, but met his end at Renfrew.

Somerled's lands were divided amongst three surviving sons, Ranald or Reginald, Angus and Dougall. Ranald ruled in Islay and Kintyre and adopted the title 'of Islay', then styled himself 'dominus insularum' and 'dominus de Argil', king of the isles and lord of Argyll.[23] By the mid-thirteenth century the three lines of Somerled held the islands from the king of Norway and the mainland from the king of Scots.[24] Angus' lands subsequently came to Donald, the son of Ranald and to Dougall, Somerled thus being the progenitor of both Clan Donald and Clan Dougall. Politically the region remained largely unaffected by the policies of the Scottish kings until early in the thirteenth century when the Scottish king, Alexander II, campaigned against this grandson of Somerled, Donald, mounting expeditions to Argyll in the 1220s.

Alexander II died in 1249 and was succeeded by his son, a minor. Later, wanting to consolidate his kingdom, Alexander III moved against the Norse and the rulers of the islands. The thirteenth-century rivalries and feuds among the descendants of Somerled helped to ensure that while the MacDougalls co-operated with the Scots Crown in the 1260s, the MacDonalds did not. They seemed closer to their Norwegian overlords, even joining King Haakon's 1263 expedition against Scotland. Whilst retaining the Northern isles in the Treaty of Perth in 1266, the Norse finally ceded the Sudreys and Man to Scotland and Alexander III formally added the isles to his Scottish dominion. The diocese of the Isles was also transferred to the king of Scots in 1266. The former vassals of the king of Norway were left in possession of their islands, now held by the king of Scots, and the MacDougalls were favoured.

Alexander III's Scotland, instead of being split between Celt and Norman, or Gael and Gall, was a hybrid country, with hybrid kingship, hybrid institutions, hybrid law, a hybrid church and an increasingly hybrid landowning class.[25] While Alexander had introduced the feudal system and created four great baronies in the Scottish Highland area, Highland society continued to be based on kinship, modified by feudalism.[26] The application of feudalism to Islay initiated a changed basis on which the local chiefs held their land. Charters in Latin included that given by the king to Donald's son, Angus Mor, for Islay and elsewhere, acknowledging him as feudal Baron of Islay. But he and his successors continued to view their attachment to territory and kin by older Celtic laws and customs and paid uneasy homage to the kings of the Scots. When creating the baronies, Alexander III had had a general assessment made for Scottish taxation purposes. In Islay this list of all lay lands became known as the 'Old Extent', traces of its use still existing in the estate documents and place-names of the eighteenth and early-nineteenth centuries.[27]

The relationship between the centre and localities always depended essentially upon the Crown's relations with the local magnates. The ideal was to have loyal, responsible magnates controlling outlying areas on behalf of the king; that was the foundation of the Crown's success in the twelfth and thirteenth centuries.[28] In the 40 years between the final winning of the west in 1266 and the outbreak of civil war caused by Robert Bruce's seizure of the throne in 1306, the MacDougall lords of Lorn acted as the main royal agents in the task of governing the west. By the last decade of the century the MacDonalds of Islay were serving Edward I of England, whilst the MacDougalls were upholding the Scottish cause. But in 1306, when the MacDougalls sided with the English in opposing Bruce, Angus Og (the Younger) chose to help the Scots king. Unfortunately for the MacDougalls, they took what turned out to be the losing side in the civil war. The Clan Donald, by supporting Bruce, had their position strengthened at the expense of the pro-Balliol Clan Dougall. Robert I destroyed the MacDougalls and granted much of their territory to the MacDonalds, though much of the western seaboard was still under the hegemony of the Bruce family. After Angus Og died, and following infighting amongst the kindred, his son John emerged in the 1330s as chief of the Clan Donald. At Perth in 1336 he signed letters of indenture with Edward Balliol which conferred title to all the lands inherited from his father, as well as Kintyre, Knapdale, Lewis and Skye.

The late-thirteenth century Campbells had also been feuding with the MacDougalls and also supported Bruce. After the 1307 turning point in Highland history, a new balance resulted from the Bruce-Balliol civil war. Campbells, MacDonalds and others became prominent instead of Lowland lords. Over the following centuries the Campbells would become the most feudal of Celtic kindreds, basing their expansion on royal patronage, judicious marriage, feudal charters, the newly-created Sherrifdom of Argyll and aggressively adopting Lowland ways. The MacDonalds, by contrast, while becoming the greatest magnate house of the medieval Scottish west, fostered a self-conscious, pan-Celtic Gaeldom.

Notes and references

[1]   E. E. Evans, 'The Atlantic Ends of Europe', *Adv Sci*, 1958–9, 15, pp. 54–64.

[2]   V. G. Childe, 'Notes on some duns in Islay', *PSAS*, 1934–5, 69, pp. 81–4; S. Piggott and C. M. Piggott, 'Field work in Colonsay and Islay 1944–45', ibid., 1945–6, 80, pp. 83–103; Islay Archaeological Survey Group, *The Preliminary Handbook to the Archaeology of Islay*, (Keele, 1960); and G. Ritchie and A. Ritchie, *Scotland: Archaeology and Early History*, (London, 1981).

[3]   RCAHMS, *Argyll Inventory, V*.

4　Ibid., p. 2.

5　B. D. Osborne and R. Armstrong, *Scottish Dates*, (Edinburgh, 1996), p. 5.

6　W. F. Skene (ed.), *Adomnàn: Life of Saint Columba*, (Edinburgh, 1874).

7　W. D. Lamont, *Ancient and Mediaeval Sculptured Stones of Islay*, (Edinburgh, 1972), p. 4.

8　RCAHMS, *Argyll Inventory*, *V*, p. 27.

9　Graham is reputed to have made plaster casts of the majority of Islay stones from papier mâché moulds, which he dried on the spot in a tent, and transported back to base on stretchers and in crates specially designed for the purpose. These accurate replicas were then photographed in the studio under special lighting designed to emphasise the ornamentation. Lamont, *Sculptured Stones*, p.9.

10　*Argyll Inventory*, *V*, p. 28.

11　Lamont, *Sculptured Stones*, p. 19.

12　C. M. Macdonald, *The History of Argyll up to the beginning of the Sixteenth Century*, (Glasgow, 1951), p. 52.

13　RCAHMS, *Argyll Inventory*, *V*, p. 32.

14　Lamont, *Sculptured Stones*, p. 22.

15　J. Trevorrow, *Celtic Foundations*, (Islay, 1985); *Norse Invasion*, (Islay, 1987) and *Parish Churches*, (Islay, 1988).

16　R. A. McDonald and S. A. McLean, 'Somerled of Argyll: A New Look at Old Problems', *SHR,* 1992, 71, p. 7.

17　Clan Donald Lands Trust, *Ceannas nan Gàidheal*, (Skye, 1985), p. 9.

18　Munro and Munro, *Acts of the Lords*, p. xx.

19　A. Grant, 'Scotland's "Celtic Fringe" in the late Middle Ages: the MacDonald lords of the Isles and the kingdom of Scotland', in R. R. Davies (ed.), *The British Isles 1100– 1500: comparisons, contrasts and connections*, (Edinburgh, 1988), p. 122.

20　McDonald and McLean, 'Somerled of Argyll', p. 10.

21　RCAHMS, *Argyll Inventory*, *V*, p. 274.

22　A. Grant, 'To the Medieval Foundations', *SHR*, 1994, 73, p. 8.

23　Grant, 'Scotland's "Celtic Fringe"', p. 133.

24　Munro and Munro, *Acts of the Lords*, p. xx.

25　Ibid., p. 119.

26　T. C. Smout, *A History of the Scottish People*, (London, 1969), p. 47.

27　W. D. Lamont, 'Old Land Denominations and "Old Extent" in Islay', *SS*, 1957, 1, pp. 183–203 and 1958, 2, pp. 86–106.

28　Grant, 'Scotland's "Celtic Fringe"', pp. 121–2.

CHAPTER 4

Lordship of the Isles and aftermath

The lordship of the Isles has long engaged the attentions of historians: it encompassed a highly aristocratic and civilised society in a semi-independent kingdom, eventually covering almost the entire seaboard of west Highland Scotland and Antrim and stretching as far as Dingwall on the Moray Firth. The hegemony and power of the lordship was based on control of the sea. The West Highland galleys (or birlinns or nyvaigs) were the most advanced of their kind in Scotland, having replaced the Viking steering oar with a rudder. Perhaps nowhere is the importance of the galley in the organisation of the lordship more clearly indicated than as a motif on the legal seals and on the funerary monuments of the area. As well as a potent image for a lordship, the fast, flexible ships gave the Hebridean lords a new mastery of their sea kingdom.

The descendants of Somerled's grandson Donald, the Clan Donald or the MacDonalds, remained the focus of military and political power in the west and Islay continued to be the main seat of power in the west. The relations between the lords of the Isles and the Scottish Crown varied greatly during the fourteenth and fifteenth centuries, depending on the relative strength of the parties. The lords of the Isles frequently appear in English records, related to the changing state of English relations with the Scottish Crown. The Isle of Man came under English control after 1346. Ireland was also under English dominance and the distance from Antrim to Islay was short, so direct communication by sea with the lords of the Isles was relatively easy. The lordship thus presented a challenge to the Scottish kings, often acknowledging only token allegiance to the Crown and frequently acting independently of the Crown in relations with England.

It was Finlaggan, on shore and island sites of the eponymous inland loch surrounded by good land, that became the focus for the activities of the sea realm of the lords of the Isles for over a century and a half. The court at Finlaggan became a centre where there was a significant concentration of population with council meetings, inaugurations, fairs and markets.[1] A stone and timber causeway led to Eilean Mòr where the lord had his hall, with a timber-sprung floor, a large open fire and serving

The aerial view of Loch Finlaggan, its islands and surrounding lands, looking westwards, provides a palimpsest of several thousand years of settlement (Royal Commission on the Ancient and Historical Monuments of Scotland).

Eilean Mòr (the big island) and Eilean na Comhairle (the Council Island) in Loch Finlaggan, were the focus for the many activities of the lords of the Isles in the fourteenth and fifteenth centuries (After D. H. Caldwell).

area for food. Claret was brought from France and pilgrim and other badges from the continental mainland suggest wide-ranging connections. The hall, chapel and other living quarters were linked by paved roads. Another causeway was constructed to a nearby artifical island or crannog, eponymously the Eilean na Comhairle, where some of the peripatetic Council meetings were held, and to which chiefs of cadet branches travelled.

Conciliar government

The administration within the lordship was conducted by the Council of the Isles, a body which advised the incumbent lord of the Isles. The exercise of MacDonald lordship was peculiarly effective and cohesive, applying male primogeniture, giving charters and, especially, through the Council of the Isles. The heads of major kindreds were associated with all matters of rule to do with succession, inauguration, acquisition of territory, marriage, relations with the Scots Crown and with England, finance, justice and patronage. Through the Council, the dependent chiefs were closely tied into the lordship. After the middle of the fourteenth century the MacDonalds were exercising something approaching sovereignty, implied in the word "dominus", 'a notoriously difficult word to translate'.[2] The lords of the Isles arranged 'inaugurations' on the main island of Eilean Mòr with much ceremony.[3] The bishop of Argyll, the bishop of the Isles and priests were present, along with the chieftains of all the principal families. There was a square stone, seven or eight feet long, and the 'trace of a man's foot thereon, upon which [the lord] stood . . . clothed in a white habit', with a white rod and his sword. The ceremony being over, mass was said.

Throughout Scotland law and order was still largely a local concern. The supreme court of appeal in the lordship of the Isles was the lord's council through its judges. The law administered within the lordship almost certainly had Celtic features. In 1357 a new system of taxation was introduced, based on a revaluation of agricultural yields.[4] While it is not known how much of the land the lords granted to their followers, military service usually consisted of the provision of galleys and crews rather than men for the king's army.

The lordship brought relative stability to the Western Isles and over the century and a half of its existence created the context for a veritable golden age of Gaelic culture. The lordship was almost a state within a state, an independent kingdom and an overtly Gaelic institution with a distinctive culture.[5] No other region of Scotland can be so clearly distinguished by its material culture as the lordship of the Isles: in many ways it was a unique and culturally distinct phenomenon.[6] Much has been written about the cultural and social influence of the lordship of the Isles. The lords were the chief patrons of a renaissance of Gaelic culture and art, preserving traditional links with Ireland, yet developing a distinct identity. Among the learned orders, poets held pride of place as the intellectual leaders of medieval Gaelic society. The MacMhuirich family were the hereditary seanachies (genealogists), poets and bards to the lords of the Isles.[7] Most of the early poetry was conventional praise poetry, which sung the virtues of chiefs and warriors. Poetry was recited to a harp or clarsach accompaniment and harpists were sometimes poets and singers in their own right. Hereditary harpists to the lords of the Isles were the MacSenach family and harp pins have been uncovered at Finlaggan. Other professionals attached to the courts included the chief judge and lawyers of the Clan Morrison, the medical MacBeths or Beatons who had come from Derry about 1300 and had settled at Ballinaby.[8]

The association of church and state in the lordship of the Isles was a close one. The lords became builders of the abbeys and chapels, turning their backs on the Columban church and introducing great medieval orders to their lands, such as the Augustinians in Oronsay Priory and the Benedictines in Iona Abbey. Benedictines were also given abbey lands and churches in Islay, such as at Ballinaby. The second lord, Donald, and his grandson may even have adopted the monastic life. Priors and canons were supplied to Islay from Iona and Oronsay. Society was reasonably well served by its church in the century and a half before the Reformation, but it is difficult to establish who said mass when and where and many chapels supplemented parish churches.[9] These places of worship were especially thickly spread in well-populated Islay, a few at least being endowed with specific lands, as at Finlaggan, Texa and Orsay.[10] There were three independent parishes in fifteenth-century Islay with secular clergy. Communities were well supplied with clergy in fifteenth and early-sixteenth centuries and links with the Vatican were strong in a kin-based society where marriage was closely monitored. Islay became notionally Protestant in the inaugural year of Reformation. In general the first two centuries of reformed worship saw the old parish churches still in use, with the possible exceptions of the buildings at Ellister and Kilbride.[11]

The Aberdeen chronicler, John of Fordun, recorded in 1380 that John, first of the lords, had two places of residence or 'mansiones' in Islay.[12] One of these is traditionally said to have been at Kilchoman, the other on an island in Loch Finlaggan.[13] Two centuries later Dean Monroe was to confirm 'the town of Kilchomain in which the Lords of the Ules dwelt offtymes'.[14] The architecture of medieval secular lordship in this group of islands exhibits a character that is different from much of the rest of Argyll. Dunyvaig and Finlaggan apart, there is a notable absence of recognised fortified houses. The first specific reference to a castle of Dunyvaig, castrum Dounowak, was also that of John of Fordun. About then, possession of the stronghold passed from the lords of the Isles to a cadet branch of the family, the MacDonalds of Dunyvaig and the Glens of Antrim, who held the castle until after rebellion and forfeiture in 1493.

The importance of the patronage exercised by the MacDonald lords of the Isles is particularly illustrated in the monumental sculpture.[15] Craftsmen were highly skilled workers in stone, metal and wood. Of their work in metal and wood very little remains, but from the hereditary stonemasons there remain many examples of their artistically sophisticated and unique style of decoration. The commissioned crosses and graveyard slabs commemorated heads of kindreds, their families and members of professions and crafts. The typical character of the sculptural renaissance in Argyll and the isles produced late-medieval stones that had no ancestry in the ancient Scots-Irish tradition but were, rather, a unique West Highland and Hebridean product, whose initial inspiration came mainly from monumental sculpture in northern England. Tall, freestanding crosses reappeared after nearly four centuries and Islay today is still unusually rich in them. There were at least a dozen, of two types: those devoid of human figures and, better known, the disc-headed crosses displaying the Crucifixion. Especially notable is the unbroken Kilchoman cross, now standing over 2.5m above the ground. It is one of the finest of the group of medieval crosses in the western Highlands and Islands that are dated about 1500, many of the others having been subsequently broken during the Reformation. Some were carved in low relief with no human figures, but with a sword and scroll. Others, up to the middle of the sixteenth century, depicted effigies of warriors or churchmen.

Lords and Kings
The four lords of the Isles between 1336 and 1493 were John, Donald, Alexander and another John, each the son of his predecessor. Rì Innse Gall came to be reflected in the Latin designation 'dominus Insularum', though it did not always apply to all of the Hebrides. The title was not the result of a royal creation, but was adopted by the first lord, whose great-grandfather was Donald, the eponymous founder of the Clan Donald.[16] In the fourteenth and fifteenth centuries the designations 'de Ile' and 'de Insulis' came into use. The designation 'de Ile' or 'de Yle' was normally reserved for the lords of the Isles, for their sons who did not succeeed to the lordship and for their daughters. The chief families of the various branches of the Clan Donald designated themselves 'de Insulis' (a form

The MacDonald lords of the Isles, their successors, and the MacDonalds of Dunyvaig and the Glens of Antrim (Munro and Munro, *Acts of the Lords*).

sometimes used by the lords themselves) or else used a name derived from the forenames of their progenitors. The name MacDonald or MacDhomnuill rarely appeared in official documents before about the middle of the sixteenth century, the most notable exception being a Gaelic charter of 1408. Though self-styled lords of the Isles, they were not in fact officially recognised as such until 1476.[17]

The first of the lords of the Isles succeeded near the end of the reign of King Robert I, during which Clan Donald and Clan Ruari had supported Bruce and so prospered, while Clan Dougall, by taking the Balliol side, had lost much of its power in the Hebrides. John was at first hostile to Robert I's west-coast policy but later made agreements with Edward Balliol and David II over MacDougall lands.[18] Relations were often strained but several family marriages indicate that in the middle of the fourteenth century John was establishing links with his former rivals. This first John, a benefactor of the church, referred to by his contemporaries as 'Good John of Isla', made two ambitious and auspicious marriages. His first wife was the sister of the McRuari chief and when her childless brother died in 1346, John took over his lands.[19] By 1350 he was sailing to the Clyde with three score longships, each of some twenty or more oars, to marry Lady Margaret Stewart. She was daughter of Robert the Steward who became king as Robert II in 1371. The children of this second, royal, marriage displaced those of the first and after Robert II's succession to the throne the lands of the lordship of the Isles and those of Kintyre were made into a jointure for John and his wife.

John's death in the 1380s, however, was the signal for an acrimonious dispute between his widow and his sons over the jointure of Kintyre, a jointure being alien to Gaelic society. The result was a dispute between the lordship and the Crown which lasted for two generations, the Stewart kings intermittently trying to tackle their problems in the north and west. John's first son of his second marriage, Donald, followed him. Harking back to older customs, it was the second son who was Donald's deputy or tanist, John Mòr, progenitor of the section of Clan Donald which became known as the MacDonalds of Dunyvaig and the Glens of Antrim.[20] The MacDonalds' dealings with the Crown included a sequence of confrontations and crises, several pitched battles and, eventually, the long-drawn-out forfeiture. Donald is notable for having granted the only extant Gaelic charter, written on goatskin and now preserved in Edinburgh, and for his efforts in trying to secure the earldom of Ross.[21] In 1411 he fought to uphold his wife's claim to the earldom in the inconclusive battle at Harlaw. James I launched an assault on the Highland problem between 1428 and 1431, but retreated and came to an accommodation with MacDonald power.

It was Donald's heir, Alexander, who was eventually confirmed as earl of Ross in 1437 and while he was often at loggerheads with central authority, he lived to become a mainland magnate as well as island prince. Alexander's acquisition of Ross brought the MacDonald possessions right across Scotland to the Moray Firth. Grant's view is that they were now by far the most dominant power in the whole of the Highlands and in terms of area, the greatest landowners in the kingdom.[22] Alexander held public office as Chief Justice north of the Forth in the minority of James II (1437–60). He and his son John, with their followers, spent more and more time in Ross. With hindsight, the acquisition of the earldom of Ross was perhaps over-ambitious. MacDonald power was over-extended and the preoccupation of the lords of the Isles with establishing authority over this earldom probably contributed to their gradual loss of political

The maximum extent of the sea-based lordship of the Isles in the middle of the fifteenth century, when it included the earldom of Ross (McNeill and Nicholson, *Historical Atlas of Scotland*).

influence over the province of Argyll and to deteriorating relations with the Crown. This becomes evident towards the end of the fifteenth century with the growing power of the Campbells.

The fourth and last lord, John II, was involved in several confrontations with the Crown, going as far as signing the secret Treaty of Westminster-Ardtornish in 1462 with Edward IV of England, agreeing the division of Scotland in the event of a successful English invasion.[23] In 1475 James III condemned John for treason and the earldom of Ross, Kintyre and

Knapdale were forfeited, though not the lordship of the Isles. Created a Parliamentary Peer of Scotland in 1476 with the formal title of Lord of the Isles, John II was confirmed in his rule of the lordship, Kintyre being added again to his lands subsequently. But disagreements arose with his illegitimate son Angus over the management of the lordship and the latter's attempts to regain the earlship. A sequence of raids seems finally to have provoked the Crown. In 1493 James IV directly attacked the lordship of the Isles and imposed forfeiture on the lord.[24] John II was deposed as Rì Innse Gall and lost all of his considerable influence and possessions, dying as a Crown pensioner ten years later.[25] In his published collection of Gaelic oral literature reflecting the accomplishments of the lords, the Dean of Lismore summed up the contemporary view:

Nì h-eibhnas gan Chlainn Domnhaill,	It is no joy without Clan Donald,
nì comhnairt bheith 'na n-èagmhais;	it is no strength without them;
an chlann do b'fhearr san gcruinne:	the best race in the round world:
gur dhiobh gach duine cèatach.	to them belongs every goodly man.[26]

Aftermath in the long sixteenth century

For most of the fourteenth and fifteenth centuries the MacDonald lordship of the Isles had been a force for peace rather than a destabilising influence, relative to the century which followed. When the lordship collapsed, a long period of turmoil ensued which endured through the sixteenth century into the early-seventeenth century. The forfeit has been considered to have been 'a political mistake for Scotland' because the MacDonald supremacy was not replaced by an equivalent supremacy for many generations'.[27] After the final forfeiture in 1493 the next 50 years witnessed many serious rebellions by west coast chiefs, aimed at restoring John's heirs. Finlaggan was abandoned about 1494 and Dunyvaig and Castle Gorm were increasingly used.[28] Even after forfeiture in 1493, however, the MacDonalds survived the assaults of both the Crown and its agents for a further 50 years.

Royal minorities in the sixteenth century added to Scotland's internal strife and in Islay from the time of the forfeiture 'there was a bewildering spate of charters, leases, cancellations and regrants of land'.[29] James IV and James V made strenuous efforts to control affairs in the north and west and did not hesitate to play off clan against clan. James IV journeyed to confront the islesmen in person at least five times after 1493. Of the half dozen major risings in the Isles between 1494 and 1545, the fact that the most serious was the last one reiterated the failure, even of James V, to 'daunt' the Isles.

This monumental slab in the Kildalton churchyard dates from the first half of the sixteenth century. Two men in armour wear high pointed bascinets, aventails and knee-length aketons. One carries a sword at his waist while the other bears one on his right shoulder. Below is a galley or birlinn with spread sail (Royal Commission on the Ancient and Historical Monuments of Scotland).

In 1493, King James IV gave charge of Islay to the earl of Argyle's son-in-law, John MacIan of Ardnamurchan, already tenant of Proaig and other lands in Islay, and a MacDonald. A charter of 1494 extended these lands, and by 1506 MacIan held more than three-quarters of the lay lands of Islay, as well as being bailie of all Islay. The Rinns of Islay were disputed by the MacLeans of Mull. John MacIan was by now the most powerful chief in the western isles. He was given the task of undertaking a valuation of Islay, creating bailie courts to replace Celtic law with feudal law and reforming the church. One of his earliest actions was the valuation of all church and lay lands which resulted in the 1507 list of the 'Fermes of Islay'.[30] This has become known as the 'MacIan Extent' and it continued as a basis for valuation and taxation into the nineteenth century. Church lands occupied about one-fifth of the island and were the responsibility of various orders, including Iona Abbey, the Bishop of Isles, local churches, Oronsay Priory and Derry Monastery (Nerabus). Between 1514 and 1516 MacIan took measures for the supply and defence of the castle of Dunyvaig in face of a MacDonald insurrection.[31]

When MacIan was killed in 1519, the earl of Argyll became guardian of his sons and the administration of his Islay estates was entrusted to Sir John Campbell of Calder or Cawdor, brother of the 3rd earl of Argyll, and the first Campbell to bear the Cawdor title, by marriage. By 1520 Alexander MacDonald of Dunyvaig and Sir John Campbell of Cawdor had entered into a bond of gossipry, fostering each other's children.[32]

The MacDonald fortress of Dunyvaig in Lagavulin Bay, from which the seas between the mainland and Ireland could be scanned or crossed.

Cawdor also made bonds with tenants in Islay.[33] He was forced to give up guardianship in 1528 and Alexander MacIan took sasine. The new earl of Argyll fell out of favour in 1531, after which James V acquired most of the lay lands in the island, and the Crown rental of 1541 is still used to establish feu duties. By 1542 Argyll was given a ten-year lease of Islay. The MacDonalds made one last bid to restore their lordship in the rebellion of 1545 led by Donald Dubh, grandson of the last lord of the Isles. But on his death, with no clear successor, the last hope for restoration of the lordship disappeared.

Dunyvaig castle became a direct possession of the Crown but was regranted to James MacDonald of Dunyvaig.[34] He married the earl of Argyll's sister, became closely allied to the Argyll Campbells and when he died in 1565 had received royal charters for widespread possessions covering almost all the lay lands of Islay, much of Kintyre and extensive holdings on Jura, Colonsay, Gigha and Ardnamurchan. James MacDonald's heirs engaged in quarrels with MacLeans over the Rinns of Islay, although in 1585 Angus married Lachlan McLean's sister. The feuds between the MacDonalds and the MacLeans finally reached their culmination in the Battle of Gruinart in 1598; the trouncing of the MacLeans is still a folk memory that comes alive at each retelling.

Campbell tactics
The downfall of the MacDonalds and the loss of their hegemony left a vacuum from which the Campbells were to benefit. Royal patronage and judicious marriage through the fourteenth century had brought them

The first detailed map of Islay, compiled by Timothy Pont in the 1580s, and published in 1654, was not superseded until the following century. Whilst the representation of the eastern part of the island is recognisable in this extract, the Rinns is not only truncated, but includes Finlaggan Castle.

extensive lands; they were the sheriffs in the new sheriffdom of Argyll. From 1383 they were also royal lieutenants of part, and eventually all, of Argyll. By the early-fifteenth century they had developed from local magnates into national ones. They held that position for centuries, but also kept their grip on their local power base, indeed strengthening it as much as possible, knowing that local and national power went together. Colin Campbell was created earl of Argyll in 1457 and went on to become Chancellor of Scotland in 1483.[35] The title, earl of Argyll, itself is important; unlike the other new and honorific peerage titles of the fifteenth century, it was a territorial designation like those of the old provincial earldoms. It probably reflected the Rì Airir Goídel, one of Somerled's titles in the twelfth century, which was used until the early-fourteenth century by his descendants. It has been suggested that when the Campbells became earls of Argyll, they were claiming a place in the Gaelic world roughly equivalent to that of Somerled's main descendants, the MacDonald lords of the Isles.[36]

The tactics of the Campbell family caused a further confusion of aims; cadet MacDonald clans and others turned to them to intercede on their behalf at court.[37] The Campbells found themselves 'colonial governors, torn between going native and representing the values of "civility"'. They found themselves trapped in the same set of pressures as the last lord, fluctuating between their roles as agents of central government and natural spokesmen of the values of the local community. Stewart government exacerbated rather than solved the problems of the Isles; every reign between James II and James VI faced a rebellion in the West.

Clanship and kinship were supremely important in this tempestuous period and the internal decline among the MacDonalds is a more satisfactory explanation of their downfall than theories of Campbell manipulation, although external influence was undoubtedly a factor.[38] By the middle of the sixteenth century Campbell leadership and influence were on the way to filling the vacuum created by the suppression of the lords of the Isles in 1493. This was so at all levels, cultural and intellectual as well as political and military.[39] Through the sixteenth century the Cawdor Campbells had built up extensive holdings in the north of Scotland. From the later-sixteenth century the government of James VI was seeking to impose more political and administrative control on the Highlands, especially after the Union of the Crowns in 1603. The clans were then confronted by the naval and military might of an expansionist British state which could co-ordinate strategy much more effectively against the two Gaelic societies of the Highlands of Scotland and Ireland.[40] The government of James VI and I did not pursue wholesale annexation in the Highlands as in Ireland. Instead, wayward clans had their lands appropriated. The main victims included Clan Donald South and the MacIans of Ardnamurchan. The Statutes of Iona in 1609 were a comprehensive attempt to impose lowland values on Gaeldom.[41] Campbell cohesion was the key to their successful expansion as a clan and it provided a sharp contrast to the internecine quarrels which ruined the southern branch of the MacDonalds.[42] The Campbells continued to encroach and in the early-seventeenth century annexed the southern isles including Islay and only the rump of lordship remained in Crown possession.

That Islay was a prized possession Ortelius had recognised in 1573, referring to it as the greatest and most renowned of the Hebrides, 'fertile for grain and rich in minerals'. Timothy Pont compiled his map during the 1580s. It is among the less accurate of his maps since the overall shapes of the islands with their large sea loch indentations were 'clearly difficult for Pont to determine with precision'.[43] Islay was depicted as a relatively densely settled land. The island, however, was devastated during the MacDonald-MacLean feud of the last quarter of the sixteenth century. Dunyvaig was besieged on at least one occasion after 1586, and James VI finally took the castle into royal custody a decade later. Early in 1606 Angus MacDonald was subjected to an act of caution for the maintenance of a royal garrison in the castle for a period of three months. However, direct royal control was considered to be the best solution and, under threat of siege in 1608, Dunyvaig was handed over to the royal lieutenants, lord Ochiltree and Andrew Knox, Bishop of the Isles. A garrison consisting of a captain and 24 soldiers was housed there.[44]

By the beginning of 1612 Angus MacDonald was in financial difficulties and had to wadset or mortgage his lands in Islay for 6,000 marks to the then Sir John Campbell of Cawdor, though this was later redeemed.[45] Sir Ranald Macdonald, later earl of Antrim, acquired Islay on the death of Angus Macdonald of Dunyvaig in 1614, but he 'had not peaceable possession of it'.[46] 'The Scotch Privy Council . . . turned in search of someone, of power and means sufficient, to reduce the castle and island, and to pay a high rent to the Crown for the possession afterwards. The Thane of Cawdor offered the required rent, and satisfied the Council that he could perform the task of bringing the Islesmen to obedience . . . and set forth on his expedition to win his island kingdom'.[47] In 1614 a Crown charter was conferred on the second Sir John Campbell of Cawdor. The Macdonalds attempted to resist this and there followed much taking and retaking of the castle by various members of the family, especially Sir James Macdonald, Angus' son. In accordance with the terms of the charter issued to Sir John Campbell of Cawdor in November 1614 Dunyvaig Castle became the principal messuage of the newly erected barony of Islay. In October of that year Coll Ciotach, who then held the castle for Sir James, readily ceded possession of it to the earl of Argyll as a punitive royal expedition under the overall command of Sir John Campbell of Cawdor was planned. In order to avoid a protracted siege an additional force of 200 soldiers and heavy ordnance were shipped from Ireland. The besieging force under Sir Oliver Lambert completed their artillery platform at the end of January 1615 and on February 1 the bombardment of the castle began. Despite its nine-metre thick walls, 'three dayes batterye with the ordnance . . . was powerful to ruyne the whole howse'.[48] Sir John Campbell finally took possession of most of the island in 1615.

The house of Dunyvaig had finally fallen in 1615 to Campbell of Cawdor and over 450 years of Macdonald rule appeared to have ended, although feuding continued sporadically through the seventeenth century. The Campbells of Cawdor were especially important agents of the expansion of Argyll hegemony and the acquisition of Islay at the beginning of the seventeenth century thus continued an established policy of expansion on the west coast, though most of the Cawdor Campbells' lands lay on the opposite side of the country.[49]

Notes and references
1 D. H. Caldwell and G. Ewart, 'Finlaggan and the Lordship of the Isles: an Archaeological Approach', *SHR,* 1993, 72, p. 160.
2 Grant, 'Scotland's "Celtic Fringe"' p. 133.
3 Clan Donald, *Ceannas nan Gàidheal,* p. 12.
4 See Lamont, 'Old Land Denominations'.
5 T. M. Devine, *Clanship to Crofters' War,* (Manchester, 1994), p. 4.
6 Caldwell and Ewart, 'Finlaggan', p. 164.
7 After the dissolution of the Lordship, they served the chiefs of Clanranald in South Uist. See D. S. Thomson, *The Companion to Gaelic Scotland,* (Oxford, 1983).
8 J. W. M. Bannerman, *The Beatons,* (Edinburgh, 1986).
9 J. W. M. Bannerman, 'The Lords of the Isles', in J. M. Brown, (ed.), *Scottish Society in the Fifteenth Century,* (London, 1977), p. 231.
10 Ibid., p. 228.
11 RCAHMS, *Argyll Inventory, V,* p. 35.
12 Idem; Munro and Munro, *Acts of the Lords,* p. xxiv.
13 J. W. M. Bannerman, 'Lords of the Isles', p. 238.
14 RCAHMS, *Argyll Inventory, V,* p. 36.
15 See RCAHMS, *Argyll Inventory, V* and Lamont, *Sculptured Stones.*
16 Grant, 'Scotland's "Celtic Fringe"', p. 133.

[17] RCAHMS, *Argyll Inventory*, *V*, p. 36.

[18] Grant, 'Scotland's "Celtic Fringe"', p. 126.

[19] Idem.

[20] Munro and Munro, *Acts of the Lords*, p. 293.

[21] W. D. Lamont, 'The Islay Charter of 1408', *PRIA*, 1960C, pp. 163–87.

[22] Grant, 'Scotland's "Celtic Fringe"', p. 127.

[23] Thomson, *Companion*, pp. 156–7.

[24] Grant, 'Scotland's "Celtic Fringe"', p. 129.

[25] Bannerman, 'Lords of the Isles', p. 213.

[26] From 'Giolla Colum mac an Ollaimh', in the *Book of the Dean of Lismore*, quoted in Osborne and Armstrong, *Scottish Dates*, p. 42. Orthography of old Gaelic is variable.

[27] Lamont, *Sculptured Stones*, pp. 206–7.

[28] Caldwell and Ewart, 'Finlaggan', p. 165.

[29] W. D. Lamont, *The Early History of Islay*, (Glasgow, 1966), p. 30.

[30] Ibid., p. 32.

[31] RCAHMS, *Argyll Inventory*, *V*, p. 274 .

[32] E. J. Cowan, 'Clanship, Kinship and Campbell acquisition of Islay', *SHR*, 1979, 58, p. 135.

[33] Ibid., p. 156.

[34] RCAHMS, *Argyll Inventory*, *V*, p. 274.

[35] Grant, 'Scotland's "Celtic Fringe"', p. 121.

[36] Ibid., p. 122.

[37] M. Lynch, *Scotland: A New History*, (London, 1991), p. 168.

[38] E. J. Cowan, 'Clanship', p. 157.

[39] J. Dawson, 'The Fifth Earl of Argyle', Gaelic Lordship and Political Power in Sixteenth century Scotland', *SHR*, 1988, 67, p. 20.

[40] Devine, *Clanship*, p. 12.

[41] Ibid., p. 13.

[42] Dawson, 'The Fifth Earl of Argyle', pp. 11–12 .

[43] J. Stone, *Illustrated Maps of Scotland*, (London, 1991), pp. 84–5.

[44] RCAHMS, *Argyll Inventory*, *V*, p. 274.

[45] Lamont, *Early History*, p. 49.

[46] Innes, *Thanes of of Cawdor*, p. 228.

[47] Bannerman, 'Lords of the Isles, p. 228.

[48] RCAHMS, *Argyll Inventory*, *V*, p. 274.

[49] Dawson, 'The Fifth Earl of Argyle', pp. 12–13.

CHAPTER 5

The Cawdor Campbells in Islay

In the hundred or so years after 1615 Islay and other isles were at last being integrated into the life of Scotland as a whole. Motivated partly by exaggerated notions of the wealth of the Western Isles and partly by a desire to bring them effectively under the power of the Crown, James VI tackled the problem from a number of different angles.[1] When compared to other parts of the Hebrides, Islay may well have seemed of 'fabulous fertility' even in the seventeenth century.[2] As an economic investment, viewed from Edinburgh or the Moray Firth, it probably seemed much less desirable. To begin with, in any case, its possession was mainly for political rather than economic ends.

In the early-seventeenth century, the first Sir John Campbell of Calder or Cawdor, held 'large and still increasing' lands in Argyll.[3] With subsequent additions, the Cawdor Campbells came to own nearly all of the island.[4] The main exception comprised the old Beaton lands centred on Ballinaby, bought in 1619 by lord Lorne, afterwards marquis of Argyll. In Lamont's view 'if Islay had to go to a Campbell, the Calder family was, on a short term view, the worst possible choice. Sir John was utterly reckless in accumulating land in widely separate parts of the country and it was impossible, quite apart from the financial difficulties in which he had become involved, to rule all these properties efficiently'.[5] The present Cawdor family's view is that 'Cawdor's new acquisition proved to be a millstone which all but drowned him in debt'.[6]

After Sir John's impecunious start in a devastated Islay, there were few times when any of the Cawdor lairds had long periods of effective management in Islay. The Cawdors were frequently handicapped by family and financial difficulties. Although there were only six lairds in 112 years, there were long periods when the lairds were minors and the Campbell lands were then managed or neglected by a succession of legal tutors, commissioners and administrators. Their residence on the island was also only sporadic. Only Sir Hugh, who came of age in 1660 and resigned in 1689, had a long-lasting adult lairdship; it was during that period that some changes were introduced that can still be seen. On a longer view,

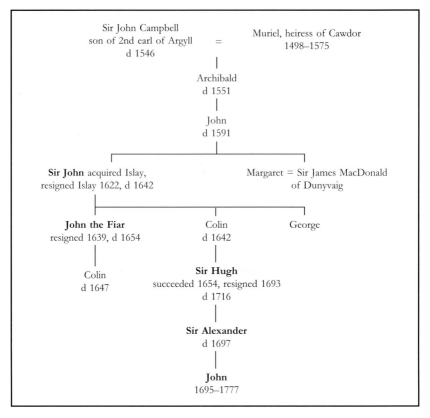

Outline genealogy of the Campbell of Cawdor lairds in Islay (Innes, *Thanes of Cawdor*).

Lamont has argued that the grant of Islay to the Campbells of Cawdor was fortunate and 'was probably even an event of major importance in its economic history'.[7] This view is based on the belief that the more advanced farming methods around the Moray Firth may have been useful examples for the Argyll lands. Despite their difficulties, the new proprietors were pioneers in the development of modern Islay and, among other innovations, Lamont mentioned the mine explorations of 1619 and the droves of cattle through Jura to the mainland and England.

There was also the seventeenth-century background of little change in the agrarian economy of Scotland. With the restricted market for agricultural products at both local and national levels in the first half of the century, much of Scotland experienced low agricultural yields and high fixed rents, the latter paid mainly in grain. Records from eastern Scotland suggest that there were between fifteen and twenty seasons of grain failure between 1600 and 1660 when the price of grain was exceptionally high.[8] More often there were complaints of gluts or low prices. Stock-raising was more important in the west and during the century, farming for external sales increased at the expense of subsistence farming, particularly in the cattle trade. The Union of the Crowns in 1603 led to a growth in droving for the London market such that the black cattle sometimes accounted for more than half the total value of Scottish exports to England, in some years reaching tens of thousands of head.[9]

That affected Islay only gradually and the early difficulties in undertaking agricultural changes on the island in the first part of the seventeenth century are understandable. Capital accumulation was hard and results were small. Most landowners were undermined by their increasing state of indebtedness.[10] The Cawdor Campbells had to meet the expense of winning and keeping the island, fighting Civil War campaigns, paying Crown and feu duties, appearing annually at the Privy Council in Edinburgh, as well as the administrative costs and family expenses included in living in style with other establishments in London, Cawdor and Muckairn in Argyll. There was a growing dependence on lowland merchants for bonded loans and a more commercial approach to the management of lands.[11] Chiefs and their gentry had to extract more income from their lands and their wadsetting or mortgaging increased.[12] Rentals in kind were gradually being converted to a cash value.

Although Innes has gone so far as to aver that 'With the acquisition of Isla began the misfortunes of the family', Sir John's difficulties were not limited to the island, nor was he unusual for the times.[13] Numerous wadsets, or mortgages, covered almost every portion of his northern estates. Creditors of every degree were clamouring for payment, the letters of the Edinburgh doer or agent 'mostly taken up with the pressing demands for money to satisfy them'.[14] The embarrassments on Islay were no less, as is evident in a letter to Sir John Campbell from his agent James Mowatt in March 1618, calling attention to the unpaid Crown Rents for Islay.[15] By that time 'The rebels hes spoilled mightilie the land that the poore tennents is almost undone'.[16] Some time between 1620 and 1622, a meeting of various of Sir John Campbell's friends made several suggestions to help resolve some of his debts; by 1623 these had reached the scale of a proposal to sell Islay or Muckairn.[17] The 'erll of Mar and the Clandonald' had expressed interest and several years later in 1627 there was renewed interest from the earl of Antrim.[18] But Islay remained in Cawdor hands.

Minorities and tutorships
The hands, however were different ones. Islay was given to the son of Sir John Campbell on the occasion of his marriage in 1622. Subsequently

Holdings with two or more tenants named in the rental of 1633 are indicated here (Cawdor Papers).

By 1644 the numbers of holdings with two or more tenants had increased, and the numbers in these multiple tenancies had also tended to increase (Cawdor Papers).

known as John the Fiar, he had been a heretic from his youth and in 1624 and 1625 he received an Irish Franciscan missionary, Patrick Hegarty from Louvain.[19] Two of Cawdor's sons and 50 other relatives were among over 500 islanders converted or baptised by Father Hegarty. There are some signs that John the Fiar also intended to take a more direct interest in Islay's other activities. Indications of this are to be found in the rentals and other documents relating to Islay that survive among the Cawdor records. 'With certain exceptions' there is a general lack of material concerning the agrarian history of Scotland before 1760.[20] The Cawdor papers certainly form one of these exceptions and contribute to what Dodgshon has referred to as a 'fine run of rentals' for Islay in the sixteenth and seventeenth centuries.[21]

Rentals for Islay survive in the Cawdor archives from 1626, though it is not until 1633 that they show in some detail the character of Islay's landholdings and agriculture. By then these holdings were probably held on long leases or tacks by men who were frequently Campbell kinsmen of the laird. Sir John's son explained that when Islay was acquired, it was 'not weel plenished with civile people' and his father had now 'peopled the said ylland with a nomber of his awne freindis'.[22] These tacksmen held the large grazing areas in the quartzitic hills of the north-east of the island as at Killinallan, in the south-east at Proaig, or in the western Rinns at Ardnave. A handful of holdings were leased as multiple tenancies, mainly concentrated in the Oa peninsula, each with up to four or five names responsible for paying the rent. On both tacks and joint farms there may also have been subtenants and possibly other families not responsible for any share of the rent, although they do not appear in the rentals. Cattle formed the major portion of the rental payments in kind; droves of cattle were collected and despatched annually to the south from Islay and Muckairn.[23]

Whatever the precise character of the domestic buildings such as the 'weill furnished duelling place at Mulindrie' described in 1586 by Dean Monroe, the incoming lairds of the early-seventeenth century seem to have brought with them a different attitude towards the style and setting of landowners' residences.[24] John the Fiar declared his intention of replacing Dunyvaig, the only 'sure place of residence' available to his father on acquiring Islay in 1614. Dunyvaig had remained a symbolic focus for local disaffection; this can be measured by the amount of destructive treatment it continued to receive, particularly during the first half of the seventeenth century. What survived the devastating siege of February 1615 and later attacks is thus but a shattered fragment of the one-time fortified residence of the MacDonalds of Dunyvaig. April 1615 also saw the construction of the island castle on Loch Gorm and one at Dùn Athad near the Mull of Oa.

After an unsuccessful assault by a group of local rebels in 1630 the Privy Council agreed in the following year to John Campbell's petition to 'demloisce and cast downe the said hous to the ground, so as it serve not theirefter for a beild, resett, or starting holl to the rebellis of the Ylles', a recommendation that King James VI had previously made to the Fiar's father, Sir John.[25] In 1631 the Fiar talked of building 'a more commodious hous . . . in a more proper pairt of the yle'. The proposal remained unexecuted, and the Cawdors continued to use their Kilchoman residence until the long-cherished proposal to replace the castle as a dwelling was finally effected by Hugh Campbell in 1677.

John the Fiar had one son, Colin, and two daughters.[26] In 1639 he was pronounced insane and the island's management nominally passed to Colin, at that time a minor. The Fiar's brother, Colin Campbell of Kilchoman, became Tutor in charge of the island, but he died in 1642 and another brother, George, took over. Both Colin and George, according to Innes, 'seem to have looked to Islay or their possessions in the far west, as their securest place of dwelling during the troubles of the civil war'.[27] Meanwhile the family continued to have its own troubles. The heir, Colin, died in 1647 whilst a student at Glasgow University and the Fiar himself died in 1654. Islay passed then to Hugh Campbell, son of Colin Campbell of Kilchoman, again a minor.

During these minorities and tutorships, financial difficulties were almost inevitable. The rental for 1644 shows that the proportion of single tacksmen had declined to less than three-fifths and there was a consequent increase in the joint tenancies, and in their numbers of tenants.[28] The Oa again predominated but more multiple tenancies appeared in Kilchoman parish than in 1633. The real significance of these shifts is difficult to determine. Tacksmen as a group tended to inhibit agricultural change and their decline was often a desirable feature of Highland improvement. In mid-seventeenth century Islay many of the Campbell tacksmen had been 'planted' on Islay and should have brought to it their experience of farming in the better lands of the north-east of Scotland. More obvious as an indication of financial difficulty is the low rental which the Campbell family obtained from their lands in Islay and Muckairn. Innes averred that by the middle of the seventeenth century 'the troubles of the time affected the Highland and Island territories, even more than the rest of Scotland'.[29] Whereas the usual rent previously derived by Cawdor each year from Islay and Muckairn was about £20,000 to £22,000, in 1651 only one-tenth was collected, followed by one-third in 1652.

Because of Hugh Campbell's minority, his uncle George continued to act as Tutor, to be followed by another uncle, James of Kilbrandan. Hugh was also a student of the University of Glasgow and as Innes put it:

> In this generation we arrive, as it were, by one step from a state of society and feeling which we cannot rightly appreciate, so different does it seem from ours; and find ourselves among the habits, manners, feelings and motives – even the language of our own time. To this effect the great Civil War serves as the line of demarcation between the old world and the new.[30]

Hugh came of age and was knighted in the Restoration year of 1660 and two years later married Lady Henrietta Stewart, sister of the 3rd earl of Moray. He served in several Parliaments as Member for the shire of Nairn and lived a parliamentarian's life in Edinburgh during part of the year, as well as embarking on major building work at Cawdor Castle. But Sir Hugh took an active interest in country occupations. In 1677, for example, he set down instructions concerning a visit to Islay.[31] He was concerned with stock and other estate affairs and his sporting interests were apparent in his instructions concerning deer, rabbits and blackcock. It was this visit that led to the construction of a new house at Lag Buidhe, 'a beautiful stretch of velvety sward at the head of Lochindaal, the first portion of what is now called Islay House'.[32] Sir Hugh ordered that lime, timber and all materials were to be got on the spot, but he proposed to take skilled masons to the island.

After the Restoration the Scots became interested in escaping agricultural stagnation. Acts of the Scottish Parliament to encourage better husbandry were numerous after 1660, culminating in the well-known enabling act of 1695 which made it relatively easy for individual landowners to divide commons and to sort out land lying in runrig for the purpose of enclosure. In the last decade of the century too, the first published Scottish tracts on the improvement of farming methods appeared. Yet the fundamental changes in agriculture that might have taken advantage of this permissive legislation and technical advice were in fact delayed for many years, due to frequent low prices and to continuing successive gluts and famines. The later Cawdors were also interested in the development of salt pans at Ardlarach and in lead-mining, bringing miners in from England.[33]

Sir Hugh Campbell and his son Alexander were among the few seventeenth-century landlords in the Western Isles who took a keen interest in the general improvement of their island properties and were prepared to invest heavily in it themselves, if necessary.[34] The 'once troublesome island' gradually became less of a burden after Sir Hugh sent the 'tough

1737 | 1677 | 1737 | 1760 | 1841/2

The earliest part of Islay House, to the left of centre, was started by imported masons around 1677 for Sir Hugh Campbell of Cawdor. 'Great' Daniel Campbell of Shawfield added the flanking wings with crow-stepped gables. The western tower, here hidden, belongs to Daniel the Younger's time, along with the eastern stair-tower, itself later replaced. In the 1840s Walter Frederick Campbell asked William Playfair to design 'offices' for Islay House. Detailed architectural drawings, including designs of monograms intertwining his initials with those of his second wife, Catherine I. Coles, are in the Library of the University of Edinburgh. This Victorian addition was later partially remodelled and screened by a mock-Georgian wing designed by Detmar Blow (MacNeill, *New Guide*).

and implacable' Sir Duncan Campbell of Ardnamurchan to sort things out and send 'huge droves of oxen, shod with horse-shoes' annually to the Falkirk Tryst.[35] In 1677 Sir Hugh had asked one of his agents to make a list of his debts since 'I purpose to tak all the readiest wayes to clear my affairis. I find my selff infirm' and he wanted to arrange his children's affairs.[36] There were further negotiations about the lead mines in Islay at the same time. The main contribution made to the landscape of today by Sir Hugh and his successor is in Islay House. On marriage in 1689 his eldest son, Alexander, took over the estates, and despite his infirmities, Sir Hugh survived until 1716.

Further difficulties

Probably the most important development in Islay in the time of Sir Alexander Campbell was the gradual evolution of the 'town' of Killarow at the head of Loch Indaal to become the administrative and commercial centre of the island.[37] In 1693 an Act of the Scottish Parliament conferred the right to hold free fairs twice annually, for two days each in July and in August, and a general weekly market on Thursdays. The same year, Sir

Alexander became a member of the Scottish Parliament for Nairnshire, taking the place of his infirm father. In 1689 he had married Elizabeth, only daughter of Sir John Lort and co-heir with her brother of Stackpole Court in Pembrokeshire. They spent most of their time in London and Wales and left the Nairnshire and Argyllshire properties in the hands of their agents. Very little else is known of Sir Alexander's period in Islay except that financial difficulties continued and were not solved by raised rents, about which there was much complaint. When he died in 1697, his heir and second son John was only two years of age, and the estate was probably run by John's uncle, Archibald Campbell of Clunes and of Kilchoman. Between 1697 and 1716 when John came of age, matters deteriorated still further, with famines frequent in the island and on the mainland, Scotland undergoing hard times. There were, however, a few improvements in Islay during this period. By 1722 it was possible to say that 'Killchomman is a choice large good possession, having many parks and enclosures in it . . . a large malt kilne and change house and a good corne mylne upon it and many other improvements'.[38]

The Anderson Papers in the National Library of Scotland include many letters concerning the management of the Islay estate carried out for the later Cawdor Campbells by James Anderson, W.S., his son Patrick and his son-in-law John Allan, sometimes referred to as the bailie [local magistrate] of Islay.[39] By the second decade of the eighteenth century, many of these letters were concerned with the difficulties of arrears of rents. In 1714–15 Patrick Anderson was writing to his father that as Mr Campbell had 'lodged the sole power in your hands it will make them repent they have been so backward and obstinat and I hope it will cause them pay their rents and arrears better'. In February 1715 James Anderson reported that Mr Campbell was 'mightily displeased at their backwardness', but by May 1716 he was telling his son 'I approve of what you have done in the Sett and hope you have finished it to contentment. When that is done I hope money will be got in & a good Drove sent out'. By the following month he was even more approving. 'Considering the backwardness of people and the artful ways of the Chamberlains I think strange you have gott so much done & am persuaded if you had not been there I had gott nothing'. He next made further mention of weak tenants, the loss of income from the 1714 rent and the 1715 one only partly lifted. Patrick wrote to his father 'I'll take care rent for 1714 be made up by the Drove & for 1715. You won't lose'.

Despite this optimism, it is clear that when John Campbell succeeded in 1716 it was to a heavily-burdened property. The Islay rent was then equivalent to £15,978 11s, Scots (about £1,332 Sterling). But arrears preceding 1714 had amounted to £4,875 18s. 8d. Scots, (£406.35) and those that accrued between 1714 and 1720 were £5,519 15s. 8d. Scots (£460) making a total of £10,395 14s. 4d. (£866.35). The Andersons' difficulties continued; in July 1716, in the aftermath of the Jacobite rebellion, Patrick Anderson was writing to his father:

> Yesterday the Act of Parliament for the better securing the peace of the Highlands was sent here by the Sheriff and published which has perfectly enraged the people here who would as soon part with their wives and children as with their arms but I hope it will be a means of humbling them . . . weather cold and wett and I'm perfectly starved for want of Tea.

By December of that year John Allan was reporting to Patrick Anderson that he had 'sett Killerow and Kilhoman paroches; the crops had been gathered'. The year 1717, however, was worse. There were many troubles with tacksmen and with the traik or cattle plague: 1717 became 'the worse paid rent that has been in Islay these 100 years'. Patrick Anderson described the conditions in May 1717, when he wrote to his father about the dismal conditions, 'these that were rich and had great flocks having lost more than the half and the small tenants are next to beggary'. Tenants had fed their meal to cattle that subsequently died and had none left to sow. They had no milk if they sold their dairy cows to buy 'meall in order to preserve their families from starving. Of the gentlemen, 'the Traik fell heaviest upon Archie and Lauchlane the latter, who had absolutely the best and the greatest stock in Isla, having lost both what he had in Ardneave and Kentra'. He thought his father would scarcely believe him when he wrote that 'I cannot gett so much butterr and milk in this place as serves my tea and the muttons are not worth the eating and it's with difficulty we can gett as much bread as serves us. I would realy thought it impossible Isla could have been brought to such a low pass'.

Further descriptions included the observation of a higher than usual death rate which he attributed to the 'stench of the dead carcasses which the fields are overspread with'. After discussing how many of the tenants had left their lands altogether, Patrick tried to forecast that even when he did achieve a very difficult sett, the loss might be 'upwards of £6,000 sterling'. In a reply dated 20 June 1717, his father showed suitable distress at the state of Islay and her people; more practically he advised Patrick to send a boat to Ireland for wheat or bread. Two years later, things were not much better. There was 'not one cow out of Isla . . . not 30 were droveable . . . there is no money in this countrey just now'. In July 1722 the same phrase was being reiterated, though an addendum said 'the only fonds they have is Cattle which do not make money till the latter end of the next month that the trist holds at Falkirk'. There were complaints on Islay at that time of tenants having to pay raised rents, with the alternative of being removed.

Apart from these local difficulties the writing was on the wall elsewhere for young John Campbell. He was apparently in financial embarrassment outside Islay, for it was probably James Anderson who wrote to him in 1720 suggesting the sale of Muckairn to 'clear this Woman' – a reference to another subject![40] This advice was probably not taken much to heart and in the summer of 1720 John Campbell was again being admonished by James Anderson, but John Campbell was heedless; next he was writing to Anderson that he had a 'most pressing & unforeseen occasion to pay £300 ster: into the Exchequer tomorrow morning by eight a clock; I earnestly desire you if . . . possible to let me have it'.

Negotiations with the more experienced Shawfield
On 8 December 1721, John Campbell of Cawdor's doer again wrote a Memorial for his consideration in which he talked of pressing debts, including a particularly large one to a Mr Brodie, and made further suggestions about raising loans or selling off lands in Argyll (but not in Islay) and in the North of Scotland.[41] The Memorial was clearly designed, also, to preserve the *amour-propre* of a difficult man. 'Nor can a sale be anyways dishonourable to him, being payment of the debts contracted by Sir Hugh and Sir Alexander . . . The sooner Mr Campbell Enters upon measures for settling matters with his Creditors, it's the better'.

By 1723 Daniel Campbell of Shawfield had acquired a wadset of Islay for £6,000 and in 1726 he purchased the right of reversion for a further £6,000.[42] These financial transactions were neither so prosaic nor straightforward as they appear at first sight. In November 1772, John Campbell had entered into some form of financial negotiation with Daniel Campbell of Shawfield, from whom he expected to receive 'the £1,500 which your obliging care has furnished me with. You may be perfectly easy about the people from Islay and Jura. Having gone so far with you, I shall, you may be assured, think myself bound in honour not to make any bargain . . . till you and I meet . . . Jura is the door to Islay and [I] shall reserve it accordingly'.[43]

A further letter from Cawdor to Shawfield on 7 March 1723, took the proposition further, with a postscript admitting that 'for one who knows so little of busyness as I it is better to receive than to make proposals, but I do assure you, Sir, that upon equall terms I had rather let it to you than to any other'. It is fascinating to conjecture a reconstruction of what must have happened between March 7 and April 9 in 1723. On the latter date, three advocates in Edinburgh wrote to John Campbell, noting his letters of March 26 and 29 to Mr Archibald Campbell W.S., which had asked him to raise from the bank, or through wadsets, 'The sum of £1,800 sterling to pay Shawfield punctually by the 5th May next and advising that you have received his proposals for a Leas of Isla'.[44] The advocates emphasised that there seemed no chance of raising a loan from the banks in Edinburgh unless the estate was clear of all debts. They also offered to act for Campbell in regard to the Shawfield lease. To gain time they suggested that Campbell of Cawdor should cover himself in the short term by raising the £1,800 on his own credit in London. In three months or so other arrangements could be made to pay this money back. The advocates strongly encouraged Cawdor to lease Islay only for one year at a time until a more stable solution to his affairs could be found. Unfortunately Campbell's actions seem to have ignored or overtaken such advice. He advised them on April 20 that he had concluded a bargain with Shawfield for a lease of his Islay lands for 21 years at £500 yearly, in return for Shawfield's advancement of the increased figure of £6,000, with Shawfield taking interest 'out of the yearly duty'.

On April 30, after the advocates had indeed tried to raise some money by wadsetting lands elsewhere, somewhat miffed about not being consulted, they worded two very strong paragraphs to the hapless young man:

> You are certainly better acquainted with the gros of your affairs . . . than we can be presumed to be, and therefore however disadvantagious this bargain . . . may appear to us, We must submitt to what you have been pleased to determine in your own affairs. This far only we expect that before you finish the agreement in writing, which hitherto you say is only verball, you'll please to send to us a further particular of the articles, such as Shawfields terme of entry to the Estate, terme of payt of the duty and when interest is to commence upon the £6,000, when it is to be repaid him . . . in parcells or all at one terme, and with any other articles and powers in favour of Shawfield.
>
> It would likewise tend to the management of your affairs with greater advantage That we were apprys'd of the time when the money to be advanced by Shawfield, was to be paid, and to what use you design it should be applyed.[45]

It was, however, already too late to influence events; added to this letter was a postscript indicating that they had now learned that an agreement in writing had been completed with Shawfield, 'so we can say no further to it, but only desire you'd send us the original agreet. or a literal copie of it'. Further advice from Mr Archibald Campbell W.S. was contained in a letter from Edinburgh on 15 June 1723, in which Cawdor was told that his commissioners thought that the articles of agreement 'are most disadvantagious and destructive, and that you have been so greatly impos'd upon'. They suggested that he make a soft approach to Shawfield to try to reverse the process of law, otherwise Campbell of Shawfield could easily and rapidly reimburse his outlay.

So it appears that without recourse to his lawyers at all, young John Campbell of Cawdor, desperate for ready cash and, unable to raise any in London, must have met Daniel Campbell of Shawfield there. With the advantage of age and certainly with more business experience, the older Campbell managed a satisfactory business deal for himself. A wadset of Islay from John Campbell to Shawfield dated 3 August and 7 October, 1723, mentioned an 'agreement entered into betwixt the said John and Daniel Campbells of the date at London the Twenty second day of Aprile last' in which Daniel Campbell had advanced and paid John Campbell £6,000 (and £500 per annum); and John Campbell of Cawdor bound himself to repay the said sum, with interest. For Shawfield's security he agreed to deliver a wadset to all his lands for 21 years or longer until the £6,000 was repaid.[46] Shawfield was also granted the rights to redeem other wadsets granted in the past on Cawdor property in Islay and Jura.

Three years later the Islay arrangement had changed in character from lease to outright sale. The terms were clear and wholly to the advantage of Daniel Campbell of Shawfield:

> The disposition follows on a contract of wadsett, dated 3rd August and 7th October 1723, whereby the said John sold for £6,000, with power of redemption, all and whole of his lands and estate, "lying within the islands of Islay . . . as in the 1614 charter, with the addition of Knockransaill, Ardaright, Ardalisyn, and Ardagarie and Jura." The said Daniel became bound to pay £6,000, over and above the previous £6,000, as the price of the right of reversion of the said lands, and John thereby renounced the right of redemption and the feu-duty of £200.[47]

John Campbell retained his Cawdor and Pembroke lands and went on to enjoy a full parliamentary career before dying in 1777 at Bath.[48] Almost the whole of Islay and part of Jura were acquired by Daniel Campbell for not much more than £12,000.[49]

Selling the island may have been the best thing that Joyless John or any of the Campbells of Cawdor ever did for Islay.[50] They had owned the island during a period when even the most competent landlord would have found it difficult to make Islay prosper. The Campbells of Shawfield were very different and, in Lamont's words, 'There is a sense in which the history of Islay as we know it today begins with the purchase of the island by the Campbells of Shawfield in 1726'.[51]

Notes and references

[1]   F. J. Shaw, *The Northern and Western Islands of Scotland: their Economy and Society in the Seventeenth Century*, (Edinburgh, 1980), p. 4.

[2]   Innes, *Thanes of Cawdor*, p. 226.

[3]   Ibid., p. xxiii.

[4]   Smith, *Book of Islay*, pp. 353ff and p. 380; Lamont, *Early History*, p. 60.

[5]   Lamont, *Early History*, p. 60.

[6]   *Cawdor Castle Guide*, (Cawdor, n.d.), p. 27.

[7]   Lamont, *Early History*, p. 65.

[8]   T. C. Smout and A. Fenton, 'Scottish Agriculture before the Improvers — an Exploration', *AHR*, 1965, 13, pp. 75–93.

[9]   Devine, *Clanship*, p. 15.

[10] Shaw, *Northern and Western Islands*, p. 43.

[11] Devine, *Clanship*, p. 15.

[12] Shaw, *Northern and Western Islands*, p. 43.

[13] Innes, *Thanes of Cawdor*, p. xxvii; F. J. Shaw, 'Landownership in the Western Isles in the Seventeenth Century', *SHR*, 1977, 56, p. 45.

[14] Ibid., p. 253.

[15] Innes, *Thanes of of Cawdor*, p. 245.

[16] Smith, *Book of Islay*, p. 343.

[17] Ibid., p. 370.

[18] Ibid., p. 378.

[19] C. Giblin (ed.), *Irish Franciscan Mission to Scotland 1619–1646*, (Dublin, 1964), p. 79.

[20] G. Donaldson, 'Sources for Scottish Agrarian History before the Eighteenth Century', *AHR*, 1960, 8, p. 87.

[21] R. Dodgshon, 'Mediaeval Settlement and Colonisation', in M. L. Parry and T. R. Slater (eds.), *The Making of the Scottish Countryside*, (London, 1980), p. 61.

[22] Innes, *Thanes of Cawdor*, pp. 273-4.

[23] Ibid., p. 278.

[24] RCAHMS, *Argyll Inventory*, *V*, p. 38.

[25] Ibid., p. 274.

[26] J. Foster, *Members of Parliament, Scotland, including the Minor Barons, the Commissioners for the Shires, and the Commissioners for the Burghs, 1357–1882, on the basis of the Parliamentary Return 1880, with genealogical and biographical notices*, (London, 1882), p. 53.

[27] Innes, *Thanes of Cawdor*, p. xxxi.

[28] CP, Bundle 655.

[29] Innes, *Thanes of Cawdor*, p. 303.

[30] Ibid., p. xxxii.

[31] Ibid., p. xxxiii and p. 334.

[32] MacNeill, *New Guide*, p. 67.

[33] Shaw, *Northern and Western Islands*, pp. 160–1.

[34] Idem.

[35] *Cawdor Castle Guide*, p. 28.

[36] Innes, *Thanes of Cawdor*, p. 338.

[37] Lamont, *Early History*, p. 67.

[38] Smith, *Book of Islay*, p. 541.

[39] James Anderson Papers, NLS. The papers referring to Islay are catalogued under Advocates MSS. 29.1.2.

[40] Advocates MSS., 29.1.2. (V).

[41] CP, Bundle 654.

[42] Lamont, *Early History*, p. 68.

[43] Smith, *Book of Islay*, pp. 424-26.

[44] CP, Bundle 657.

[45] Idem.

[46] CP, Bundle 654.

[47] Smith, *Book of Islay*, p. 429.

[48] Burke's *Peerage, Baronetage and Knightage*, (London, 1967), p. 476.

[49] This excluded Sunderland and Ballinaby farms. See Macdonald, *General View*, p. 615.

[50] *Cawdor Castle Guide*, p. 28.

[51] Lamont, *Early History*, Preface.

Shawfield House, Trongate, in Glasgow (Mitchell Library, City of Glasgow).

Allan Ramsay's portrait of
'Great' Daniel Campbell of
Shawfield and Islay, who was
'a very canny Scot. By his
indomitable energy and
general shrewdness . . . he . . .
amassed a large fortune'
(Russell, 'A Canny Scot').

CHAPTER 6

Hints of change: the first Shawfield Campbell

When Daniel Campbell of Shawfield came to Islay in the third decade of the eighteenth century, the landscape that he saw was one that had changed only slowly through the preceding centuries. He, and particularly his successors, introduced changes in the economy which profoundly affected the appearance of the island and the lives of those who lived there. These alterations did not take place all at once. Although the landscape changes were ultimately quite widespread, the new methods and ideas that constituted the agrarian revolution were initiated gradually, and at different times in different parts of Islay. The old patterns and methods continued to exist alongside the new throughout the rest of the eighteenth century and well into the nineteenth.

The first Daniel Campbell of Shawfield and Islay was born about 1670, the second son of Walter Campbell, Captain of Skipness in Argyll; his mother had Islay connections.[1] In 1692, in his early twenties, he went to New England and became a shipowner and merchant, defying the English ban on Scottish transatlantic trade. On his return to Scotland he built up an exporting business with Sweden, exchanging American tobacco for iron ore. He also became involved in the slave trade, with the ill-fated adventure to establish a Scottish colony at Darien, on the isthmus of Panama, became a collector of Customs at the new Port Glasgow and was one of the early Scottish financiers. By his first marriage to Margaret Leckie of Newlands he had three sons (all of whom predeceased him) and three daughters. In 1702, when just over thirty, he was elected to the Scottish Parliament as the Member for Inveraray Burgh in Argyll. Five years later, he was one of the Commissioners in that Parliament at the time of its dissolution. His vote was one of those in favour of the 1707 Act of Union and he continued to sit as the Member for Inveraray in the united Parliament. He had purchased the Lanarkshire estate of Shawfield, on the banks of the Clyde between Glasgow and Rutherglen. Shawfield House, his fine town house in spacious grounds on the north side of the Trongate facing Stockwell Street, was the first commission for Colen Campbell, the nephew of Sir Hugh Campbell of Cawdor, and was finished

	Laird in Islay	Succeeded by
'Great' Daniel (1670–1753)	1726–1753, aged 56 to 83	Grandson
Daniel the Younger (1753–77)	1753–1777, aged 16 to 40	Brother
Walter (1741–1816)	1777–1816, aged 36 to 75	Grandson
Walter Frederick (1798–1855)	1816–1848, aged 18 to 50	Sequestrated

Campbell of Shawfield Lairds in Islay, 1753–1848.

by 1711. In the following year Daniel Campbell also became the owner of Woodhall estate in Lanarkshire.[2]

Widowed in 1711, he married again three years later; his second wife was Lady Katherine Erskine, daughter of Henry, 3rd Lord Cardross and widow of Sir William Denholme. They had one daughter, Katherine. As member for the Glasgow Burghs in the Union Parliament from 1716 to 1734 and Deputy Lieutenant of Lanarkshire, he 'raised himself to . . . great importance, not only in Glasgow . . . but also in Westminster, where he had considerable influence', according to one of his descendants.[3] A Whig and great personal friend of Sir Robert Walpole, he was called 'Great Daniel' partly from his stature and build, partly from the position he achieved. His biographical vignette summarised his abilities by saying that he 'far surpassed all his brothers in business capacity, and proved himself a very canny Scot. By his indomitable energy and general shrewdness, combined . . . with a certain amount of what his countrymen call "pawkiness", he, from a very small beginning, amassed a large fortune', with which he began to acquire his estates.

In 1725 Shawfield House was severely damaged by a mob in reprisal for Campbell's unpopular political action in voting for the 1725 Malt Tax, which Scotland had been spared since the Union of 1707. He was not in residence and had removed valuables beforehand, even requesting General Wade's help in anticipation of trouble. The £9,000 he received in compensation from Glasgow may have helped him to pay for the purchase of Islay and part of Jura. At the time he acquired Islay, Daniel Campbell was already 55 years of age. He remained a Member of Parliament for almost another decade, entailing considerable travelling between London, Glasgow, Woodhall and Islay, at a time when such journeys were measured in days. Even so, during almost three decades from the purchase of Islay until his death in 1753 he was probably much less of an absentee landlord on Islay than his Cawdor Campbell predecessors. His large family was probably one reason for adding the flanking wings and a western part to Islay House in 1731.

N

1733
Number of tenants
• 3–4
● 5–9

10 km

In 1733, just after 'Great' Daniel Campbell of Shawfield acquired Islay, much of the island was still in the hands of the tacksmen. Tenancies with more than two tenants responsible for paying the rent were concentrated in 'The Glen' and in the Oa (Smith, *Book of Islay*).

Tacksmen and joint farmers

When Daniel Campbell came to Islay in the 1720s times had been hard. Much of the land had been mortgaged to kinsmen of the Cawdor Campbells, often distinguished from one another in rentals as Dallas, Calderach and so on, according to where they came from. The rental for 1733 in the *Book of Islay* shows that, in general, the large grazing lands were held by tacksmen in the north-east, the south-east and in the Rinns, whereas joint farmers were found on the mixed grain and stock holdings in more accessible and more productive areas along river valleys and on well-drained beach deposits.[4] There may have been tacksmen who were interested in farming for its own sake and there were tacks in Islay that had arable land of consequence. Some of these were enclosed and improved quite early, as shown in the mid-eighteenth century by Stephen MacDougall's maps of Coul, Cladavill and others.[5] But in most of the tacks, grazing areas were more extensive than arable land.

It is perhaps not surprising that tacksmen were among the first to be affected by the change in ownership. The 1730s saw the start of an

Tacksmen on Islay built conspicuous houses, such as this Georgian one at Ardnave.

emigration of some of the disaffected tacksmen from Islay. The colony of New York had advertised for Protestant settlers from Europe, with the promise of improved land for each family. Captain Lauchlin Campbell of Islay visited the colony in 1737 and returned there the following year with his own and thirty other families. A further 40 families emigrated in 1739 and still more in 1740.[6] In all, he encouraged 423 people to move there from Islay, many at their own expense. The venture was not a great success for Captain Campbell, although he was able to purchase a modest tract of land in southern Ulster, afterwards Orange County, N.Y., and erected a dwelling for himself and his family, calling it Campbell Hall. There he remained, except for a return to Scotland to fight for the Hanoverians in the 1745 rebellion. While some eventually settled in Washington County, others went their own ways, some joining North Carolina pioneers. Subsequent rentals of the century recorded a gradual decline in the number of tacksmen and their tacks became single farms or joint farms.

Apart from these large tacks or single farms, the other areas of the island were farmed communally by joint tenants. Some of these had subtenants and there were probably also some cottars or squatters who had no formal share in the land and did not pay rent. The tenants of the joint farms seldom had equal shares of either rent due, or of the shares or soum of grazing capacity or of arable land. The rental for 1733, for instance, shows that Keppolsmore, with eight tenants each holding a six-pennyland directly from the landlord was one of the few exceptions.[7]

Even there, of course, these equal shares may hide the existence of subtenants with smaller subdivisions of the six-pennylands. Much more characteristic was a joint township like Ballychatrican in the Oa, where two tenants shared an eight-pennyland, two shared a four-pennyland and five each had a four-pennyland. The rent was thus payable jointly by nine tenants, some of whom may in turn have obtained part of their rent from subtenants.

As elsewhere in the Highlands and Islands, it was not until surveyors were employed by the lairds during and after the eighteenth century that landholdings were reckoned for rental purposes in terms of area rather than by value, i.e. their capacity to support stock and to produce crops. Long after such surveys were available, the old denominations or assessments of worth sometimes continued to be used in Islay, as shown in documents connected with the sale of parts of the island even in the late-nineteenth century. From the time of the colonisation of Islay from Ireland in the sixth century until the end of the Norse connection in the Western Isles in 1266, the chief land denominations in Islay appear to have been the davoch, valued at ten marks and the quarter at two and a half marks.[8] After 1266 an assessment subsequently known as the Old Extent was imposed by King Alexander III, replacing the earlier denominations with poundlands, marklands, ten-shillinglands and cowlands. With the forfeiture of the Lordship of the Isles to the Scottish Crown in 1493, yet another system of land valuation was attempted. The 'bailie' of Islay, MacIan of Ardnamurchan, was ordered by the Crown to bring the island into line with what was then the prevailing national system of quarterlands valued at 33s. 4d. Scots. This reconciliation was only partially accomplished in Islay and the local system of denominations belonging to the Old Extent continued side by side with the newer MacIan denominations right up to the early-nineteenth century. For example, the 1733 rental contains remnants of the Old Extent system, although the majority of holdings were reckoned for rental purposes under the MacIan system of quarterlands, and eighths. The picture was still further complicated by the conversion of the Scots reckoning of the MacIan system into sterling equivalents; the latter became known in Islay as the False MacIan Extent.

Early-eighteenth century farming
The way that the land of Islay was worked in the early-eighteenth century must for the most part be deduced from accounts written by visitors later in the century.[9] Although the term 'openfield agriculture' is the subject of some controversy, it is an acceptable description of the system in Islay, as

elsewhere in Scotland.[10] The eighteenth-century leases and tacks indicate that the land of the island was organised into wintertown, common pasture, muir and shielings or summer grazings. The term 'infield', frequently met with elsewhere and indicating the area of best soil that was cultivated regularly, was not often used in connection with Islay. It may in fact have been part of the wintertown, the latter phrase perhaps either an indication that the stock grazed the stubble in winter or a direct translation from the Gaelic 'baile-geamhraidh'. It has also been suggested that the term 'wintertown' may describe the township settlement from which people removed in summer to shielings.[11] Another term that only infrequently occurs in Islay manuscripts is 'outfield'; elsewhere this indicates land of lower productivity that is normally grazed and cropped only periodically. It is possible that the pressure of population in eighteenth century Islay was not sufficient to require such periodic cultivation of the grazing area.

MacDougall's surviving estate maps of Islay between 1749 and 1751, like those of Gemmill in the early decades of the nineteenth century, only occasionally show a well-marked division into infield and outfield.[12] Instead, as in the township of Ballichlavan, the arable and pasture parts of each holding are shown as intermingled in the area near the settlement, depending on the topography, rocky outcrops and soils. The manner in which the openfield was cultivated in Islay up to the mid-nineteenth century is described in the *New Statistical Account* of the 1840s.[13] Mention is made several times in other sources of periodic reallocation of each tenant's strips in the openfield or commonfield, with the field itself probably enclosed by a dyke of turf or stone.

Apart from these areas of enclosed and improved land, each township possessed communal grazing on the muirs and hills, perhaps with temporary shielings on summer pastures. The small area of improved land around the house of the township's herdsman on the common muir of Ballichlavan is shown in Gemmill's plan. The number of stock that each of the joint tenants could graze on the muir was defined by his share in the rent and was called his soum. Earlier reference to shielings in Islay is found only in the rental of 1722, where Toradill's 'shielding in the muir' is listed.[14] Other indications can be found in the Gaelic *airidh* and its variants in the original namebooks of the Ordnance Survey and on the maps and plans from which these were compiled in the later-nineteenth century.[15] Their location can nowadays also be identified on air photographs and through field investigation. They were an important supplement to the grazing capacity of townships that depended on the sale of cattle for monetary income, but the use of common grazings and shielings in Islay appears to have ceased almost entirely in the nineteenth century.

In the 1770s Thomas Pennant reported that Joseph Banks had allowed his artist, Moses Griffith, 'to copy as many of the beautiful drawings in his collection, as would be of use' for Pennant's *Tour*. This one depicts 'sheelins' or temporary dwellings used after transhumance to summer pastures in Jura. Cheese from the cows' milk matured in baskets (Pennant, *Tour*). Ground plans of shielings in Islay conform to the same pattern (RCAHMS, *Argyll Inventory, V*).

The Welshman, Thomas Pennant, commented on the shielings in Islay and Jura which formed a prominent feature of the landscape. His account of one particular group is probably the best eye-witness account of transhumance in the Hebrides during the mid-eighteenth century. A drawing of shielings in Jura complemented Pennant's description:

> . . . a bank covered with sheelins, the habitations of some peasants who attended the herds of milch cows. These formed a grotesque groupe; some were oblong, many conic, and so low that entrance is forbidden, without creeping through the little opening, which has no other door than a faggot of birch twigs . . . covered with sods; the furniture a bed of heath, placed on a bank of sod, and above, certain pendent shelves made of basket-work to hold the cheese, the produce of the summer.[16]

Details of the productive capacity of the early-eighteenth century tacks and joint farms are given in the *Book of Islay*. The grazing capacity and the amount of grain sown on each 'town' or 'land' were supplemented by remarks on the nature of each holding and its suitability for grazing and crops. Some of the figures for the soum or grazing capacity and similar crop data were omitted for certain towns or lands in the Rinns not held by the Campbells. The remoter and hillier parts of the island in the north-east and south-east were mainly used for grazing. Adjacent to these areas were holdings that generally had more land capable of producing crops for human and animal consumption. Grain cultivation was more important than stock grazing in the larger river valleys, especially the Sorn and on the better-drained parts of the raised beaches around Loch Indaal.

The total soum for Islay for 1722, excluding much of the Rinns, amounted to 6,645 cows and 'the product thereof yearly, such as thair two year old stirks and calfs with the cows'.[17] A rider was added to the effect that 'with each cow there are two sheep with their year olds and lambs to be grassed. As for extent ther, a toun is allowed to have fourtie cows: they are also there allowed to have eightie sheep with there product'. The number of horses or mares each land was allowed to graze, together with 'thair product also of two year olds and foals', amounted to 2,232, again with the Rinns excluded. Substitutions in the soums were permitted; usually two cows could be substituted for a horse and five or six sheep for a cow. Sheep were specifically mentioned only on three lands in Islay in the 1722 rental: Taycarmagan [sic], Ballevicar and on the Losset lands in the north-east. At that time, sheep were less important than cattle for rearing and export; their main use was probably to meet local needs for mutton and wool.

In 1722, again excepting the same townships, the total soum for 'corn' (Scots oats) amounted to 5,428 bolls, a boll being the size of container used in a particular area at a given time. The size of a boll varied from crop to crop, area to area and period to period. The rental mentions that this corn soum was sometimes exceeded on the island and this was also true of barley, for which the total soum was 798 bolls. Barley accounted for only about one-eighth of the cereal crops in the soum, which seems a low proportion on an island that was presumably already distilling whisky 'Pees, ry, pottatoes, as they [sic] think fit, or thair convenience can allow them' were also mentioned as additional crops. Interesting remarks on the 'present capabilities' were given for each of the holdings with a few hints at potential capability. These included such phrases as 'Kilcherrans [Kilchiaran] a very good possession, alike for sowing and holding', 'Leack, Sannaigbeig, Grannard and Caspellen . . . the best land in the wholl countrie', 'Daill, Octonafreitch, Kilbrannan, & Surn a good wadset . . . the most of it lying exposed for good improvement'.

The rental of 1722 is some indication of the worth of the island that Campbell of Shawfield got for his £12,000; in 1722 the total rental was about £15,980 Scots, equivalent to about £1,332 sterling. Amortised at even ten per cent for ten years, he could easily have paid off the £12,000 and by 1733 the rental had gone up. It must, however, be remembered that the lands were not free of encumbrances and by the middle of the century many Islay lands were still wadset to various Campbells, as shown in the Valuation Roll for Argyll in 1751.[18]

Surveys and plans for agrarian change

An important legacy from the period of the first Daniel Campbell's lairdship of Islay comprises the estate documents of the time that still survive, including some of Stephen MacDougall's maps and plans. Immediately before going to Islay, MacDougall had in 1747 surveyed the estate of Taynish on mainland Argyll and the island of 'Giga' or Gigha, both owned by Roger McNeil of Taynish.[19] William Roy's Military Survey of Scotland did not include the islands, so the few extant MacDougall maps for parts of Islay are of considerable interest. It seems likely that MacDougall was brought to the island by Daniel Campbell in order to determine the areal extent of the holdings, as a basis for assessing the improvements already carried out and to identify areas where other improvements could be initiated. These surveys, showing the agriculture and settlement pattern before enclosure and sometimes also indicating the form of the intended reorganisation, are fascinating and valuable historical documents. The seventeenth-century Enclosure Acts of the Scottish Parliament remained valid under the terms of the Union. Each landlord could therefore set about planning his estate with considerable freedom of action.

Although few maps or plans of individual holdings on Islay survive, those that do can probably all be ascribed to MacDougall's period and they are drawn at a scale of about 1:10,000. They show the marches or boundaries, enclosures, fields, buildings and areas capable of improvement for a few holdings in the Rinns. Also illustrated are the large houses in which tacksmen lived and the clustered houses of the subtenants or others. More of these maps may have formed the basis for a generalised, smaller-scale map that covers the whole island. This, though drawn by MacDougall between 1749 and 1751, was not published until a century later, when preparing for the sale of the island. Many townships that have disappeared from subsequent rentals can be located on Stephen MacDougall's map.

For Islay it is unfortunate that only a few maps of this period remain. The possibility that additional maps were drawn is suggested in a surviving list of the contents of the Islay House library in 1777, which contains the entry 'Book of Maps of Islay'.[20] Much estate material relating to the island is also known to have been lost in a fire at the Campbell mansion at Woodhall in Lanarkshire in the middle of the nineteenth century. John

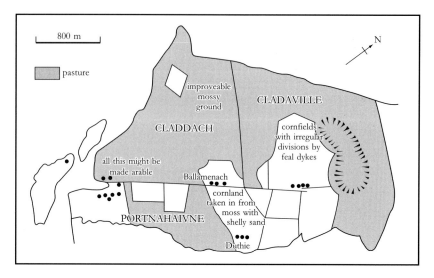

The surveyor, Stephen MacDougall, worked for various Argyll estates in the mid-eighteenth century. For 'Great' Daniel Campbell of Shawfield, he assessed present and potential land use in plans such as this one, redrawn, for the southern tip of the Rinns peninsula. Each dot may represent one occupied building, and pastures are shaded (Islay Estate Papers).

Simple realignments on tacks such as Coul were typical of 'evolutionary' landscape change (Islay Estate Papers).

Francis Campbell, about the same time, also remarked that much of the family's collection of documents had been 'plundered'.[21] One map acquired by Sir Joseph Banks on his way to Iceland in 1772, may have been the same 'beautiful map of Islay' that Pennant saw the same year.[22] Another map that appears to have been lost is that to which Arrowsmith made reference in 1807 when he said that he had obtained a complete map of Islay by Robert Campbell, Esq.[23]

Great Daniel's tentative innovations

Although the main changes that were to transform Islay did not come until later, the first Daniel Campbell of Shawfield and Islay was responsible for a number of innovations during his thirty-nine years as principal laird or landlord. Writing in 1777, more than twenty years after Daniel Campbell's death, his grandson and successor declared that from the time his grandfather had acquired the estate

> . . . he immediately began, and zealously carried on, extensive plans for the improvement and civilisation of that corner. Every encouragement to Agriculture as the basis of his own and his tenants prosperity, was his great Object: To the branch of the flax husbandry and manufacture, he particularly turned his care and attention. He laid out in building Lint Milns, bringing to the Island, Manufacturers, Hecklers, Weavers etc. considerably above £2,000 Sterling.[24]

The emphasis on flax for linen-making is significant. It was part of a general growth of the flax industry in Scotland at this time and was one of the characteristic ways in which individual landlords attempted to improve Scottish agriculture. Islay became a laboratory for agricultural experiment and later in the century it was to become a showpiece of success. Daniel Campbell was an 'agricultural improver' and the Honourable Society of Improvers in the Knowledge of Agriculture in Scotland, the first of its kind in Britain, had been established only three years before he acquired Islay in 1723. As his grandson had pointed out in 1766, improvement was not only a matter of new crops and new techniques. It also involved social changes and alterations in the pattern of land management. His grandfather had introduced

> . . . a Spirit of Industry into the Island of Isla, as the most proper means to Divert from, and if possible, to Eradicate the Idel-Loving and Clanish Spirit that prevailed, particularly he attended to the Raising of Flax, Built Flax Milns, Provided Flax Dressers, Hecklers, and Spinning Wheels, he encouraged Weavers, Gave Premiums to Importers of Flax Seed, and Dealers in Yarn, and to accelerate a Change to Industry, he gave his Tennants Leases for 31 years, a Term unknown to their Predecessors.[25]

MacDougall probably used his large-scale plans in the mid-eighteenth century to compile a small-scale map of the whole island, although it was not to be published for another century. This redrawing omits the blocks used to represent settlement but locates many of the names of holdings mentioned in the text but no longer to be found on modern maps (Smith, *Book of Islay*).

Writing in 1808, Walker suggests that flax was probably the limit of Daniel Campbell's experimentation, whereas his grandson credited him with attempts to encourage agriculture in general, fisheries, as well as better education provision.

The use of leases was comparatively new in Highland Scotland. In the seventeenth century they were generally very long leases, usually for life and for nineteen additional years after death. By the eighteenth century, the normal period was between eleven and nineteen years, with most of the leases or tacks on one estate arranged so as to terminate in one year. Then the whole estate would again be 'sett' or let for another term. Walker mentions that the Campbells of Shawfield had let all the estate in three nineteen-year leases from 1720 to 1777.[26] He perhaps meant that Islay had been let in 1720 by the Cawdor Campbells and Daniel Campbell had taken over the leases.

Great Daniel's son, John, born in 1696 and later a Commissioner of the Inland Revenue, also married twice. His first wife, Lady Margaret Campbell, daughter of Hugh, 3rd earl of Loudon, died without issue a few years after their marriage in 1728. In 1735 he married Lady Henrietta (or Harriot) Cunninghame, daughter of the 12th earl of Glencairn. As John Campbell died in 1746 before his father, it was Daniel, the eldest of his four sons from this second marriage, who eventually succeeded, still a minor, to the estate of Islay, part of Jura and to the mainland estate, when the redoubtable Great Daniel died at Woodhall in 1753, aged 83, having sadly bemoaned the 'Infirmatys attending old age'.[27]

Notes and references

[1] The Shawfield Campbell biographical material used for this chapter has been obtained mainly from the following sources: Burke, *Peerage;* J. B. Burke, *Genealogical and Heraldic Dictionary of the Landed Gentry of Great Britain and Ireland,* (London, 1843–9); L. Stephen (ed.), *Dictionary of National Biography,* (London, 1908); J. D. Duncan, 'Notes on an Inventory of Articles which escaped the hands of the mob on the occasion of the sacking of Shawfield Mansion, 1725', *TGAS,* 1868, I, p. xxiv and pp. 388-397; Foster, *Members of Parliament;* S. Forman, 'Islay House', *SF,* 1960, May, pp. 37-40; J. M. Reid, 'A New Light on Old Glasgow: The Shawfield Papers of Daniel Campbell', *GH,* 1, 2 and 3 June, 1959; Lady C. Russell, 'A Canny Scot', *Three Generations of Fascinating Women and other Sketches from Family History,* (London, 1905), pp. 154–82. The Shawfield Papers in the Mitchell Library, Glasgow, mainly relate to the period before Islay was bought by Daniel Campbell of Shawfield.

[2] *Cawdor Castle Guide,* p. 28.

[3] Russell, 'A Canny Scot', p. 154.

[4] Smith, *Book of Islay,* p. 550.

[5] S. MacDougall's maps and plans of 1749–51: a few extant MS. plans are in the IEP. The reduced smaller-scale map of Islay, lithographed in 1848, is printed in Smith, *Book of Islay,* pp. 552–3.

[6] G. F. Black, 'Early Islay Emigration to America', *OT,* 27 March, 2, 23 and 30 April, 1927; D. Barclay, 'Lauchlin Campbell of Campbell Hall and his Family', *Historical Papers of the Historical Society of Newburgh Bay and the Highlands,* 1902, 9, pp. 31–6; D. Meyer, *The Highland Scots of Carolina,* 1732–1776, (N. Carolina, 1961); J. M. Patten, *The*

Argyle Patent and Accompanying Documents, excerpted from The History of the Somonauk Presbyterian Church, (Baltimore, USA,1979); G. S. Pryde, 'Scottish Colonisation in the Province of New York', *Proceedings of the New York State Historical Association,* 1935, 33, pp. 147–50.

7   Smith, *Book of Islay*, p. 550.

8   Lamont, 'Old Land Denominations'; J. MacQueen, 'Pennyland and Davoch in South-Western Scotland: a Preliminary Note', ibid., 1979, 23, pp. 69–74; B. Megaw, Note on the above, ibid., pp. 75–7.

Pennylands were derived from subdivisions of quarterlands, which by the early sixteenth century were valued at 33*s*. 4*d*. Scots, popularly known as 32/-. In sterling these became 32 pennylands and were divided viz:

Ceathramh	Quarterland	33*s*. 4*d*.	32/- 32*d*.
Ochdamh	Eighth or Auchtenpart	16*s*. 8*d*.	16/- 16*d*.
Lewirheis		8*s*. 4*d*.	8/- 8*d*.
Kerrowrane or Cota ban		4*s*. 2*d*.	4/- 4*d*.
Da Sgillin		2*s*. 1*d*.	2/- 2*d*.

9   Pennant, *Tour*; Anderson, *Account*; Sinclair, *OSA*; Walker, *Economical History*.

10 See also R. A. Dodgshon, *The Origin of British Field Systems: An Interpretation*, (London, 1980).

11 Shaw, *Northern and Western Islands*, p. 91.

12 W. Gemmill's MS. plans are in the IEP and relate mainly to the 1820s and 1830s. Photocopies are in the SRO.

13 *The Statistical Account of Scotland, by the Ministers of the Respective Parishes (NSA)*, (Edinburgh, 1843-6), 33 vols., *Argyleshire*, (1845), p. 654.

14 Smith, *Book of Islay*, p. 528.

15 MS. name books, maps and plans of the Ordnance Survey, Edinburgh.

16 Pennant, *Tour*, p. 246.

17 Smith, *Book of Islay*, pp. 521–44.

18 IEP, Attested Account of the Valued Rent of Islay, 1751.

19 S. MacDougall, *A Map of Taynish . . . in Argyll, 1747*, The British Library, Map Library, K. Top. XLIX 28. Also, *A Map of the Island of Giga, 1747*, XLIX 37. 1.

20 Smith, *Book of Islay*, p. 473.

21 Reid, 'Shawfield Papers'; Ramsay, *John Ramsay*, pp. 50–1.

22 Pennant, *Tour*, p. 261.

23 A. Arrowsmith, *Memoir relative to the construction of the Map of Scotland published by A. Arrowsmith in the year 1807*, (London, 1809).

24 Daniel Campbell the Younger petitioned the Annexed Estates Commissioners on several occasions for grants of money to aid his plans for the development of Islay. See SRO, E727/60 and E728/47. This particular reference is E727/60/1.

25 SRO, E728/47/4(2).

26 Walker, *Economical History*, p. 68.

27 Saltoun Papers, SRO, SB74.

CHAPTER 7

More comprehensive development

In virtually every European country in the eighteenth and nineteenth centuries, the rural economy had to produce more food to support the growing towns and land was now seen as an asset to be managed for profit rather than for supporting rural population.[1] From the 1760s there was an increasing demand in the rest of Britain for such Highland produce as cattle, mutton, wool, linen, kelp, whisky, timber, slate and many other commodities.[2] Labour was required in Lowland agriculture, the Clyde herring fishery and in the bleachfields around the textile towns and villages. Recruitment into the Army and Royal Navy for the Seven Years War, the American War of Independence and the Napoleonic wars also created a demand for labour. Rentals increased to capitalise on the surplus from rising prices. The traditional tacksman class was gradually reduced in number and social significance, with subtenure forbidden. The conventional eighteenth-century assumption was that a rising population was an economic benefit. Between the end of the Seven Years War in 1763 and 1775, there were further emigrations of about 1,300 people from Islay to North Carolina, perhaps encouraged by the Islay pamphleteer, 'Scotus Americanus'.[3] But the view of a correspondent to the *Edinburgh Advertiser* was that 'the loss of useful hands must soon impoverish any country'.[4] Another also pointed out that 'the poor deluded farmers that went away some years ago from Islay . . . wanted a passage back'.[5]

It was against this background of accelerating change in economy and society that Daniel Campbell the Younger succeeded, aged only sixteen, to the Islay estate, on the death of his grandfather in 1753. After reaching his majority, he too became a member of Parliament, representing Lanarkshire from 1760 to 1768. Daniel Campbell the Younger is reputed to have been a 'great character in his day, but of a totally opposite sort to his grandfather. The first Daniel Campbell of Shawfield had a genius for making money and accumulated a large fortune which his grandson helped largely to diminish. Daniel the Younger is described as 'living in great style . . . And he spent his money right and left, even more on others than on himself'.[6] A well-informed man, who travelled widely in Europe, he

collected rare books and musical instruments. He spent summers and
autumns on Islay and continued to implement and expand many of his
grandfather's ideas of agricultural improvements, involving leases, stock
and crops. In 1760, though still only a bachelor of 23, he added two stair-
towers, extending the south front of Islay House.[7] He also had the
ornamental and octagonal East Tower constructed, with his monogram
alongside that of his king.[8] Eight years later, one of the most impressive
and enduring results of his management was to be seen in the construction
of Bowmore, one of the earliest planned villages to appear in the Highlands
and Islands. He was also an instigator and shareholder in the first regular
sailing packet in the Hebrides which plied weekly between Islay and West
Loch Tarbert in Kintyre.[9]

Such innovations were not merely far-reaching in their effects; they
were part of an overall vision that entitles Daniel Campbell the Younger
to be counted among those on whom much of the success of the agricultural
revolution in Scotland ultimately depended. In his early twenties he was
already thinking hard about his island estate and by 1759 had begun
'particularly to inquire into the Situation of Isla, the Disposition and
Genius of its Inhabitants, whom he found still to Retain a Bias to the
Clanish manner of their Ancestors, averse to Industry and Intercourse'.[10]
So he 'Therefore Examined the Schemes Employed by his Grandfather,
and began to pursue them with more enlarged views In regard to
Agriculture, Manufactures, Trade and Police'.

Financing Islay's improvement
Daniel Campbell's vision was expressed implicitly; it did not constitute a
development plan in the modern sense of the term. He himself described
it as an 'Outline of a Plan, rather than a Minute and tedious detail'. But it
is significant that he used the term 'plan' at all and fortunately a substantial
amount of evidence survives in the landscape and in writing, which enables
much of that minute and tedious detail to be reconstructed. Daniel Campbell
needed extra finance to accomplish his ambitions. Islay did not become
an Annexed Estate, as its owner had remained loyal to the Hanoverians
during the 1745 rebellion. Nevertheless, funds at the disposal of the
Annexed Estates Commissioners could be used in other parts of the
Highlands and Islands to promote 'the Protestant Religion, good
Government, Industry and Manufactures . . . to Erect publick Schools . .
. for Instructing Young Persons in Reading and Writing and English
Language and in Several Branches of Agriculture and Manufactures'.

The first application by Daniel Campbell the Younger for assistance
of this kind seems to have been made in February 1766.[11] His 'Memorial

and Petition', a more colourful forerunner of present-day application forms, showed that Daniel Campbell was an early advocate of regional development policies, jointly financed by public and private sources. He urged that to establish linen manufactures and fisheries in the Western Islands, 'the proper Plan is that the publick and the proprietors of such Islands, go Hand in Hand.[12] He also reminded the Commissioners that feu duty of £500 had been paid annually to the Crown for many years back, arguing that some of this ought to come back to assist in the improvement of conditions on the island. Similar arguments are still frequently heard, as islanders calculate the excise duties levied on the whisky exported from Islay's distilleries! The laird maintained that, if encouragement were given, 'this island might soon become of infinite Utility to the Nation in General' and he requested £600 to carry on and complete the building of his parish church in what was to become the village of Bowmore, as well as a schoolhouse with an annual salary for the schoolmaster, a prison and a further £600 towards the establishment of linen manufactures and fisheries.

This first application was unsuccessful; the Commissioners objected to giving aid for his suggested 'General purposes'.[13] Daniel Campbell apparently thought they had missed his point and renewed his request in further memorials.[14] These are much more interesting than the first and help to establish the position of both 'Great' Daniel and Daniel the Younger among leaders of change and improvement in the Highlands and Islands. The memorials discuss his 'Schemes and Plans of Improvements' under several headings: agriculture, fishing, linen manufacture, trade, roads, bridges, sailing packet, fishing, religion, education, and law and order. He requested £1,000 in the first instance and added an assurance (the lack of which in his first memorial had apparently troubled the Commissioners) that 'notwithstanding the large Sums he had already Expended, he would still advance out of his own pocket, a sum Equal to that which should be Granted'. The result on this occasion was more successful and the Commissioners granted him half the sum that he had requested.[15]

A decade later, in 1777, Daniel Campbell again went in search of development aid. Writing to the Secretary of the Board of Trustees of Annexed Estates he recalled that after his previous successful application and the award of a grant for £500 he had 'assiduously pursued my plan of the improvement of that Island. Large sums have been expended, I may say at least £2,000 Sterlg, exclusive of what was laid out by my grandfather'. He then requested another £500 from the Board and promised to 'lay out a like sum for the improvement and prosperity of that Island'.[16] £300 was to be used to send farmers to Northumberland and other parts of England to study the new practices there and to give premiums to certain farmers in the form of new and improved types of seed. Another £200 was to be spent on two mills, one for 'making' grass or barley, another for wheat. A further £200 would be used to purchase a vessel for training fishermen and £300 towards completing quays at Bowmore and Port Askaig.

This time the Board members were immediately sympathetic.[17] The public good, they decided, was best served by giving Daniel Campbell £500 to help promote the fisheries and improve the quays. They considered that the agricultural proposals were best left to Shawfield himself. It was the opinion of the Commissioners that 'they have a gentleman to deal with, who, for activity and public spirit may be safely trusted with the management of the sum promised by them, without the least doubt of his being a faithful Stewart for the good of the public as well as for his own'.[18] It is sadly ironic that, having so successfully mastered the difficult art of obtaining government aid, Daniel Campbell the Younger died almost immediately afterwards. It was left to his successor to put the money to its intended use.

Optimistic agrarian plans

Daniel Campbell's thoughts and plans for agriculture, as they are set out in the memorials, are based on an optimism characteristic of the Scottish Enlightenment. He had gone so far as to suggest that nine-tenths of the surface of Islay was capable of improvement. The island, he added, contained 'most types of soils', which were able to produce 'Grains and Grasses, Cultivate in Britain, Comparative with the Continent. It has little Frost or Snow, so that Wheat and Sown Grasses, often make a Progress in Winter. It is a Country remarkably adapted for Flax, and bounds with Efficatious and lasting Manures, The hard and soft Marles, Lymstone and Shell Sand'. He also pointed out that he had been

> . . . endeavouring to abolish certain Old hurtfull Customs, at the same time as he has been Introducing the most approved methods of the Old and New Husbandry, Summer Fallowing, the Use of the manures and laying down the Grounds in Good Heart, with Grass Seeds, Also has introduced the Turnip Husbandry, Wheat, the two Rowed Barley, White Oats, Beans, Pease, Hemp, Veitches, and Tare Seeds with Clover, Rye, St. Foin, Lucern, Burnet and Timothy Grasses, and has introduced all the different Ploughs, Machinery and Tools now used in the New and Old Husbandry, and has . . . experienced that all those Seeds and Grasses are Cultivate in Isla of equall perfection and Advantage with any part of Britain'.[19]

Envisaging that there was good reason to expect that his tenants 'would soon become of very considerable Publick Utility, by exporting Great Quantitys of Wheat and other Grains', he also reminded the Commissioners that Islay's farmers would 'Rear up and export more Live Cattle, than at present, But also to Fatten for Export, and for the Use of Traders upon the Coast'.

Unfortunately there are few archives or published sources that can provide an objective review of Daniel Campbell's expansive claims. What seems probable is that some improvements were taking place, but that these were mainly confined to the larger farms, perhaps those on the best lands, those near the laird's mansion and those of the gentlemen farmers. Tacks or leases granted in 1768–9 by Daniel the Younger and in 1779 and 1802 by his successor, survive in archives.[20] Those for 1769 did not require tenants to make improvements; the 1779 leases, however, saw the introduction of 'improving' clauses. The absence of such clauses in the earlier leases was commented on in 1769 by Daniel Campbell's factor.[21] There was clearly scope for improvement and one way to do this, as both landlord and agent recognised, was through leases containing the new clauses 'productive of new and better effects'. At that time Islay was

> . . . occupied by two classes of tenants – the gentlemen possessing several Quarterlands extending to three and four thousand acres and upwards. They mind husbandry very little, only the yearly sett of these large farms to a sett of poor people, whom they call their farmers. The small tenants, four, five, six or eight of them, enjoys a Quarterland promiscuously among them . . . These manner of holdings the proprietor is determined to alter.[22]

The word 'promiscuously' strikes oddly on the modern ear, but the basic problem was little incentive for an individual to attempt improvements. Reorganisation of landholdings was essential, but for this patience was necessary:

> In regard to the first class tenants . . . each is only to enjoy such an extent of land as may rationally fall under cognizance and management of a good improver. As to the second class or small tenants, their farms are to be new modeled, each to have an establishment for himself, and to occupy individually . . . But, as these cannot be carried into execution till the expiry of the current leases, that circumstance becomes the chief and principal argument for delaying the sett till the expiry of current leases . . . Shawfield has lately granted nineteen year leases of a considerable part of his estate from Whitsunday 1768 last, and part does not commence . . . till Whitsunday 1779, the period when all his tacks of the Argyllshire state expires.[23]

It is ironic that this major obstacle to Daniel Campbell's improvements was probably caused by the nineteen-year leases that had been one of the earliest agricultural advances made before his grandfather's time. Since the existing nineteen-year leases on his estate did not expire until 1787 or 1798, not much could be done until that time. It was therefore not Daniel the Younger who would achieve the reorganisation and agricultural improvements meanwhile could be only piecemeal.

Village planning

Daniel Campbell was not the first to envisage a new element in the eighteenth-century landscape in Scotland, but he was one of the first and, as it turned out, one of the very few to act on this vision in the Highlands and Islands. Throughout Scotland as a whole, in little more than a century from about the time his grandfather had bought Islay in 1726, over 150 completely new planned villages were established at the instigation of individual landlords. They were developed 'in response to and also to assist a revolution in the economy of the estate and of the nation'; and they were 'expected to provide a completely new framework for human life in the countryside . . . part of a still larger ideal of promoting economic growth in the kingdom'.[24] The movement also had its social and aesthetic aspirations: the village was usually designed 'street by street, house by house, and garden by garden with certain social, economic and architectural considerations always in view'. The landowner generally exercised control over the appearance and layout of the village but the houses were seldom built at his expense. He was normally responsible for providing facilities such as inns, a church and sometimes also a courthouse and a school. Daniel Campbell's Bowmore, begun in the late 1760s, seems to have followed this general pattern. Often, the landowners also exercised complete control over the affairs of the village through a baron bailie who was frequently also their agent or factor.

Like many others of its kind, Bowmore was based on a geometric plan, with a broad main street, running south and uphill to the newly-constructed church. Daniel Campbell had applied in particular for financial help in building Bowmore's church, as 'a very necessary and expedient measure, upon an Island so populous and extensive as Isla, for civilising and promoting the protestant Religion amongst the present Inhabitants, exclusive of the great increase that may be reasonably expected, in a very short time, from the Encouragement offered by the Memorialist to Settlers and the plans of Improvement now under execution'.[25] He added that plans of this church as well as of the proposed schoolhouse and prison could have been exhibited with his Memorial, but he did not consider it imperative as he 'must necessarily contribute largely to this work himself'.

The church conspicuously dominates the top of the wide Main Street. Its architecture is unusual, but it stands in good proportion to the rest of the street and the village. It was probably inspired by the various projects for a church at Inveraray designed between 1747 and 1760 by William Adam and his son John, in particular John Adam's scheme of about 1758.[26] This undermines the belief that a 'French architect who, doubtless influenced by tradition, was determined to eliminate any corners for the devil to lurk in'.[27] Another suggestion has been that 'its exterior was in imitation of a church in Rome'.[28] The simple internal layout, with a central pillar supporting the roof-structure, indicates the gap between the ambitions of the patron and the limited experience of the unknown mason-architect.

Over a short period, Daniel Campbell spent £1,660 on church matters, compared to an annual income from Islay rents of about £2,700.[29] The new church and manse at Bowmore cost about £500 (a restoration appeal launched in 1980 was for £200,000) and two new manses had become necessary at £200 each. There were also other expenses including the yearly stipend for a minister of £32 6s. 2d.[30] Daniel Campbell also maintained a school in each parish 'for instructing Youth in Reading and writing the English language', clear emphasis was placed on what, for Islay, was then a foreign language. He also wanted 'One Schoolmaster at least Qualified in teaching Grammar, Arithmetic, Book-keeping and practical Mathematics', for whom a school or schoolhouse was necessary, and whose salary the public should pay. A prison was needed on Islay 'especially in a Country where the partiality of Family Attachments does in part still prevail'.

The main street in Bowmore was intersected by others and along the streets single-storey or two-storey houses were constructed, built directly on to the street with no front gardens. To encourage people away from the land and to make subsequent land reorganisation easier, whilst also recognising that those so displaced retained an attachment to land, he planned his village so that each family had a 'feu' consisting of a house site and a little land for a 'garden', potatoes, oats, flax and cow's grass. The village was thus intended for farmworkers or day-labourers and also for non-agricultural workers. Creation of suitable non-agricultural employment was apparently as difficult then as it is now, perhaps even more of a problem for island than mainland landlords. Fishing was not yet as important in Bowmore as Daniel Campbell had perhaps implied in his first memorial that it would be and the main national drive to reorganise and improve the fishing industry was still fifteen years or so in the future. Apart from an incipient service sector, distilling and other industries based

The later-eighteenth century period of renewal in many aspects of Scottish life included similar events, albeit different in scale, such as the creation of Edinburgh New Town and Islay's village of Bowmore, both started in the 1760s. 'Designed street by street, house by house, with certain social, economic and architectural considerations always in view', Bowmore's wide Main Street is dominated by the unusual round church with its conical roof. In the 1980s the prize-winning Ayrshire herd returns for milking to McKerrell's Dairy.

The fishermen's buildings beside Bowmore harbour were partially remodelled in the late-twentieth century, but the staircases seen in nineteenth-century watercolours still remain.

on agriculture were the only possibilities. Linen-weaving in particular had to be introduced and encouraged if Bowmore was to succeed economically. Half a century later, when another phase of village-building on Islay was undertaken by Daniel Campbell's successors, there were more opportunities.

Linen manufacture, fishing and mining

In Daniel Campbell's memorials there seems to be a tacit assumption that flax-growing was required, not merely to provide a basis for village industry, but that it represented in itself a significant agricultural improvement. In 1777 he wrote that 'Agriculture and the Flax husbandry in particular, have been my favourite objects.[31] By 1776 he had contracted a Linen Manufacturer from south of the border to settle in Isla to carry on 'the Branches of Weaving and Bleaching, to whom he hath promised to advance a Considerable sum of money . . . and . . . hath already set up above Twelve Looms'. The laird also laid out ground which he offered rent-free for seven years to persons 'skilled in any Branch of the Linnen Manufacture as an Encouragement to Settle there'.[32]

This enthusiasm for flax-growing, before cotton from the American colonies reduced its importance, was apparently shared by someone else on Islay. Even before Daniel Campbell's first memorial, Mrs Margaret Campbell of Lagganlochan petitioned the Commissioners and Trustees for Improving Manufactures in Scotland for assistance in January 1765. Her request was sent the following month to the Commissioners of Annexed Estates as 'this Board's Funds are too narrow even for the low Countries'.[33] In passing on the request, the Board recommended 'the Island of Islay as remarkably fit for Flax Raising and Spinning' and also recommended Mrs Campbell as a 'proper person to be intrusted with the Distribution of any Encouragements the Commissioners may think fit to bestow'. In Mrs Campbell's opinion, for £60 to £80 per year for three years, it could be practicable 'to have Sixty Girls annualy taught Spinning, as many Wheels & Reels given them – and a Competent Allowance of good Flax seed given to the Farmers'. Thereafter she hoped 'they would be able to carry on the trade themselves'. Whereas the spinning was usually an occupation for the womenfolk, weaving was more likely to have been done by men, since it was much heavier work. Finishing, washing and drying would probably also have been done by women. The finished product was probably intended at first mainly for local consumption, but in 1772 Pennant noted that £2,000 worth of flax yarn was exported, which 'might be better manufactured on the spot to give employ to the poor natives'.[34] In 1777 Daniel Campbell could claim that 'Manufacturers have been brought, public marketts for the sale of yarn have been instituted and large quantities of Yarn sold'.[35]

As with other developmental opportunities, the scope for improvement in fishing seemed almost unlimited to Daniel Campbell. His first memorial in 1766 declared:

> The Shoars of this Island abound with most kinds of Fish known in the Scotch Seas; There are Several Rivers abounding with Salmon, and in Lochindale . . . great quantities of Herrings have been taken. There are Cod Banks on every side of the Island, most of which were of late discovered by Fishing Vessels from Liverpool and other parts of England. The Inhabitants know no Art of Fishing but by the Hand Line and Rod; wherewith they take Cod, Haddock, Whiting, Flounder; and a great Variety of other kinds particularly a Delicious Fish which they call the Merry Fish . . . But for want of method no great quantities are Caught.[36]

On his own initiative, he offered house sites and other attractions such as three acres of land, peat rights and free rent for seven years to encourage those 'skilled in the Cod and Herring Fishing, willing to settle in the said Island'. He had introduced the 'Long Lines, Salmon and Herring Netts', instead of the simple hand rods. The fish resources within and adjacent to the island had been explored and this suggested that there was 'very great Encouragement towards a profitable and lasting fishing'.

The most successful mode of fishing up to the time was buss fishing and its success depended on the bounty paid. Daniel Campbell remarked that Islay already had ten busses, but that they were used only in the herring fishery from September to January. For the remainder of the year some or all of these busses were taken out of the water and the 'hands return to work on the land or are idle'. Daniel Campbell's intention was to convert this activity from a convenient off-season supplement to agriculture to a full-time occupation. He proposed to establish other branches of the 'Curable Fish that fall from January to September and thereby to secure Employment for the whole year and a Moderate Degree of profits on such as will Engage to Continue the Fisheries, when the Bounty is withdrawn'. But he had scarcely had time to effect much progress before his premature death.

According to Pennant as many as 700 men were employed in mining and fishing in Islay in 1772. Islay's mineral resources had been recognised by the Cawdor Campbells and they seem to have been of at least equal interest to Daniel Campbell the Younger, although government assistance was not available for mining and there is therefore no mention of it in the memorials addressed to the Commissioners. In July 1770 a report on the 'State of the Mines in Isla' was prepared for Daniel Campbell.[37] At that

Silversmith Adam Graham made this goblet about 1780 from Islay silver, mined from Dalradian limestone veins about 1780 (Glasgow Museums).

Lead-smelting furnace at Freeport, 1772 (Trustees of The British Library).

time there were eight mines open, all fairly near to each other and near the present village of Ballygrant. Seven exploited lead-ore veins (Mulrees, Portnealon, Shenegart, North and South Ardachie, Belligrand, Gartness) and one a copper vein at Killslaven. Technical problems of drainage and power were described in each case, as well as the apparent richness of each mine. The general tone of the report was optimistic; the mines could be worked 'with considerable profit both to the Proprietor & Undertaker'.

This optimism was echoed by Pennant in the 1770s:

> The ore is of lead, much mixed with copper . . . the veins rise to the
> surface, have been worked at intervals for ages, and probably in the time
> of the Norwegians . . . The lead-ore is good; the copper yields thirty-
> three pounds per hundred; and forty ounces of silver from a ton of the
> metal. The lead-ore is smelted in an air-furnace, near Freeport . . . Not
> far from these mines are vast strata of that species of iron called bog-
> ore, of the concreted kind: beneath that large quantities of vitriolic
> mundic.[38]

Pennant's optimism, however, was not shared by Shawfield, who claimed
that mining on Islay was only about half as profitable as it was in the
better-known and richer veins at Leadhills in Lanarkshire. This view was
endorsed by John Williams in the 1780s.[39]

The first half century of Shawfield Campbells

For the Campbell of Cawdor period of management in Islay, the main
problem for us today is a relative shortage of material and evidence. But
from 1726 to 1777, when the first Daniel Campbell of Shawfield and his
grandson were making their improvements and planning others, the problem
is rather an excess of enthusiasm, most evident in the boundless optimism
of the memorials. In assessing the extent to which the Shawfield Campbells
had brought real benefits to Islay, it seems reasonable to conclude that,
taking population increase into account, the island was economically more
advanced in 1777 than it had been in 1726. A flax industry had been
established and was apparently thriving; the mines near Ballygrant provided
substantial employment and fishing was entering a phase of expansion.
The new village of Bowmore offered a lifestyle and opportunities that
was immensely different from any that had been available to the island
people before the 1760s. Encouragement of religion and education was
scarcely more important than the institution of a ferry to the mainland; all
changes brought Islay and its inhabitants into closer contact with a Scotland
that was itself in the ferment of the eighteenth-century 'enlightenment'.

This exchange of ideas was exemplified in the visit to Islay in July
1772 of the distinguished topographer, Thomas Pennant. He was a native
of Flintshire, an antiquarian and naturalist with an 'unusual flair for
accumulating historical information about whatever places he visited'.[40]
The Islay visit took place during his second tour of Scotland; his first had
taken him no further than the Lowlands. Even Samuel Johnson awarded
Pennant a good mark: 'He's the best traveller I ever read; he observes
more things than anyone else does'.[40] Thomas Pennant was far less critical

of things Scottish than was Dr Johnson and was duly rewarded. Both Edinburgh and Glasgow made Pennant a Freeman of their cities, an honour that Glasgow has not felt called upon to accord to any other Welshman except David Lloyd George.

Travelling with Pennant on his second tour was the draughtsman Moses Griffith. It was Griffith who drew or copied the illustrations that, engraved by Mazell, were included in the published account of Pennant's tour; some of the original drawings survive in the British Library.[42] The two men visited Islay from the 2nd to the 6th of July 1772 and, despite unpleasant sailings, they found much to interest them and thoroughly enjoyed the hospitality of various Campbell lairds. Apart from Shawfield himself, with whom they dined at Islay House, Pennant eulogised over Campbell of Sunderland's northern part of the Rinns:

> The improvements of his lands are excellent, and the grass so good and the fields so clean, as to vie with any place. Near the house, in a well-sheltered nook, is an apple-orchard, which bore plentifully: these with strawberries, are the fruits of these remote islands; the climate denied other luxuries of this nature: and even in these articles, Pomona [Roman goddess of fruit trees and fruit] smiles but where she finds a warm protection.[43]

He made similar comments about Campbell of Ballinaby's estate:

> His land is quite riante [pleasing]; his pastures in good order; and his people busily employed in hay-making: observed one piece of good grass ground, which he assured me was very lately covered with heath, now quite destroyed by the use of shell-sand. Perhaps it may seem trifling to mention, that some excellent new potatoes were served up at dinner; but this circumstance, with the forwardness of the hay harvest, shows what may be effected by culture in this island, when the tenure is secure, for both Sunderland and Balnabbi are proprietors.

Because of the size of Islay, it was scarcely possible for the visitors to cover the entire island in four days and they do not appear to have ridden anywhere south of Bridgend. Pennant only mentions that he looked across the loch to Bowmore. From Sunderland, he explored 'the unspeakably savage' scenery to the north and west and rode into the 'fine cave of Saneg-mor . . . of an august length and height'. Not everything that Pennant observed on Islay could be described as 'riante'. He also recorded

> . . . a set of people worn down with poverty: their habitations scenes of misery, made of loose stones; without chimnies, without doors, excepting

The cruck-frame cottage illustrated in Pennant's *Tour* can still be recognised in Islay's rural buildings, both ruined and occupied (Pennant, *Tour*).

Weaving of flax into linen was one of the major innovations of the Campbells of Shawfield. The interior of a weaver's cottage, however, merited Pennant's description of the Ilich as 'lean, withered, dusky and smoke-dried' (Pennant, *Tour*).

the faggot opposed to the wind at one or other of the appertures, permitting the smoke to escape through the other, in order to prevent the pains of suffocation. The furniture perfectly corresponds: a pothook hangs from the middle of the roof, with a pot pendent over a grateless fire, filled with fare that may rather be called a permission to exist, than a support of vigorous life: the inmates, as may be expected, lean, withered, dusky and smoke-dried.

This picture, Pennant hastened to add, was one that was not limited to the island of Islay. It is easy to forget that famine was still never far off even in the eighteenth century, whether from overpopulation, bad weather, crop disease or other causes. Pennant himself mentioned that in the summer of 1772 famine had only just been averted by the arrival of a ship, bearing part of the £1,000 worth of meal annually imported to the island. He described the natural effects of bad food and the related epidemics on the island, together with 'dropsies and cancers'. Other comments, for example on social customs and superstitions reinforced his general picture of an island still only in the early stages of what was to be a social and economic transformation.

The rural squalor that Pennant described is, paradoxically, probably the best testimony to the vision of the first Daniel Campbell of Shawfield and even more to that of his grandson. 'I have assiduously pursued my plan of the improvement of that Island', wrote Daniel Campbell the Younger just before he died in 1777.[44] The social, economic and educational gap between the Shawfield Campbells and the vast majority of Islay's inhabitants was great. Although, or even because, the island offered better physical resources than in many parts of the Highlands and Islands, it would not have been surprising if the Shawfield Campbells had seen improvement wholly in terms of economic benefit, especially to themselves, and resorted to the technique of clearance used elsewhere. It was Islay's good fortune that its owners saw improvement in social as well as economic terms and that they set out to improve the quality and condition of Islay's inhabitants. When Daniel Campbell the Younger died in 1777, aged only 40, the main task of landholdings reorganisation was still in the future, but the humanitarian character of the changes had been established as the pattern to follow. The step from Pennant's cottages, 'scenes of misery', to the fine new village of Bowmore was a magnificent beginning and Bowmore continues to be a fitting memorial to the humanity of its founder.

Notes and references

1   Devine, *Clanship*, p. 39.

2   Ibid., p. 42.

3   I. H. Adams and M. Somerville, *Cargoes of Despair and Hope*, (Edinburgh, 1993), p. 211 *et seq.*; W. R. Brock, *Scotus Americanus: a survey of the sources for links between Scotland and America in the eighteenth century*, (Edinburgh, 1982); Meyer, *Highland Scots, 1732–1776*, p. 84.

4   *EA*, 17 July 1772.

5   *EA*, 5 May 1772.

6   Russell, 'A Canny Scot', p. 176.

7   Forman, 'Islay House', *SF*, p. 40; Glasgow Testaments, 13 February 1778, 604, NLS.

8   RCAHMS, *Argyll Inventory*, *V*, p. 294.

9   Smith, *Book of Islay*, p. 469.

10 Daniel Campbell the Younger petitioned the Annexed Estates Commissioners on several occasions for grants or money to aid his plans for the development of Islay. These requests are in the Annexed Estates Papers, SRO, E727/60 and E728/47.

11 SRO, E728/47/2 (2).

12 SRO, E728/47/1.

13 SRO, E728/47/4 (2).

14 SRO, E728/47/2(2).

15 SRO, E727/60/1.

16 SRO, E727/60/1.

17 SRO, E727/60/2.

18 SRO, E727/60/2.

19 SRO, E728/47/4(2).

20 IEP, Leases to tenants.

21 Smith, *Book of Islay*, pp. 469–71.

22 Idem.

23 Idem.

24 T. C. Smout, 'The Landowner and the Planned Village in Scotland, 1730–1830', in N. T. Phillipson and R. Mitchison, *Scotland in the Age of Improvement*, (Edinburgh, 1970), p. 76.

25 SRO, E 728/47/3:

26 RCAHMS, *Argyll Inventory*, *V*, p. 35.

27 Weir, *Guide to Islay*, p. 34.

28 Forman, 'Islay House', p. 38.

29 Rental in 1779, according to Macdonald, *General View*, p. 619.

30 SRO, E728/47/4(2).

31 SRO, E727/60/1.

32 SRO, E728/47/1.

33 SRO, E728/19/7.

34 Pennant, *Tour*, p. 261.

[35] SRO, E727/60/1.

[36] SRO, E728/47/ 1.

[37] Professor John Walker Papers, Edinburgh University Library (EUL), MS. D.c.i.57.

[38] Pennant, *Tour*, p. 249.

[39] J. Williams, *The Natural History of the Mineral Kingdom,* (London, 1789).

[40] Pennant, *Tour*, pp. 249–68; G. V. Jones, 'Pennant, The Observant Traveller', *SF*, 1971, June, p. 23.

[41] Jones, 'Pennant', p. 23.

[42] According to Pennant, 'Joseph Banks, Esq. . . . permitted my artist to copy as many of the beautiful drawings in my collection, as would be of use in the present work'. The originals are in the British Library Map Library K. Top XLIX. 37. 3a and b.

[43] Pennant, *Tour*, p. 254 *et seq.*

[44] SRO, E727/60/1.

CHAPTER 8

Consolidation in momentous times

Walter Campbell of Shawfield shared his predecessors' concern for the islanders. In this Islay was fortunate: there were enough landlords elsewhere in the Highlands during this period who possessed vision and drive in abundance, but who were notoriously lacking in humanity. Walter's elder brother had set a pattern that seemed to require consolidation and extension after his death. In regard to agricultural improvements, for instance, it was becoming clear that the system of improving leases could only bring results if, instead of the older communal method of farming, every tenant had his own holding. This inevitably meant that fewer people should be dependent on agricultural employment, at a time when the population as a whole was growing. Sources of non-agricultural employment were therefore needed.

When Daniel Campbell the Younger died in 1777, he left a large amount of personal and heritable debt, though probably little was directly related to the Islay estate. He also left closets full of dandy clothes and well-stocked cellars and libraries.[1] His next brother John had died a year or so earlier, also a bachelor. The succession of the Shawfield and Islay estates therefore passed to the third son, Walter Campbell of Skipness, born in 1741 and an advocate. Under the 1770 Law of Entail, Walter was initially unable to sell off parts of the estates to help clear debts of over £90,000. His difficulties were summarised in a petition sent to Parliament by Walter and some of his cousins, and a private Act enabling them to sell and realise some of the money was passed.[2] The Shawfield and Jura estates were sold, but Islay was retained in the family, along with Woodhall, Skipness and Ardpatrick. This decision was almost certainly in the best interests of Islay's inhabitants.

Walter Campbell unexpectedly became laird of Islay at the age of 36, beginning with considerable difficulties and only slightly fewer responsibilities, since he never became a Member of Parliament. He spent more time on his Islay estate than did many other Highland lairds, between three and four months each year and in 1788 extended it by purchasing the Sunderland estate for £10,000.[3] In the thirty-nine years from 1777 to

1816 that he was responsible for Islay, changes in the island's economy and, to a certain extent in the landscape, continued, although perhaps the greatest number of changes that remain visible today did not occur until after his death. He came to be much admired by other improvers, travellers and visitors interested in the agriculture and changing social economy of the Highlands and Islands, in times that were often difficult for the nation as a whole.

Relentless population growth
Innovation, improvement and change in a rural landscape are seldom easy to achieve on a large scale, though the more kindly environment and less acute population pressure in Islay made them easier and more rewarding than in many other parts of the Hebrides. Nevertheless, as elsewhere in the Highlands and Islands, the increasing population of villagers, tenants, subtenants and landless cottars was making a reorganisation of the system of agriculture simultaneously both more essential and more difficult to achieve. The Rev Dr Webster undertook the first comprehensive estimate of the population of Scotland in the middle of the eighteenth century. Alexander Webster was born in 1707 and was elected Moderator of the General Assembly of the Church of Scotland in 1754. Acting on behalf of the government, he persuaded the Society for Promoting Christian Knowledge in the Highlands and Islands to require every minister in those presbyteries where the Society had erected Charity Schools, to enumerate his parishioners. In default the minister was threatened with withdrawal of the school. The total for Islay in 1755 was 5,344 persons, a figure that was to increase considerably over the next half century.[4] Dr. Webster's 5,344 islanders of 1755 had risen by the late 1760s to over 7,000. The clerical authors of *The Statistical Account* provided details of each Scottish parish in the early 1790s and estimated that the total population of Islay was then about 8,400, composed of the parish of Killarow with 2,500, Kilmeny 2,000, Kilchoman 2,300 and Kildalton l,600.[5] One of the ministers even gave a total of 9,500 for the island; the laird himself claimed over 10,000, although the figure at the first official census in 1801 indicated an island population of 8,364.[6] Using this latter figure, there had been a growth of between 50 and 60 per cent in less than 40 years.

With some justification the rise in numbers was regarded for much of the eighteenth century as a sign of progress and Daniel Campbell the Younger and his brother Walter looked forward to further growth. The latter claimed that there had been no emigration in his time, 'though there are more inhabitants than are industriously employed. 'My great object has been . . . to retain at home and render usefully employed those hands that have heretofore been less productive than they ought to have been'.[7] By the end of the century, however, at the national scale Malthus published his *Essay on the Principle of Population* and national census-taking was instituted.[8] There were serious food crises in 1782–3, 1795–6, 1806–7 and 1816–17.[9] By then on Islay the concern had changed to the problem of relating the island's population to available resources and to creating non-agricultural means of employment. Here, as in other respects, Islay's main landlord reflected, or even slightly anticipated, national trends.

In the latter part of the eighteenth century and the early years of the nineteenth, similar increases in population had occurred for several reasons over most of the West Highland seaboard: the cessation of civil warfare after the 1745 rebellion; after mid-century also, the spread of the potato as a human foodstuff that could be grown in increasingly marginal environmental conditions; end-of-century inoculation and vaccination against smallpox; and the existence of supplementary sources of income in linen manufacture, fishing, whisky distilling, mining and the manufacture of kelp from seaweed. The full reason for this rapid population increase is still not completely understood. The rate of increase varied from one part of the region to another and in Islay the lack of a substantial kelp industry, together with the relatively greater ease of outward migration to the mainland and emigration beyond Scotland, meant that the rate was probably not so great as elsewhere, or as it might otherwise have been.

Nevertheless the minister of the parish of Killarow and Kilmeny was able to comment 'the whole population of Islay has increased greatly within these 40 years, owing principally to the tenants, who are in possession of large farms, dividing their possessions among their children, which encourages marriage. Some, however, who are reduced in their circumstances, are obliged to emigrate'.[10] This theme of emigration was further developed by the writer of the Kildalton parish account, when he observed that 'the females are more numerous than the males, a great number of young men having left the parish, and gone to the Low Country [i.e. the Scottish Lowlands] for employment. Some have gone to America and other places; so that the number of inhabitants has diminished within these forty years'.[11] With the institution of regular decennial censuses in 1801 it becomes possible, despite defects in the early censuses, to be more precise about changes in numbers, age structure, occupation and other characteristics.

While in all the parishes of Islay the population increased dramatically during the second half of the eighteenth century, agrarian change maintained and even improved standards of life, partly because of natural endowment.

But it was often achieved by the exodus of people. Highlanders and Islanders had left for Europe, England and Ireland for centuries long before the 1700s and from the 1730s transatlantic emigrations to New York and North Carolina involved substantial numbers. After the Seven Years War there was a renewed increase in emigration in the years between 1763 and 1775. More left from the Highlands and Islands than from any other British region except the London area.[12] Almost one-fifth of all British emigrants in these years came from the Highlands and Islands of Scotland, one of the most sparsely populated areas of the United Kingdom.

Transatlantic emigration all but ceased during the American War and when it resumed, was less frantic. After the outbreak of war with France in 1793 emigration again slowed down, but after peace in 1801 the exodus rose to the high levels seen before the American War. Landowners and government were concerned about the potential loss of labour and army recruits and rushed through a Passenger Vessels Act in 1803 to increase the costs of transatlantic voyage.[13] The number of emigrants fell drastically again, though individual parties of Highlanders continued to leave during the Napoleonic wars.

These waves of emigration, consisting mainly of small tenants with some means, were a reaction to the many changes in land settlement, rentals and tenure which were destroying the old way of life. The reasons why so many people should seek to emigrate are far from clear. The 'pull' factors involving 'chain migration' to the expanding settlement and economies of the transatlantic colonies were important. The 'push' of Malthusian population pressures in a rising population may have led to the outflow of 'surplus' people. Population loss was inevitable because the Highland and Hebridean economy could not always generate enough work. However, the picture between 1769 and 1815 is considerably more complex and it is by no means certain that the demographic explanation is entirely satisfactory for that earlier period. Economic activity was often expanding, despite years of crisis. This was not an exodus born of the stress of hunger and destitution. Rather it was a movement which involved a degree of choice in which the the Highlanders and Islanders chose to go to the New World to improve their situation, as 'makers and masters of their own destiny'.[14] This emigration was one of rising expectations.

Changes in the rural scene

The three main aspects of the agrarian revolution in Scotland were enclosure, consolidation of holdings into single farm units and the separation of agricultural and industrial activities. Depending on population pressure and other factors, these occurred at different times in different areas of

the Highlands and Islands. The general enclosure acts enabled the Scottish
lairds to make these improvements more informally and not necessarily
all at once. It has been claimed for Islay that 'towards the end of the
seventies . . . the dominant personality, Campbell of Shawfield, a landowner
with control of almost the whole island, had driven through a complete
agrarian reorganisation with the aid of a band of farmers who combined
elegant manners with professional assiduity'.[15] However, other writers
had different views and from archive evidence it seems clear that such a
sudden and wholesale reorganisation did not take place. One of Walter
Campbell's inherited difficulties was that other leases did not expire until
1787 or 1798.[16]

By 1785 James Anderson was reporting that it was difficult to imagine
the degree of improvement that could be achieved in the islands. They
had been 'hitherto so entirely neglected [except] for the island of Islay
which has been for a few years past under the care of a judicious proprietor,
who has studied to augment his own revenue by promoting the prosperity
of his people'.[17] Walter Campbell himself described what he had achieved
by the beginning of 1791.[18] Over thirty miles of good roads had been
built, with bridges and milestones, two quays erected, small inns built,
regular packet and post established, and two villages begun. Land was
being reclaimed, Shetland sheep imported (with plans for Spanish sheep
as well), and exports included horned cattle, horses (including one 'bred
by me' which was being ridden by the Prince of Wales), fish, kelp, yarn
and even grain.

The writers of *The Statistical Account* in the last decade of the eighteenth
century were local ministers who compensated for their lack of wider
experience by their ability to give precise information about specific places
in their parishes. The Rev Archibald Robertson of Kildalton bewailed the
lack of attention given to agricultural improvements by the small tenants
and the gentlemen farmers of his parish alike. He contrasted this situation
with the parish of Killarow where people 'are encouraged to improve a
little in agriculture, by the example of Mr Campbell of Shawfield, who is
one of the best farmers in the west of Scotland: and perhaps his Islay
estate is capable of as much improvement as any in the kingdom'.[19] Only
a small part of the Kildalton parish was described as being enclosed and
this deterrent to improvement was emphasised. Kildalton's relative isolation
from the main centre of activities at the head of Loch Indaal was probably
one major factor delaying improvements. The only route from this parish
to the others was along the beach of Laggan Bay; no roads over the peat
bogs had yet been built.

The Rev John Murdoch, minister of the united parishes of Killarow and Kilmeny, also paid tribute to Mr Campbell, who 'has improved large tracts of moor ground, within view of his own house, which lies about three English miles from the village; and from his method of cultivation, they have produced large crops. He spares neither pains nor expence; and in this respect several of his tenants attempt to imitate him'.[20] Mr Murdoch estimated that about £700 to £1,000 annually was spent by Walter Campbell on improvements, compared to an island annual rent several times that amount.[21] The same approving attitude was adopted by the Kilchoman writer:

> Within these dozen years, the present proprietor has more than doubled his rents; yet the tenantry, as well as himself, are better off than ever. They have given him, as it were, an addition to his estate, by rescuing many acres of moor and moss, from a state of nature, and bringing them to yield good crops of corn and grass. On the other hand, the proprietor has given the tenants such advantageous leases, that they have greatly bettered their circumstances, as well as increased their numbers, and are enabled to live much more comfortably than formerly.[22]

One might suspect that some of this praise by the Islay ministers was generated by the knowledge that the proprietor was not only responsible for their appointment and for paying their stipend, but was likely to read their comments when the Account was published. Their accuracy is, however, evident from the independent appraisals of more expert witnesses. Contemporary writers and analysts, experienced in assessing estate management, recorded the improvements that had taken place despite population and other difficulties. The general impression that improvements were taking place in some areas of Islay but not in others is also corroborated by contemporaneous estate documents and rentals. Leases and rentals indicate that by the end of the eighteenth century, the earlier pattern of large single holdings and joint farms had been altered in several respects, particularly in their relative distribution. There is also evidence that tenants were becoming mobile, going within the island from one township to another, or from townships to single holdings. They were also moving into the village of Bowmore and were migrating to the mainland, especially to the Scottish lowlands and emigrating abroad.

Even more striking was the smaller number of large areas rented by a single farmer: by 1798 there were only 32.[23] Some of the large tacks had become single farms. Others, instead of being worked by subtenants, had become joint farms with tenants who rented directly from the laird but still farmed in common. The large holdings were still in the north-east and south-east and there were some medium and small-sized holdings near the laird's mansion at the head of Loch Indaal. But the distribution of joint holdings with more than two tenants had considerably expanded in area. Multiple townships existed over the whole of the Oa peninsula and in the interior valleys of the eastern hills. Indeed between 1779 and 1802 the leases showed an increase of about one-third in the numbers of legal small tenants per holding. Subtenants too may have increased in like proportions, although the new leases were supposed to debar tenants from subletting.

The Hebridean model

Into the new century, Fraser recorded that the improvement of Islay had been going on ever since Anderson's time, in an 'accelerated ratio in every kind of improvement'.[24] During his tour in the following decade, the surgeon-geologist, John MacCulloch, considered that Islay retained 'so few of the Highland manners, as scarcely to excite any feelings different from the Low Country'.[25] The most complete record of the agricultural situation and changes in Islay, however, compared to the rest of the Hebrides, during Walter Campbell's lairdship, is that of James Macdonald.[26] Born in North Uist in 1777, Macdonald later gave up the struggle to be a sedentary minister of a Fife parish church and became a much-travelled companion to the Clanranald heir at the turn of the century.[27] He was commissioned by Sir John Sinclair to write a *General View of the Agriculture of the Hebrides* and in 1808 spent the months of May to September gathering information in the islands. His payment was £300 in three instalments and his work was highly praised: 'No better report has ever appeared on any special subject'.[28] Macdonald recalled the time spent on Islay in 1808 as one of the happiest periods of his life, 'and equally interesting, whether recollected as dedicated to the contemplation of a sequestered island in a state of rapid improvement, and unlooked for approaches to a high state of refinement; or as enjoyed in the conversation and company of a most polished and hospitable class of his Hebridean countrymen'.[29] He described the island as 'the most improved of the large Hebrides, and as the leader and model of the other isles, [it] deserves particular attention'.[30]

Macdonald's systematic analysis and text of 700 octavo pages, covering the Hebrides as a whole, are accompanied by an appendix of regional Hebridean descriptions, adding another 200 pages. Throughout both parts there are recurrent references to Islay as a Hebridean model. His style is varied, but his use of sources and attempts at quantification, analysis and explanation are impressive. In his preliminary references to Islay and to Walter Campbell, Macdonald inserted a careful disclaimer, saying that he was going to 'make frequent mention of this gentleman, and always to his advantage, it is but justice to him and to myself to state (in order to prevent the imputation of partiality), that, at the time of writing this, I have not the honour of his acquaintance, and have never as yet even seen him'.[31]

Macdonald also paid due and sometimes considerable praise to other improvers in Islay and elsewhere. These included the other main improving proprietor of the island, Campbell of Ballinaby, as well as some of Shawfield's tenants, 'thirty gentlemen farmers'. Concerning Campbell of Ballinaby's efforts, he explained:

> Mr Campbell of Ballinaby, in Islay, is fast improving both soft peatmoss and hard hill ground, for the purposes of aration. He rears excellent horses of the real west or Hebridian breed on his own property, rather larger than the common Gearran [gelding], but with the same properties of strength, activity, durability, and hardiness. A pair can draw the plough, with proper management, for twelve hours every day in the week. Three pairs of these ploughed regularly, each working day, from the 6th till the 24th of May 1808, and with singular vigour and correctness, without any driver or leader but the ploughman. They had done the same for months before. We have never seen a more beautiful furrow in Norfolk, East Lothian or Holstein than behind the Gearrans, bred in Islay, and conducted, both plough and horses, by one Islay boy.[32]

A decade earlier, the Kilchoman minister had noted that the Islay folk were said to keep too many horses at the expense of 'the system' of black cattle. There was a lively trade in horses across the North Channel, culminating in the annual Ballycastle Fair.

Macdonald set out clearly his reasons for emphasising the roles of individuals in the island, rather than that of their environment. He argued that the state of property was neither very favourable nor very adverse to agricultural improvements. More depended on the landlord's disposition: every improvement of consequence owed its origin and success to 'some spirited and intelligent' proprietor, especially one who resided regularly on the spot and who understood business. Although Macdonald seems to have regarded Walter Campbell of Shawfield as the most important improver in all the Hebrides, many parts of the southern islands, including Gigha, Colonsay and parts of Mull, were farther ahead than most of the Outer Hebrides. This was attributed mainly to the influence of the landlords, but Macdonald suggested that there were other more complex reasons, such as the lairds' interest in, or an area's ability to produce kelp from seaweed. He was particularly impressed that there were never any arrears of rent on the estate of Islay, though he later contradicted himself on this point.

In Macdonald's comparisons, Campbell of Shawfield found himself in distinguished company of the great estates of 'Lord Macdonald, Shawfield, Clanranald, Seaforth, Duke of Argyll, Hamilton, &c.', managed by resident stewards or factors, who usually lived on the spot. Lord Macdonald and Campbell of Shawfield were able to demonstrate that 'a large rental is not incompatible with the other duties of a landlord'. He claimed that Shawfield had always distinguished himself since he succeeded to the Islay estate as

> . . . the first of the Hebridian improvers. He resides in that island for three or four months of the year, and spends among a tenantry, who love and respect him, a very large portion of the rents which they pay. He plants trees, and they grow where it was supposed none could thrive. He incloses, drains, embanks, and has shut out the sea from several hundred acres of fine land; employs nearly one hundred labourers all the year round, and teaches practically regular industry, good order and perseverance . . . He encourages, in the most judicious and effectual manner, all those tenants who exhibit active industry, and a desire for improvement. By these means he has within a period of thirty-four years tripled the rents, and the intrinsic value of his fine island; and . . . has bettered the situation of his tenants beyond description, and at the same time doubled their numbers. Most of the other great proprietors are at present non-residents, and spend very little of their time upon their estates.[33]

Macdonald did point out that the environment of Islay may have encouraged experiments in agricultural improvements. His field observations of the soils, for example, led him to conclude that substantial areas of the island showed

> . . . judicious management, rational industry, and rapid improvement. The principal proprietor, as well as Mr Campbell of Ballinaby, sets a good example, which a very respectable tenantry are anxious to follow. Green crops are generally introduced – lime stone is burned for manure with peat fuel, even by the small tenants, who pay no more than eight or ten pounds of rent; and inclosures, roads, and draining, give the soil an air of sheltered richness and comfort rarely witnessed on this side of Scotland.[34]

This contrast with other parts of the Hebrides could be measured in different ways. Macdonald reckoned that Islay had just over 8,000 hectares of arable and meadow land, after the Uists and Barra (16,000), Skye

(12,000) and Harris and Lewis (10,500).[35] Islay had twelve per cent of the arable and meadow in the islands, although the island represented a much smaller proportion of the total area. Rents for part of Islay represented about 30s. (£1.50) per year for each person, compared to 23s. (£1.15) for the Hebrides as a whole, or 120s. (£6.00) for Berwickshire.[36]

The agricultural system that gave such encouraging results was an interesting blend of the traditional and the novel; the major visible changes in landscape and agrarian reorganisation in Islay were yet to happen. Though there had been some changes in landholdings, the prosperity was based more on new crops and new methods. Among the novelties was wheat cultivation, in which Macdonald noted a 'fair experiment' had been made, but he also recognised that some years must elapse before the results of the experiment could be good enough to warrant encouragement. It seems to modern eyes an unlikely crop for Islay, but this was the period of the Napoleonic blockade.

Barley, used for cattle food and for whisky distilling, was a different matter. Macdonald reported that barley was grown from improved strains, instead of the old, low-yielding 'bear' or 'bigg' barley. Lime, spread to destroy the grub worms to which barley was very prone, helped to give good yields. Oats of course were grown both for human consumption and for animal fodder, as were potatoes. The latter were important also as a cash crop for export; as in Bute, Gigha and Colonsay, the potato fields were usually drilled and then hoed, in contrast to the lazybed digging of the Outer Hebrides. Similar improvements were evident in green crops. The first field of clover in the Hebrides had been sown in Islay as far back as 1761 and new grass strains had been introduced for both hay and pasture. The flax that was among the earliest innovations of Daniel Campbell was the basis of the yarn-spinning and linen-weaving, producing what Macdonald described as the staple commodity of the island of Islay.

Despite such crop improvements, the mainstay of agriculture on Islay remained livestock and, as in the past, this meant cattle rather than sheep. Some of the wealthier farmers had introduced new breeds, but black cattle still represented a large proportion of the total. The lack of sheep – Macdonald claimed there were no sheep farms as such on Islay – was unlike the situation in many other parts of the Highlands and Islands where clearances were already substituting sheep for the previous rural economy. In Macdonald's view, Islay and some of the other smaller islands could not afford room for sheep walks and were better under black cattle. Wool and mutton were imported to Islay and instead of sheep, Macdonald noted that hogs were reared in great numbers. These, like potatoes, were apparently intended partly for export to Ireland.

This pattern of slow but perceptible change, based as much on improvements to the old order as on its replacement by new techniques, became the characteristic feature of the agricultural 'revolution' on Islay. In the types of crop and breeds of animal, in the system of rotation and the patterns of landholdings, old and new methods continued to coexist until at least the middle of the nineteenth century. This evolution was in contrast to many parts of the wider West Highland region where swifter and more uniform transformation of the landscape of any one estate, resulting in a pattern of large farms and lotted crofting townships, was a true revolution.

Non-agrarian change
Unlike his predecessor, and especially his successor, Walter Campbell did not establish any new village to accommodate the growing island population. Nor did the Campbell seat at Islay House change much. It was, however, probably during this period that the source for much of the agricultural innovation was built, the Home Farm in Islay House Square. Bowmore, established in 1768, continued to develop as the main administrative centre for the island. Shore, Jamieson (reputedly named after a drover) and High Streets were laid out to the west of Main Street and School and Flora Streets east of it. It is possible that some of the single-storeyed cottages in these streets that remained thatched as late as the 1960s were among those referred to in *The Statistical Account* of the 1790s, though much altered internally.[37] Along the broad Main Street and a number of cross and side streets, are some of the survivors of the Georgian houses and cottages of the late-eighteenth century, extensively remodelled inside. A watercolour of a Fair Day in Bowmore in the 1830s shows the slate-roofed houses along the main street and there is today much similarity.[38]

One of the Shawfield Campbells' enthusiasms was the development of linen manufacture and this was a main stimulus to employment in Bowmore, along with day-labouring. With each house and garden the Shawfield landlords granted nineteen-year leases for feus of five or ten acre lots outside the village 'to be reclaimed from a wild state, the first 6 years gratis and the other 13 years at a very small rent . . . many hundred acres . . . which a few years ago were used as peat mosses, and not worth 6*d.* an acre of rent, are now covered with flourishing crops'.[39] These lots remain clearly visible today on either side of School Lane.

In the first decade of the nineteenth century Bowmore's population, according to the village schoolmaster, was about 670.[40] Around £7,000 was raised annually by the manufacture of linen, some of it exported. Little flax was grown elsewhere in the Hebrides; Islay produced three times as much as all the other islands combined.[41] One Scots acre on Islay produced thirty-two stones of lint, bringing the farmer a profit of two guineas and providing three months' employment for twelve people in its manufacture. Whatever the importance of linen manufacture to Bowmore in its first half-century, it declined subsequently as cotton and wool replaced linen and as large factories in the Lowlands and England replaced the handloom weavers of the villages. By 1841, when detailed employment information became available in the copies of the census returns for the first time, there was only a handful of handloom weavers in Bowmore, half of them making linen cloth, the other half using wool.[42]

Although less evidence survives of Walter Campbell's activities outside the agrarian sphere, he did report in 1779 to the Commissioners of the Annexed Estates on the use of the grant that they had made to his brother two years earlier. Walter had spent £250 of the grant, matched by a similar contribution himself, on the Port Askaig pier and on various unspecified coastal fishing experiments. Work on Bowmore pier had not yet begun and he asked for the remaining £250 of the grant in advance:

> Besides the Pier at Portaskeig a much larger and more expensive one is proposed to be erected at Bowmore the principal village in the Island situate upon the first harbour in the West the estimate whereof amounts to £420 Str and is to be begun the lst of March next, part of the materials being already provided and laid down. It is therefore hoped the Honourable Board will now find it convenient to advance the other £250 . . . towards erecting the Quay at Bowmore.[43]

By the time of *The Statistical Account* in 1794, the Rev John Murdoch was able to describe the fine quay at Bowmore which could take vessels of three metres' draught. In the late-eighteenth century, however, fishing was still mainly for local consumption. Every farm around the head of Loch Indaal was alleged to have a boat, but James Anderson noted that there was little attempt to utilise this resource except for family needs. Shellfish were to be found 'in very great quantities; crabs and lobsters of the largest size, and finest quality Great quantities of oysters of different kinds . . . also great plenty of mussels, cockles, clams, rasor or spout-fish, limpets, wilks, shrimps and several other sorts'.[44] Similarly there was no shortage of what he described as 'finny fish'; shoals of mackerel, the abundant haddocks, whitings, skate, halibut, sole, and flounders. As for herring, 'the quantities that might be catched on these coasts between the months of June and January, were the inhabitants in a situation that permitted them to follow that business, are so great as would appear altogether incredible to such as never have been on those coasts'.

Traditional fishermen's cottages nestle around Portnahaven harbour; the village was renowned for its many seafaring captains. Nowadays many of the houses are occupied, mainly in summer, by families based in Glasgow or beyond. (Eric Thorburn).

The British Society for Promoting the Fisheries of Scotland was encouraging landlords to set up villages expressly for fishing. Tobermory on Mull and Ullapool on the Wester Ross mainland were the two main results of this endeavour.[45] It is rather surprising that the response was not greater, in view of the importance of fishing on Scotland's east coast and the comparative shortage of land-based resources along the west coast. In 1785 the economist, James Anderson, suggested that part of the explanation was to be found in the restrictions caused by the laws on salt; he also emphasised the latent aversion to the sea of most inhabitants of the West Highlands. Anderson recommended subsidies that would encourage landlords to establish fishing villages and he argued that these villages would have to be planned on a relatively large scale if they were to be successful.[46]

On Islay, the arguments for fishery development had been heeded by Daniel Campbell the Younger. It was his brother Walter who was left to make the first significant experiments in this direction, after his purchase of the Sunderland estate in 1788. At this time Portnahaven, on the southern tip of the Rinns, was already a thriving fishing harbour and settlement. According to the Kilchoman minister, writing in *The Statistical Account*, Portnahaven was famous for its cod fishing and Walter Campbell had encouraged its development by providing boats, land and timber for houses.[47] The main problem was the lack of a market. By the first decade of the nineteenth century both local and distant markets for Portnahaven fish had expanded. Macdonald described the industry as he found it in 1808: 'The inhabitants of the village were furnished with fresh fish at a halfpenny per pound; and each of the fishermen cleared £2 sterling by one night's industry . . . they frequently run over with cargoes of [fish] to . . . Ireland, and sell them under the name of wild salmon'.[48] But development of this resource still lay in the future; it depended not merely on infrastructure and the encouragement of Islay fishermen but required parallel development of transport facilities and marketing arrangements.

At the turn of the century Walter Campbell and other neighbouring landowners, including Mr Archibald Campbell of Jura and Messrs McNeill of Colonsay and of Oronsay, approached another source of public finance. They prepared an application in 1804 to the recently-established Commissioners for Making Roads and Building Bridges in the Highlands of Scotland, asking for help with their planned overland route to the mainland through Islay and Jura.[49] Walter Campbell wanted financial help for the survey and construction of the extension to the existing road from Port Askaig to Bridgend that had been made at his expense. The proposed extension to Portnahaven was surveyed in 1805 by George Langlands and built the following year at a cost of just over £60 per kilometre for its 22 kilometres. The section through Jura suffered various complications, but was eventually built at Archibald Campbell's expense by about 1810, by which time the piers at Feolin and Lagg were also 'of the most substantial kind'.

Although kelp manufacture was never so significant to Islay's economy as it was elsewhere in the Hebrides, there was some activity, especially in the south-east where the tidal range was rather greater than on the other Islay coasts. Even there the tidal range was less than the five or so metres regarded by Macdonald as being favourable for seaweed growth.[50] A letter from Campbell of Ardmore in 1820 described some of the difficulties of reaping seaweed in Islay, including the lack of 'experts' who could increase the harvest.[51] In 1821 the Islay factor paid out £413 in about 400 individual payments, so the scale was indeed small. The individual producer retained only about one-third of the price from the mainland dealers, the other two-thirds going equally to Walter Campbell and to freight charges. Nor did mining contribute much to the island at this time; MacCulloch's report in the second decade of the century was that the lead mines had been abandoned for some time.[52]

Distilling and brewing, however, were increasing. It is difficult to estimate either the amounts of spirits produced or the numbers employed. But when the 1795 Act was passed which prohibited distilling in Britain, the farmer of the excise on Islay was supposed to have 'taken up' about 90 stills some with a capacity of over 80 gallons.[53] But the islanders were not to be outdone and replaced them almost as quickly, only to have these confiscated in turn. Even when prohibition ended, the islanders did not always bother to take out licences. The reverend authors of *The Statistical Account* frequently referred to the evils of alcohol and other less prejudiced writers observed the existence of many distilleries on the island. Macdonald, for instance, remarked that the islanders were 'fond of ardent spirits . . . They might, however be gradually weaned . . . from their obstinate prejudices in favour of whiskey, were a few breweries established among them'.[54] Walter Campbell had 'with his unwonted activity and beneficence, built a brew-house, and establishing a complete brewing apparatus at Bridgend, near Bowmore . . . some years ago'. Macdonald described its output, on the basis of his own acquaintance with it in 1808, as being 'very good strong ale and table-beer' which appeared 'already to have effected a laudable change in the taste of the whiskey-drinking classes on that island, many of whom now prefer good ale to bad whiskey, and have relinquished the detestable habits of drunkenness in which they were formerly too apt to indulge'. Even then, grain had to be imported by the distilleries.

Running like a thread through many of the contemporary accounts was the growing realisation that, however desirable or remarkable were the improvements in agriculture and other traditional activities, the growing pressure of population demanded other solutions. Macdonald noted that although spinning of yarn and weaving of cloth were carried out in Islay for local use, it was not the basis of an industry that served many markets beyond the island. There were no bleachfields in the Hebrides, 'not even in Islay, where great quantities of flax are manufactured into yarns and linens, and whence these are sent to the Firth of Clyde and Dumbarton for bleaching'.[55] There were also growing opportunities for employment in the service sector, especially through increasing transport of goods about the island and to and from the mainland and Ireland. Nevertheless there were still too many people on Islay for the available work. The Government assistance provided in the 1770s was not repeated in very large sums. Macdonald remarked that 'government has done nothing in Islay to promote the improvements carried on by the patriotic and enlightened proprietor, who . . . has done much; but he cannot do everything'.[56] Campbell of Shawfield and Islay, Macdonald indicated, was willing to sacrifice rent increases and land improvements and was willing to carry arrears of rent, to avoid clearing people from the land. But it was impossible for them all to be accommodated on the island in a manner 'consistent with his general system'. The quandary was handed on to Walter Campbell's successor.

In 1814, two years before he died, Walter Campbell sold the Sunderland estate that he had acquired in 1788 to his son, Walter, while the estates of Skipness and Ardpatrick went to his remaining sons, Robert and Colin.[57] Walter Campbell, 'the most zealous improver of all', died at Islay House on 19 October 1816, at the age of 75; his monument is in the round church at Bowmore. His first marriage, at the age of 27, to Eleanor Kerr of Newfield had produced ten children. His heir, John, was a Member of Parliament for Ayr Burghs until, in what had almost become a family tradition, he predeceased his father. John Campbell's marriage in 1796 to Lady Charlotte Campbell, youngest daughter of the fifth duke of Argyll, had produced a male heir, Walter Frederick Campbell, who was about eighteen when his grandfather died.

Notes and references

[1] IEP, Inventories.

[2] Macdonald, *General View*, p. 63 and p. 619.

[3] J. G. Smith, *The Old Country Houses of the Old Glasgow Gentry*, (Glasgow, 1880), Plate LXXXIX.

[4] Kyd, *Scottish Population Statistics*, p. 33.

[5] Sinclair, *OSA*, pp. 276–302.

[6] W. Campbell to Earl Bathurst, 26 January 1791, Historical Manuscripts Commission (HMC), *Report on the Manuscripts of Earl Bathurst,* (London, 1923), p. 20.

[7] Idem.

[8] T. R. Malthus, *An Essay on The Principle of Population*, (London, 1798).

[9] Sinclair, *OSA*, p. 293.

[10] Ibid., p. 301.

[11] Idem.

[12] B. Bailyn, *Voyages to the West*, (New York, 1986), p. 95.

[13] Devine, *Clanship*, p. 179.

[14] J. M. Bumstead, *The People's Clearance*, (Edinburgh, 1982), p. 221.

[15] M. Gray, *The Highland Economy 1750–1850*, (London, 1957), p. 81.

[16] Smith, *Book of Islay*, p. 469.

[17] Anderson, *Account*, p. 145.

[18] Campbell to Bathurst, 26 January 1791, HMC *Bathurst*, pp. 20–1.

[19] Sinclair, *OSA*, p. 287.

[20] Ibid., pp. 298–99.

[21] By 1808 the annual rental was £11,000. Macdonald, *General View*, p. 613.

[22] Sinclair, *OSA*, p. 284.

[23] IEP, Rental for 1795.

24   R. Fraser, *A Letter to the Right Hon. Charles Abbot, Speaker of the House of Commons, containing an Inquiry into the most effectual means of improvement on the coasts and western isles of Scotland, and the extension of the Fisheries*, (London, 1803).

25   J. MacCulloch, *The Highlands and Western Isles of Scotland . . . Founded on a series of annual journeys between . . . 1811 and 1821*, (London, 1824), 4 vols., IV, p. 419.

26   Macdonald, *General View*. Islay is referred to throughout the text; the main Islay account is on pp. 612–63.

27   Biographical material on James Macdonald is from A. Gillies, *A Hebridean in Goethe's Weimar*, (Oxford, 1969).

28   J. Donaldson, *Agricultural Biography*, (London, 1854), p. 103.

29   Macdonald, *General View*, p. 633.

30   Ibid., p. 614.

31   Ibid., p. 64.

32   Ibid., p. 66.

33   Ibid., pp. 63–4.

34   Ibid., p. 21.

35   Ibid., p. 27.

36   Ibid., pp. 549–50.

37   Sinclair, *OSA*, p. 301.

38   Forman, *'Islay House'*, p. 38.

39   Macdonald, *General View*, p. 630.

40   Ibid., p. 637.

41   Ibid., p. 532.

42   Copies of the Census enumerators' schedules for 1841 to 1891, New Register House, Edinburgh.

43   SRO, E727/60/3 (1).

44   J. Anderson, 1785, pp. 10–11.

45   Lewis, *Topographical Dictionary*, II, p. 546.

46   Anderson, *Account*, p. 67ff.

47   Sinclair, *OSA*, p. 281.

48   Macdonald, *General View*, pp. 630–1.

49   See *Reports of the Commissioners for making Roads and Bridges in the Highlands and Islands of Scotland, BPP*, 1805, III; 1807, III; 1810, IV and 1812–13, V.

50   Macdonald, *General View*, pp. 621–2. About twenty tons of seaweed produced one ton of kelp.

51   IEP, Factor's note about payments to kelp gatherers in Ardmore, 1820.

52   MacCulloch, *Highlands and Western Islands*, p. 419; see also R. Forsyth, *The Beauties of Scotland*, (Edinburgh, 1805-8), 5 vols., (1808), V, p. 517.

53   A. J. Youngson, *After the Forty Five*, (Edinburgh, 1973), pp. 115–6.

54   Macdonald, *General View*, p. 207.

55   Ibid., p. 53.

56   Ibid., p. 631.

57   IEP, Disposition of the Estate of Sunderland, 1814.

CHAPTER 9

Creating the landscape

Almost a hundred years had passed between the purchase of Islay by 'Great' Daniel Campbell in 1726 and the death of Walter Campbell in 1816 and during this time the basic task facing a landlord on Islay had changed. The initiative and perseverance of the Campbells of Shawfield, their factors and tenants, had yielded results that deserved and received widespread recognition among agricultural experts and social observers throughout and beyond Scotland.

By the second decade of the nineteenth century and with recession after the end of the Napoleonic wars, the need for further agricultural improvements still remained, but it had ceased to be the primary problem. Prosperity had brought its own difficulties in the form of a population that was still continuing its rapid growth, despite migration. If agricultural reorganisation was to be pursued to its logical conclusion in terms of maximising revenue, then a large number of families would have to find their primary income from non-agricultural sources. There was, in fact, no real choice: a reduced dependence on agriculture was as necessary, on a long-term view, for the tenants and cottars as for the landlord.

The scope for influence and initiative on the part of the principal laird was still enormous and Walter Frederick Campbell rose to the opportunity. Succeeding his grandfather at the age of only eighteen, over the next 32 years he initiated many of the changes in agriculture and settlement that have contributed to the present appearance of Islay. The period of Walter Frederick Campbell's lairdship of Islay was probably one with greatest evidence of change that Islay ever witnessed, as far as landscape and settlement were concerned.

In his personal life, Walter Frederick Campbell repeated several of the Shawfield characteristics. He was a Member of Parliament, for Argyll, from 1822 to 1841 and was married twice.[1] His first wife, Lady Eleanor Charteris, daughter of the eighth earl of Wemyss, was the inspiration for the names of two of the villages that he established, Port Ellen and Port Wemyss. The death of Lady Eleanor in 1832, after mental illness, was a profound shock to her husband: in a black-edged letter to Campbell of

The artist, William Heath, recorded the Islay scene in the 1830s, executing a large volume of highly romanticised watercolours for the laird. The Paps of Jura form the backdrop to this distant view of Islay House (*Scottish Field*).

A different view by Heath of Islay House and Square from the garden in the new policies established during the gentrification of the estate.

Lumsden reported in 1825 that 'Mr Campbell has lately built a very pretty shooting cottage, situated in a romantic part of the coast'. The *cottage ornée* at Ardimersay, as depicted by Heath, was superseded later in the century by Kildalton House nearby.

The second lighthouse in Islay, after the Rinns, commemorated the premature death in 1832 of Walter Frederick Campbell's first wife, Lady Eleanor, in a pious plaque.

Melfort in March of the following year, Walter Frederick wrote that he was as yet 'little able to attend to anything I am not in good health and it will be along ere I recover the shock both health and spirits have received'.[2] The lighthouse at the entrance to Port Ellen harbour commemorates Lady Eleanor's death with a rather pious inscription. She is buried in one half of a sombre black marble sarcophagus in Bowmore Church: the other half has remained empty.

Walter Frederick did recover, and his second marriage in 1837 to his cousin, Catherine Coles, produced further children. During his lairdship, considerable additions were made to Islay House, including the rear extension 'of offices' designed in Scottish Baronial style by William Playfair.[3] A second residence in the south-east, Ardimersay Cottage, was also constructed and in 1820 Foreland House was finished and surrounded with gardens and plantations by his uncle, Captain Walter Campbell. Walter Frederick Campbell's main contributions to Islay, however, were of much wider significance, taking the form of changes in agricultural extent, further separation of agricultural and other employment (including the creation of several new villages) and thorough improvements in internal and external communications and transport.

Pressures in the agrarian economy

This was the period when the population on the island was increasing to its maximum of around 15,000 about the time of the 1831 census (1841 and 1851 in Kildalton and Oa).[4] How did this happen? In the parishes of Killarow and Kilmeny for example, the numbers of marriages recorded in the old parish registers increased at a growing rate in the first decades of the nineteenth century. These were followed by similar increases in the numbers of births. As long as births were more numerous than deaths, and despite net out-migration, the population continued to increase. Between the 1750s and the 1790s, population had increased by between 50 and 60 per cent; between the 1790s and the 1830s it increased by 80 per cent to just under 15,000.

The number of multiple tenants was also at its highest. In 1824, only 49 tenants had large and medium-sized holdings, twenty had small single holdings under £20 annual rent, but 670 tenants still occupied 95 townships.[5] Land pressure and the upper limits of cultivation in Islay therefore were also approaching their maximum. Townships were divided into Upper and Lower, or West, Mid and East or whatever was appropriate. In the low sun of winter and spring the lazybed ridges which accompanied this expansion of cultivated land can still be seen in remoter parts of the upper hills and moors. Because of this land pressure, and also because of

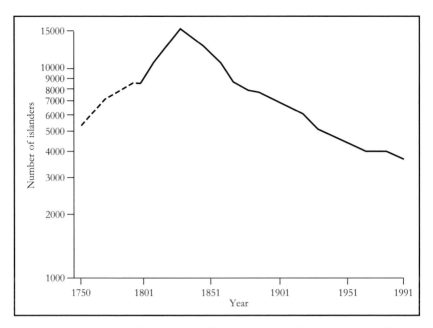

Islay's population, 1755-1991. Numbers of islanders increased by almost one-half in the second half of the eighteenth century; but in the next three decades it almost doubled. A figure of 14,992 was recorded in the 1831 Census. The subsequent decline from this peak was almost as rapid, as the semi-logarithmic graph shows. For the past century, the rate of decline has been more gradual (*Census of Scotland*).

a national decline in cattle and crop prices after the Napoleonic wars, arrears of rent mounted steadily. The tenants were not evading payment of their rents, but were simply not able to pay.

Some of Walter Frederick's views on the mounting problems were expressed in 1826 in a report to the Select Committee investigating the possibility of encouraging emigration as a means of alleviating overpopulation in the western Highland and Islands.[6] He preferred to solve land pressures by persuading the surplus population to move to villages, with enough land for potatoes and cow's grass. But some people had refused to give up their farms and, in such cases, he would have been 'very glad to have got those people to emigrate, and would have advanced a moderate sum of money'. He tried to make changes without moving islanders compulsorily from their birthplace. Walter Frederick Campbell's objective was not the total clearance of people from the land; his purpose, like that of his Shawfield predecessors, was the improvement of agriculture and an improvement in the returns from farming for his tenants and

Approaching the time of maximum population and land pressure, and, Bowmore and
Portnahaven apart, with village building still to absorb people from the land, the extent of
the numbers problem facing Walter Frederick Campbell is shown here in the map of
holdings with more than two tenants in 1824 (Islay Estate Papers).

himself. Agricultural reorganisation almost always involved a reduction in
the number of tenants.

In the Scottish Highlands and Islands landlords had virtually complete
freedom of action. An Act of the Court of Session of 1756 had clarified
the legal procedures for removal of tenants, which could relatively easily
be accomplished through the application to a local sheriff court at least
40 days before Whitsun. Most of the Highland population had no absolute
legal right to land and this made the reductions in numbers possible.
Gradual and relentless displacement rather than mass eviction was the
norm; most clearances before 1815 were not designed to expel people.
Most removals probably only involved a few people at a time until the
more drastic episodes of the mid-nineteenth century, when some Highland
landlords seem to have equated agricultural improvement with total
clearance of tenants. On Islay total clearance was still rare, perhaps partly
because the pressure of population on resources was not so great as

elsewhere, but also because the Campbells of Shawfield were both humane and perceptive enough to realise that total clearance was not a prerequisite for improvement.

During this period the laird employed the surveyor William Gemmill to produce maps and plans of some of the holdings on the island, presumably with a view to their further improvement or reorganisation.[7] Together with other surviving estate material such as annual rentals and factors' reports the maps and plans make it possible to reconstruct the nature and progress of planning and achievement of reorganisation. Although it followed the family tradition of estate improvements, this period of major reorganisation by Walter Frederick Campbell during the 1820s and 1830s was to be the last of such enterprises on Islay. Subsequent changes were slower and more sporadic, variations on a landscape theme that was established during Walter Frederick's lairdship that is still clearly recognisable.

During the 1830s improvements continued and were exemplified in the development of what is still an important element in Islay life. The Islay, Jura and Colonsay Agricultural Association was inaugurated in 1838, the first such to be established in the islands, in the early-nineteenth century.[8] By the 1830s one of the principal objectives was 'the improvement of Highland breeds of cattle and sheep' on the three islands. The Annual Show that was instituted has become one of the principal events of the Islay calendar.

Evolutionary rural change
Some of the processes of change were gradual and evolutionary. For example, evolution from eighteenth-century tacks to single farms was characteristic of some grazing areas. In Islay, some improvements had taken place from the early-eighteenth century onwards. For instance, the manuscript estate plan by Stephen MacDougall of the Islay tack of Coul shows that, even before 1749, the land had been reorganised into arable and pasture fields, enclosed by dykes or walls of stone or turf. Around the entire holding ran a stone dyke.[9] In a rental of 1795, Coul was mentioned as forming part of a larger tack comprising the six holdings of Coul, Coulererach, Foreland, Cultoon, Corgortan and Buninuilt. But by Walter Frederick's time in 1819, Coul had become a single holding with a single tenant.

Another gradual process of change was provoked by increases in numbers of tenants and the consequent subdivision of their holdings. The late-eighteenth century had seen a rapid increase in the number of legal agricultural tenants, as for example in Kendrochid.

Tenants in 1803	Tenants in 1824	Rent in 1824
J. Leitch	J. Leitch	£8 13s. 4d.
	A. Leitch	£8 13s. 4d.
J McCannell	J. McCannell	£8 13s. 4d.
	A. McCannell	£8 13s. 4d.
J. Smith	M. McCannell	£17 6s. 8d.
A. Smith	J. McCannell	£10 16s. 8d.
	Heirs D. Leitch	£6 10s. 0d.
A. McCannell	A. McCannell	£17 6s. 8d.
D. McCannell	D. McCannell	£8 13s. 4d.
	G. McCannell	£8 13s. 4d.

Changes in tenancies in Kendrochid between 1803 and 1824. Proportional shares of total rent indicate communal working of the joint farm. Halved or shared portions of rent indicate subdivision of individual shares.[10]

Continued subdivision of multiple holdings, often already too small to provide an adequate living, hindered the improvement of agricultural techniques and provided an immediate reason for reorganisation. To remedy the deteriorating situation, a reduction in the number of tenants and an informal reorganisation of the holdings so as to enlarge the individual holdings were undertaken. The total number of tenants in Nereabolls in the Rinns, for example, was reduced from eleven to eight between 1824 and 1833. From the rentals it seems that most of the eleven tenants, all of whom had been in arrears of rent, were replaced by others from surrounding townships. The equally-apportioned rents indicated for the year 1833 perhaps represent an attempt to re-establish an earlier division into eight shares that had become subdivided with population increase. But such reorganisation does not appear to have been accompanied by a physical reorganisation. The lack of any regular pattern on subsequent maps of Nereabolls, or at the present day, tends to confirm this and to imply that the creation of consolidated holdings for each of the tenants was a more informal process.

The old system of joint farms had involved annual or periodic reallocation of a large number of cultivable strips among the tenants. It seems probable that in places like Nereabolls, where small tenants persisted and clearance did not take place, the first stage in consolidation of holdings

Tenants in 1824	Rent	Tenants in 1833	Rent
A. MacDonald	£6 5s. 0d.	A. Mackenzie	£18
J. MacArthur	£6 5s. 0d.		
A. MacEachern	£12 10s. 0d.	A. McLergan	£18
Heirs Macmillan	£12 10s. 0d.	J. McDermid	£18
A. Brown	£6 5s. 0d.	D. & A. Campbell	£18
A. Johnston	£6 5s .0d.		
J. Mackinnon	£12 10s .0d.	J. Mackinnon	£18
D. Macmillan	£12 10s. 0d.	A. McDonald	£18
D. McQuarrie	£6 5s. 0d.	C. Campbell	£18
D. Lamont	£6 5s. 0d.		
A. Johnston	£12 10s. 0d.	D. Mitchell	£18

Reductions in tenants and tenancies in Nereabolls between 1824 and 1833 were perhaps to re-establish an earlier number of holdings.

may have been an agreement to abandon periodic reallocation in favour of a fixed pattern of strips.[11] This would in time be succeeded by an exchange of strips among tenants, a process of consolidation which could be initaited either by the landlord or by the tenants themselves, as their numbers began to decline. Usually a rather irregular pattern of field boundaries resulted, following the irregular limits of the former cultivated fields. Only rarely in the Islay townships where reduction of tenants took place is there evidence that a rigid system of small holdings or crofting townships was imposed by the landlord. By the gradual processes of emigration, delayed marriage or celibacy, emigration or death, informal rearrangement of the land into single consolidated holdings took place, at least when there were no more than, say, ten tenants in a township.

Revolutionary plans
There had been occasional clearances in late-eighteenth century Islay to make way for a single farm, as at Ballyclach sometime between 1779 and 1795. Similarly Octovullin had eleven tenants named in a rental of 1812, but by 1824 there was only one. In the 1820s and 1830s such clearance became rather more common.

But only in a few cases on Islay was clearance as sudden and revolutionary as it was in the more notorious 'cleared' areas elsewhere in

Echoing the round church at Bowmore were the D-shaped plans of the farmsteading at
Kilchiaran, built in the mid-1820s, and similar to the steading at Maam near Inveraray in
Argyll; and of the village of Port Wemyss, started a decade later.

the Highlands and Islands. Of the few sudden clearances that did take
place, Kilchiaran is perhaps the best example. Numbers of tenants on this
holding rose in the late-eighteenth and early-nineteenth centuries, so that
by 1825 there were seventeen direct tenants named in the rental. The
rental for the following year gives only the names of two brothers, Duncan
and James Campbell. Many of the tenants' names can be traced in later
rentals for nearby holdings and villages. Eleven of them moved into the
adjacent townships of Gearach, Olistadh and Conisby, or to the new
village of Port Charlotte. The remainder migrated further or left the
island.

    Walter Frederick's role as landscape planner is more evident in the
planned or formal reorganisation of holdings. This type of reorganisation
was carried out first by Walter Campbell of Shawfield and Walter Campbell
of Sunderland, but was repeated by Walter Frederick. Its hallmark was the
regular field patterns that it produced, often with a dispersed settlement
pattern, and it is most evident around the shores of Loch Indaal, near
Walter Frederick's Home Farm. One of William Gemmill's maps of the
lands of 'Isla House', the proprietor's mansion, shows the layout
characteristic of the Romantic approach to designing lairds' policies and

Tenants in 1802	Tenants in 1815–16	Tenants in 1824–25
J. McEachern	J. McEachern	J. McEachern*
J. McEachern Jr.	J. McEachern Jr.	J. McEachern
		D. McIntyre
R. McEachern	P. McEachern	P. McEachern*
A. McEachern	A. McEachern	A. McEachern
A. Bell	D. Bell	D. Bell (To Gearach)
	D. & A. Gillespy	A. Gillespy*
D. McNeill	D. McNeill	N. McNeill
	J. McNeill	J. McNeill **
		A.McAllister**
A. Currie	P. Currie	D. & J. Currie
		L. Currie
	D. McLachlan	P. Currie &
		D.Gillespie*
D. McLellan	D. McLellan	J. McLellan
		J. McArthur

Seventeen tenants in Kilchiaran made way for one large farm. Their names can be traced in subsequent rentals to other holdings and Rinns villages. Those marked with an asterisk moved to Conisby, while those marked with two asterisks moved to Olistadh.

estate buildings; this has remained almost unchanged to the present day. The House, garden, plantations, drives and Home Farm Square are all shown as part of the new landscape.

The pattern on Islay is very different from the formal reorganisation elsewhere in the Highlands, where the establishment of lotted or regular crofting townships was more typical. In Islay, the former joint townships were reorganised into several individual small holdings, generally with no common pasture. Unlike joint farms, where the shares of rent were usually equal divisions or subdivisions, the rents on the reorganised small holdings were not usually proportional to each other. The rental for Ballitarson in 1824 indicated this uneven apportionment of rent. Gemmill's plan of Ballitarson showed the new individual holdings bounded by stone dykes. Each holding had its own farmstead. Indications of the old order are shown by phrases such as 'old turf dykes not shown'.

Peaty moorland was surveyed by William Gemmill in 1828 for laying out 'twenty acre' holdings or lots, for tenants displaced elsewhere (Islay Estate Papers).

Another form of reorganisation was that of lotting, through the creation of small blocks or strips of land, perhaps with common pasture, which were laid out for part-time or non-agricultural workers near villages, or on waste land or muir. These village lotments form a distinctive feature of the Islay landscape; they were planned by the lairds to enable those who worked as day-labourers or in non-agricultural employment to produce their own potatoes and milk. The lots were essentially a type of land-reclamation scheme, involving drainage of the unimproved land, followed by dressing with shell sand.

Around the edges of the villages of Bowmore, Port Charlotte and Port Ellen, for example, the peaty muir was reclaimed in lots or compact blocks by village tenants. Some of these were displaced agricultural tenants from the townships, who had now become agricultural day-labourers or craftsmen with no other access to land. Each plot of reclaimed land was intended to produce potatoes for a family as well as oats and grass for a cow's milk. A less elaborate scheme was set up around the lead-mining area of Ballygrant. The fishing village of Port Wemyss in the 1830s, however, showed a pattern more reminiscent of Outer Hebridean townships laid out for crofter-fishermen much later in the nineteenth century. Each individual tenant's lot or holding was a narrow strip of land running back from a road to the hill or to the shore. On Gemmill's map of 1833 showing the lots at Wemysshaven or Port Weymss, together with the township common pasture, each of the 52 narrow strips had a different tenant's name. The tenants can often be traced through earlier rentals to townships on the Rinns affected by clearance or reduction, including Kilchiaran, Lossit and Nereabolls.

The reclamation of such land in regularly shaped lots by village tenants was paralleled elsewhere on the peaty muir or moorlands of Islay by schemes of lots for other agricultural tenants who had been displaced from joint farms. Schemes of this kind were started on the Glenegedale, Duich, Glenmachrie and Torra muirs between Bowmore and Port Ellen. The schemes were planned in 1828, based on a map of William Gemmill. They do not appear to have been settled completely as planned and, in view of the generally poor quality of the land, were probably among the least successful of the various experiments in reorganisation. It is worth remarking, however, that even these muir lots in Islay took a different form from those conceived by most Highland and Hebridean lairds. The absence of common grazing is noticeable, despite the vast areas of adjacent hill grazing. The principle of one piece of land for each tenant was maintained; the small tenant was limited to his lot and hill pasture was used for cattle and sheep farms.

Villages proliferate

Although most of Islay's villages were founded several decades later, they all owe much to Daniel Campbell's first experiment with his model village of Bowmore. Walter Campbell of Sunderland redeveloped Portnahaven in the 1820s and four new villages were established in the 1820s and 1830s by Walter Frederick Campbell as part of his overall plan for the island. Port Ellen, Port Charlotte, Port Wemyss and Kiells were all designed to provide non-agricultural employment, in fishing, distilling, weaving and the provision of services. In 1821, three-quarters of the 2,285 families on Islay were listed in the Census as being employed in agriculture.[12] But by 1831, when several of the villages other than Bowmore were still to appear or were just beginning, this proportion had already dropped to two-thirds. The villages were to help reduce the rate of population decline

Islay's Highland Games now take place in August instead of December, but the shot putt, hammer throw and caber toss are the same activities as John Francis Campbell depicted in one of his watercolours, dated 1842 (Trustees of the National Gallery of Scotland).

thereafter on Islay, in comparison to that being experienced in many other parts of the Hebrides. In most of the villages, tenants had moved from the 'country' and built their single-storeyed or two-storeyed houses that are for the most part still standing, albeit renovated.

As a substantial early example of village creation, Bowmore is really *sui generis* on Islay, the more so because of its diversity of function: the other villages tended to have a more specific economic base, though diversity has often come with the passing of time. Just as Bowmore had its counterpart on the Scottish mainland in weavers' villages like Eaglesham, so the creation of villages based on fisheries reflected a more widespread movement. During the first quarter of the nineteenth century the fishing industry seemed potentially prosperous enough to encourage the creation of fishing villages in Islay. In 1825 Portnahaven fishing boats, 'probably the finest on the west coast of Scotland', were reported to be going to the Giant's Causeway, 30 miles away in Antrim, to fish for a 'rich harvest of cod, ling and turbot'.[13] In the early 1820s Walter Campbell of Sunderland formed a new village around the creek of Portnahaven, as was later described by Lord Teignmouth, 'on the basis of an old one, which he found in a poor and wretched state'.[14] Cottages were built 'on a new plan, arranged in rows on either side of the creek, neatly slated, and furnished with windows, fire-places, and sometimes with grates'. Some of them became shops, which were well supported: bakers, grocers, and other tradesmen. The same author added that the girls of the villages were introduced to 'plain embroidery' and 'execute it skilfully'. A school for the Society for Promoting Christian Knowledge, one of Telford's Parliamentary churches, with a glebe donated by Walter Campbell and a 'neat . . . and orderly' public-house were all included in the new community of Portnahaven.

The next village to appear was started about 1821 around Leodamus Bay in the south-east of the island. Named in happier circumstances after Walter Frederick Campbell's first wife, a list of the 1821 'founders' of Port Ellen, originally Port Eleanor, was published in a later guide to Islay.[15] A distillery was established in 1827. Though partly concerned with provision for rural migrants and for fishermen, it has also been claimed by Shanks that the 'building boom' of the 1830s in Port Ellen was only partly the result of deliberate village planning, and that it was also connected with the property qualifications required for parliamentary franchise after the 1832 Reform Act.[16] Lord Teignmouth noted that 'the expectation of a fishery at Port Eleanor produced by the appearance of the herrings, has been disappointing' and this is confirmed by occupation structures of Port Ellen in 1841.[17] Then the major sources of employment were

This redrawing of Gemmill's plan of Wemysshaven or Port Wemyss in 1833 shows the D-shaped plan of the village, narrow lots and common pasture; incomers were from nearby holdings affected by clearance or reduction of tenants. Individual names were noted, with the state of progress of house building (Islay Estate Papers).

agricultural labouring, services and distilling.[18] Some of the street names in the village retain the family names given to them, such as Frederick Crescent, after the laird and Charlotte Street, after his mother.

The plans for another fishing village, Port Wemyss, are dated 1833. Despite the apparent association with east coast ports of Fife and recalling the Fife fishermen brought to Islay many decades earlier by the younger Daniel Campbell, the name is almost certainly a tribute to the family or to the memory of Walter Frederick Campbell's first wife, who was a daughter of the eighth earl of Wemyss. The semi-circular plan of the village at Port Wemyss with its accompanying lots, was drawn up by William Gemmill. Many of the tenants were encouraged to engage in the fishing industry whose outlook seemed prosperous. The factor's superscriptions on Gemmill's map demonstrate the progress of house construction in the new village: 'finished', 'building', 'commenced', or 'nothing done'.[19] Several of the new tenants came from rural areas in the Rinns and by the time of the 1834 rental there were 34 names.[20] A few years later Lord Teignmouth noted the success of those Islay fisheries, (though not the herring) despite opposition to Campbell of Sunderland's plan to convey the cured fish to market quickly in a single vessel, instead of each boat making its way to Ireland.[21]

Whereas both Portnahaven and Port Wemyss were villages in which fishing was the dominant activity, in Port Charlotte fishing was from the start only one element in the economy. Begun in 1828 on the western side of Loch Indaal, expanding the site of the earlier changehouse and malt mill at Skiba or Sgioba on Port-na-Dronnaig, in several respects Port Charlotte resembled Bowmore. The village plan and buildings were similar, though Port Charlotte's architectural focus was provided by the school rather than the church. Like Bowmore also, Port Charlotte was intended to accommodate agricultural day-labourers and craftsmen; many of these came into the new village from the surrounding townships, as happened at Port Wemyss. By 1833 a distillery had been established. It continued to live up to Lord Teignmouth's description of it in 1836, when he remarked that one's attention was easily drawn from Bowmore to the 'showy village called Port Charlotte which Mr Campbell has erected on the opposite side of the Bay'.[22] Walter Frederick Campbell's mother was commemorated in the name given to the new village. Lady Charlotte Campbell had inherited her beauty from her mother, one of the two renowned Gunning sisters of eighteenth-century society. Widowed at the age of 34, and with nine children to support, Lady Charlotte kept a diary, later published notoriously and anonymously, of her life as lady-in-waiting to Princess Caroline, wife of the Prince Regent.[23] Thereafter, while living abroad, and much to her family's annoyance, she married her son's tutor, the Rev Edward Bury, by whom she had two further daughters, before being widowed a second time. She wrote a host of minor 'silver fork' novels to supplement the income from a Shawfield annuity and continued writing almost until her death in 1861, aged 86.

It is not known exactly when the village of Kiells was begun, though the factor in 1826 noted that a stone dyke was built around the 'weavers lots' in Kiells, and there is mention in 1829 that £750 had been spent on houses there.[24] The weavers were listed then, from east to west, as William Walker, John McLelland, John Stewart, Robert White, John McLellan, William Brownlee, Andrew Young, ? Hamilton, Robert Crawford and John Stewart. These were probably the ten families that Lord Teignmouth reported as having been brought from Glasgow by Walter Frederick Campbell 'to introduce the book-muslin into Islay . . . in the hope of

An engraving by Thomas Dick
of Walter Frederick Campbell,
laird of Shawfield and Islay, after
a painting by Kenneth McLeay
(Trustees of the Scottish National
Portrait Gallery).

Walter Campbell's son, John (Jack), here
portrayed by Edridge, did not live to
succeed to the Islay and other estates.
Colonel Jack's wife, Lady Charlotte,
daughter of the 5th duke and duchess
of Argyll, was a renowned Court beauty,
notorious diarist and minor novelist of
the 'Silver-Fork School'. The eldest of
her eleven children, Walter Frederick,
named Port Charlotte after her (Russell,
'A Canny Scot').

The Kilmeny village of Kiells was built in the 1820s to house immigrant linen weavers and their families from Glasgow, in five pairs of cottages. With house improvement grants in the early 1970s, the uniformity of the cottages disappeared and the intervening spaces were filled by pairs of local authority houses.

forming a manufacturing colony, which might be recruited from the native population. It has proved not altogether unsuccessful'.[25] The original house designs for Kiells village contained no distinctive windows like those found in weavers' villages elsewhere, though they did have small attic windows. Modernisation grants have resulted in both exteriors and interiors being considerably modified.

The small, straggling and essentially unplanned settlement of Ballygrant had very different functions in its early days. When the principal link with the Scottish mainland was the drove road through Port Askaig and Jura, Ballygrant was a staging post on the journey from Killarow, Bowmore's predecessor at Bridgend and, later, from Bowmore itself. Ballygrant Inn is the modern version of that 'changehouse'. Ballygrant also served in the eighteenth and nineteenth centuries as the focus of sporadic lead, copper and silver mining in Islay: the scars and residues are still visible in the landscape, especially around Mulreesh. In Ballygrant itself, some of the former miners' houses remain as 'Miners Row', now much renovated.

The Hebridean exception

Walter Frederick Campbell's few clearances, the considerable planned reduction in the numbers of joint tenants on the farms, physical changes to the pattern of landholdings, his attempts to attract people from the land into the villages for day-labouring and non-agricultural employment,

These West Highland oxen were prizewinners at the Highland Show in 1838, the year in which the local agricultural association was established (Royal Highland and Agricultural Society of Scotland).

and even the muir reclamation schemes, all resulted in a decrease in the number of joint tenancies and joint tenants after the early 1830s. Whereas in 1821 three-quarters of the agricultural families on Islay were joint tenants, by 1831 only one-third of the smaller number of agricultural families were joint tenants.[26] This reduction in the number of joint tenants was sometimes accompanied by reorganisation of holdings as in the case of the cleared townships or reorganised groups of smaller holdings. But in other cases, the old organisation and morphology tended to remain, or changed gradually and informally. Relics of the older order of tacks and joint farms continued to exist side by side with the newer pattern of laird's policies, single farms and small holdings. Teignmouth averred that 'of farmhouses and cottages Isla attends an infinite variety'.[27] This varied landscape was, and is, in strong contrast to many other areas of the West Highland seaboard, where changes were abrupt and all-embracing.[28]

The more gradual aspect of change in Islay is also unlike the reorganisation that took place in many parts of lowland Scotland. There, earlier in the eighteenth century, revolution of the landscape had often occurred much more completely and suddenly. Even in nearby Cowal and Kintyre on mainland Argyll, sheep farming was established as early as the mid-eighteenth century by the clearance of tenants, many of whom moved relatively easily to Glasgow and the other lowland industrial centres. Islay was an exception and has remained so to this day. Though it is undeniably part of the Highlands and Islands in very many elements of its physical appearance and social character, there is also a Lowland aspect of the landscape, created mainly in the second quarter of the nineteenth century through the establishment of a varied pattern of agricultural holdings and the establishment of a number of villages, with later Victorian replacements or additions.

Notes and references

1   Foster, *Members of Parliament*, p. 62.

2   Campbell of Melfort Papers, EUL, MS. E59/2 Dk.73.151; also IEP, MS. Pedigree of Campbell of Skipness, Shawfield and Islay, 1886.

3   W. M. Playfair, Drawings of Islay Estate Offices 1841–42 (and also of East Lodge 1845–6), EUL, Special Collections Catalogue 30.
     William Heath (1795–1840) was commissioned by Walter Fredrick Campbell to record scenes of Islay and Islay life. Dated from 1829 to 1836, the rather romanticised watercolours are bound in a volume presented by Mr Ian Hunter of Laphroaig to Mr James Morrison on his coming of age in 1951. The volume was bought from the sale of the effects of Rosneath Castle, the home of Princess Louise, Duchess of Argyll. No further publication of the Heath illustrations reproduced here is permitted without the owner's agreement. See also RCAHMS, *Argyll Inventory*, *V.*

4   *Census of Scotland 1951*, (1953), Table 3.

5   IEP, Rental of 1824–25.

6   *Report of the Select Committee appointed to inquire into the Expediency of encouraging Emigration from the United Kingdom*, BPP, 1826, IV, p. 75.

7   The maps and plans by or attributed to William Gemmill are in the IEP and photocopies are in West Register House, SRO, Edinburgh. Other contemporary documents amplify them, such as the lengthy and much annotated List of Offers of Farms in 1833 in the IEP.

8   Macdonald, *General View*, p. 561; M. Storrie, *Continuity and Change: The Islay, Jura and Colonsay Agricultural Association, 1838–1988*, (Islay, 1988).

9   IEP, Stephen MacDougall's MS. Plan of Coul Park.

10   This and subsequent tables are based on various rentals in IEP.

11   M. C. Storrie, 'Landholdings and Settlement Evolution in West Highland Scotland', *Geografiska Annaler*, 1965, 47, pp. 138–61.

12   *United Kingdom Census 1821* and *1831*.

13   Lumsden, *Steam-Boat Companion*, p. 69.

14   C. J. Shore (Baron Teignmouth), *Sketches of the Coasts and Islands of Scotland and the Isle of Man*, (London, 1836), 2 vols., II, pp. 315–6 and p. 331.

15   MacNeill, *New Guide*, pp. 113–4.

16   C. M. Macdonald (ed.), *The Third Statistical Account of Scotland (TSA)*, (Glasgow, 1961), p. 345.

[17] Shore, *Sketches*, p. 314.

[18] Copies of each census enumerator's schedules for the censuses in Scotland from 1841 to 1891 are available for inspection at New Register House, Edinburgh. Those for Islay have been discussed in M. C. Storrie, 'The Census of Scotland as a source in the Historical Geography of Islay', *SGM*, 1962, 78, pp. 152–65.

[19] IEP, William Gemmill's MS. map of Wemysshaven, 1833.

[20] IEP, Rentals for 1833 and 1834.

[21] Shore, *Sketches*, p. 317.

[22] Ibid., p. 311.

[23] Biographical material from various sources. See *Diary Illustrative of the Times of George the Fourth*, attributed to Lady C. S. M. Bury or Campbell, (London, 1839), 4 vols.; and M. W. Rosa, *The Silver-Fork School*, (New York, 1936), pp. 146–58.

[24] IEP, Factor's note on tenancies at Kiells.

[25] Shore, *Sketches*, p. 324.

[26] IEP, Rentals for 1821 and 1831.

[27] H. A. Moisley, 'Some Hebridean Field Systems', *Gwerin*, 1960, 3, pp. 22–35; 'The Birth of a Crofting Landscape; North Uist in 1799', *SGM*, 1961, 77, pp. 89–92.

[28] Shore, *Sketches*, p. 308.

CHAPTER 10

Crisis and solution

The decades of the 1820s and 1830s in Islay were very busy ones, in which the population soared to between four and five times the present population, despite migration. As well as the activities in weaving, fishing, mining and distilling, construction of roads, piers, villages, dykes, farmhouses and out-buildings, distilleries and public buildings were all going on apace. But in the recessionary aftermath of the Napoleonic wars, the balance between income and expenditure deteriorated, both for the landlord and for his tenants and other islanders. The immediate consequence of the post-war price collapse was a dramatic surge in rent arrears and the need for more disposable income to service debt charges. There were difficult years of harvest failure, particularly in 1816–17, 1821–2, 1825, 1835–6 and the potato disease in the decade after 1845 was yet to come.[1] It became virtually impossible for even the best laird and his agents to handle the growing crisis. Many of the early-nineteenth century activities had been bolstered by temporary wartime conditions. With the coming of peace, the export economy of areas such as the Highlands and Islands of Scotland suffered. Cattle prices halved between 1810 and 1830.[2] Fishing encountered both erratic herring migrations and withdrawal of herring bounties. Duty on imported barilla was reduced and cheaper alkali could be obtained using common salt, so both the price and production of kelp fell drastically. Only sheep prices suffered less. The making of illicit whisky was being threatened by excise changes. Peace also led to the return of soldiers and others. The 1820s decade began the process of disintegration of the economic fabric in the Highlands and Islands. In Devine's view:

> The experience of the western Highlands is a salutary reminder that economic change is not necessarily for the better . . . The Highlands became a "problem" region where economic transformation had produced difficulties rather than benefits . . . Whether more effective management of the resources of the region by the landlord class would have resulted in a different outcome is an interesting question. Several landlords, particularly on the kelping estates, seem to be more interested in profit than in investment yet others such as Campbell of Shawfield and Islay

did try to fund relatively ambitious fishing and industrial developments. But after doing well to start with, they often came to little, suggesting that even the most imaginative of schemes, using not inconsiderable finance, faced major problems. Highland landlords were confronted with more formidable obstacles than their counterparts elsewhere in Britain.[3]

External threats

The relentless rise in population had continued and population growth outstripped traditional agricultural productivity. The old agrarian economy had been balanced annually on a knife-edge between a meagre sufficiency and periodic shortage, particularly in a climate that was almost marginal for successful grain cultivation. After the end of the Napoleonic wars the economic and demographic pressures notably increased as sources of employment and income became less certain. A large population had been vital to the labour-intensive economy of the later-eighteenth century. In Argyll and particularly in Islay agrarian change maintained and even improved standards of life, along with the outward movement of people from the region.

As the post-war recession deepened, most people learned to subsist on potato cultivation, fishing, labouring and earnings from family members temporarily in the Lowlands, or further afield. Out-migration did not keep up with the decline in employment and income. Viewed from the perspective of more than a century and a half later, the improvements made by Walter Frederick Campbell in the 1820s and 1830s, despite all the difficulties, were considerable. The external world began to influence the economy of Islay more and more, as well as the lives of its inhabitants and especially of the landlord himself. The pace of innovation slackened.

Further development of the landscape and of agriculture in Islay after the mid-1830s proceeded at a much slower rate than in the previous decade. Overall, the numbers of agricultural tenants in multiple tenancies were declining fairly dramatically: in the 1833 rental there were 95 holdings with 539 joint tenants named.[4] Twenty years later the corresponding numbers were 65 and 305. A gradual decrease in the number of tenants per holding was accompanied by an increase in the average size of the individual holdings. Only in a few areas, such as Cragabus in the Oa, did the holdings remain unconsolidated. Rentals show that the number of agricultural tenants in most parts of Islay continued to decline except in the Oa, the 'Glen' and in the northern Rinns.[5] Lord Teignmouth confirmed that all was not well when he wrote in the 1830s of the continuing existence of subletting with its 'usual mischievous effects' and also of the continuing presence of runrig tenure, especially on the 'frequented shore of Lochindal'.[6] He nevertheless paid the usual tribute to the 'meritorious exertions' of Walter Frederick, his uncle Walter, of Sunderland and their agents, Mr Chiene, the factor, and Mr Webster, the overseer.

In the normal state of affairs the problems noted by Lord Teignmouth would not have been of much importance; indeed the gradualness of landscape and social change is one of the virtues of the Islay story. But the times were becoming anything but normal. As in Ireland and other areas, excessive reliance was being placed on the potato, which had spread rapidly throughout the West Highlands and Islands after the middle of the eighteenth century, tending to replace barley and oats as a human foodstuff. By the 1830s lazybed cultivation for potatoes had extended cultivation limits to their maximum. In 1835 the potato crop throughout the region had almost failed.[7] The disease was caused by the fungus *Phytophthora infestans* and there was no contemporary understanding or cure for the blight. Maritime regions were especially at risk. The spores spread most rapidly in the moist environment during the spring and summer months. 1835 was an exceptionally cold and wet season and the crop continued to have difficulties for the next decade.

The leavers

Despite Walter Frederick Campbell's attempts to create employment in his reorganised landscape of farms and villages through the 1820s and 1830s, the mounting arrears of rent and the farming difficulties already appearing in the 1830s made migration inevitable. The previous chapter showed that, despite net out-migration from the island, Islay's population continued to increase dramatically and alarmingly to around the time of the 1831 census and even to that of 1841 in Kildalton and Oa, where numbers of marriages and births remained higher. But thereafter it began to drop as rapidly as it had risen. In the most populous part of the island, Killarow and Kilmeny, the numbers of marriages and births fell in the 1830s, and young single people and recently-married people left. For the island as a whole, net out-migration added to the fall in births. Temporary migration to seasonal work off the island partly helps explain why mass emigration did not necessarily occur when population growth was outstripping available resources. Agriculture, fishing, industry, construction, transport and domestic service in the Lowlands all needed increasing amounts of temporary and even permanent labour. Part of the income earned there helped to support many island households, indirectly discouraging further migration in the short term.

Emigration was increasingly being seen by lairds and their agents as the necessary cure for the perceived problem of 'overpopulation', although

some like Walter Frederick Campbell inclined also to the view that the
problems derived from economic difficulties as much as demographic
forces. Migration is not easy to measure, but references to its size or
impact are often found when population change was considered to be
threatening. The enumerators of the census in 1841 attributed the decrease
in Killarow not only to 'young persons leaving during the summer months
for the Low Country, in search of employment', but also 'to extensive
emigration, amounting to about 720 persons since 1831'. The minister for
nearby Kilmeny also noted that the decrease there was to be accounted
for by emigration. This theme of emigration was further developed by the
writer of the Kildalton parish account in the 1840s, when he observed
that 'the females are more numerous than the males, a great number of
young men having left the parish, and gone to the Low Country for
employment. Some have gone to America and other places; so that the
number of inhabitants has diminished'.

Migration was not wholesale or planned, but took the form of trickle
and chain migration. The population became more mobile. Perhaps the
first move was by rural displacement into an island village. In Islay this
was rarely the result of total clearance at this time. More usually it resulted
from reduction in the numbers of tenants on a landholding. The next
move was perhaps to Glasgow, Paisley or Greenock and thence perhaps
further afield, particularly to Upper Canada, i.e. what is now Ontario, the
United States of America and subsequently to South Africa and the
antipodes. Most emigrants in the 1820s and 1830s probably travelled in
family units or small parties of around one to two dozen people. *Oran le
seann Ileach*, the song of an exiled Islay pioneer, describes the way in
which, despite hardships, these settlers eventually controlled their own
lives in the townships of Ontario.[8] Some pioneer graveyards in the
townships of Oro and Nottawasaga on Georgian Bay, in Lake Huron,
have many headstones for islanders such as Campbells from the Oa, who
sailed from Loch Indaal in 1831 with their family of six. Other families
were the Bells, Curries, Dallases and many Macs.[9] Descendants of a
family of Gilchrists who had pioneered and settled Islay in Victoria County
in Ontario in the 1830s, were later to move west, homesteading and
founding Islay in Alberta.[10]

The conventional wisdom of the eighteenth century against emigration
did not change quickly, but with the very serious subsistence crisis in the
1830s, a new consensus began to emerge. It came to be regarded as
axiomatic that the Highlands were 'overpopulated' and that only through
extensive emigration could the problems of the area be alleviated. In 1841
a Select Committee of the House of Commons solemnly concluded that

there was a population surplus in the crofting parishes of 45,000 to 60,000 people. For Islay it was suggested that one-fifth, or 3,000, of the population ought to be removed.[11] But the most significant change occurred in the attitudes of many Highland and Hebridean lairds. Some became interested in 'assisted emigration', although for the most part the state was at first unwilling to play a major role in this. A scheme of assisted emigration to Australia was established, using colonial land revenues to help cover emigration costs.[12] In 1837 Walter Frederick Campbell was one of the parliamentarians involved in promoting colonisation and settlement of New Zealand.[13] But perhaps the most remarkable aspect of the period from the end of the Napoleonic wars to the 1840s is that many more did not go.

Problems mount for the stayers

One of the problems that faced Walter Frederick Campbell during these unhappy decades was that Islay's suffering was usually less than that in other areas, partly due to the earlier exertions of himself and his forebears. This meant that Islay did not receive as much government or other assistance provided elsewhere. The 1841 Select Committee was told by one witness that Islay was a comparatively fertile island 'in . . . as good a state as to provisions as Arran, and the great proprietor there has the character of being at all times disposed . . . to attending to the people's wants . . . Owing to the liberality of the proprietor and to the exertions of his principal tenants in affording employment, no public assistance will be required'.[14] By this time the landlord was scarcely in a position to share this view.

Charles Baird, the Honorary Secretary of the Glasgow Committee for Highland Relief, reported that in 1841 the Committee had sent Islay some 576 bolls of meal and 90 barrels of potatoes.[15] He added that the landlord had given donations, especially in Bowmore parish which was 'in a state of extreme misery'. Baird believed that Walter Frederick Campbell could give no more and the Committee thought it right to send some supplies to Islay, to aid him in his exertions. Walter Frederick, in a letter from 10 George Square in Edinburgh on 28 March 1842 to Sir George Clarke, asked what had become of his petition to the Treasury for a grant to help work the mines in order to relieve unemployment. He even exaggerated Islay's population by about twenty per cent while saying that without such a grant he certainly 'should not attempt to work these mines, my great object being to give employment to the Large Population (seventeen thousand Souls) resident in my Highland propriety'.[16]

When compared to similar reports on most other areas of the west

At present, most of Islay's population of about 3,500 lives in villages: rural settlement is predominantly dispersed. However, around the time of maximum population, settlement was usually clustered (Compiled from copies of Census enumerators' schedules for 1841, New Register House, Edinburgh).

Highland seaboard, it does seem that the destitution and poverty on Islay were not so great as elsewhere, little though this can have comforted the laird or his tenants. The policy of reducing the dependence on agriculture, and in some parts of Islay a real reduction in the size of the agricultural population, saved the island from the most extreme pressure on the land experienced elsewhere. An interesting survey of the agricultural situation in Islay in 1843 was presumably an effort to try to get to grips with the rental situation which was becoming less and less favourable to the landlord.[17] The amounts of barley, oats and potatoes sown were shown against their yields and the proportion expected to be sold for cash; similar data was collected for the horses, cattle and sheep kept by the 529 tenants, 499 cottars and 105 workmen engaged in agriculture.

The island could not escape the effects of the potato disease that spread from Ireland throughout Scotland in the middle of the 1840s.

Walter Frederick reported that the disease had first been observed during August 1845 in Islay in the stems, leaves and tubers of potatoes in a south-facing field near Port Ellen.[18] He added that the Rinns were still quite free, as also were the sandy areas of the island, but that the disease was spreading. Ministers of the parishes who were asked to report on the situation at the end of 1846 wrote varying accounts.[19] In Kilmeny, for example, the Rev Donald Macdonald observed the 'failure'of the potato crop and went on to say that although the average crop of oats and barley had been better that year, much of the barley was destined to the distilleries to pay for the rent owed, so that 'want, and extreme destitution, and starvation press hard on a great proportion of our people already . . . there are in the villages and other locations in Islay, upwards of 5000 souls whose pressing wants and impending starvation demand immediate relief'. If his estimate is to be believed, this meant about 40 per cent of the Islay population by that time.

The Rev James Dewar, writing about his parish of Kilchoman, was less specific, but equally alarmed. He asserted that Walter Frederick was doing 'every thing in his power . . . to alleviate our present distress, and to meet the grievous calamity with which it has pleased the Almighty as a judgment to visit us'. But prospects for the following summer were 'dark and gloomy'. Draining at Loch Gruinart to reclaim land had begun, but Dewar believed it would bring only a brief respite. Over in Kildalton, the Rev Archibald McTavish agreed that the following spring and summer would be critical periods, 'for their small stock of oats and bere will soon be consumed'. For the present, however, McTavish felt that Islay was surviving the crisis better than many other areas. The most telling illustration of the intense pressures unleashed on a population by failure of the potatoes, and the inability to buy imported food, was the increase in mass migration: Jura lost almost one-third of its population.[20]

Unfortunately the slight relative advantage of Islay continued to keep it well down the list of priority areas for such government assistance as was available. The latter was of course, not great and the appalling problems in Ireland, where perhaps a million people died of starvation or disease between 1846 and 1851, made it easy to neglect the problems on Islay. Cattle numbers were run down by selling to pay for meal or to pay some of the rent. Landowners were hit both by relief costs and by rising payments for the poor. Both the *New Statistical Account* of the 1840s and the registers kept by the Superintendent of the Poor after the Scottish Poor Law Act was passed in 1845 indicate the growing problems in Islay. Unfortunately, the landlord himself was perhaps unwilling to admit his increasing inability to control the island's affairs. Sir Edward Pine Coffin, appointed by the

Treasury to inquire into the need for government assistance, reported
that he had been in touch with Walter Frederick's Edinburgh agent, who
'expresses his belief, that although severe privation must inevitably be
caused by the failure of the potato crop in that island, the measures taken
or intended by Mr Campbell's order will suffice, without Government
interference of any kind, to prevent any absolute destitution'.[21]

During previous food shortages, emergency meal supplies had to be
imported into the western Highlands to avert starvation. But what Devine
has called the 'Great Hunger' of the later 1840s was of a quite different
order of magnitude from past scarcities.[22] The failure of the potato in
1846 finally removed the principal part of the food supply in many areas.
But disaster would not have happened if other economic resources had
been available to purchase food supplies from elsewhere. Cattle prices
were depressed and herring fishing was in difficulty. Migrant family members
brought or sent back remittances but after the depression of 1848, there
were fewer jobs available in the lowlands. Even so, the failure of the
potato in the Scottish north and west did not lead to a crisis of Irish
proportions. The problem was both more manageable and containable.

After serving in the East Indies, Charles Trevelyan was appointed
Secretary to the Treasury in 1840. He was a member of the evangelical
'Clapham Sect', a man of intense religious beliefs, renowned for his integrity,
strong principles and commitment to duty. By September 1846 he
unequivocally stated government policy to be that 'the people cannot,
under any circumstances, be allowed to starve'.[23] It was the duty of each
landowner to provide for the subsistence of his tenants. The latter, in
turn, had to pay for help or carry out work of some kind in return. Public
loans continued to be made available, under existing legislation, for fisheries,
drainage and public works. Sir Edward Pine Coffin, in charge of government
relief measures, was sent to the Highlands in September 1846 to report
on the extent of the potato failure and its social consequences. After
active service in the Napoleonic wars, Coffin had taken part in famine
relief operations in China and Mexico, and had been just been knighted
for his services in the administration of relief at Limerick. Regular tours
of inspection were carried out by Sir Edward and his officers in the
powerful steam vessels of the Royal Navy which were also used to convey
vital supplies in virtually all weathers.

A visit to Islay by Sir Edward's deputy, Captain Pole, found Walter
Frederick Campbell more sympathetic to the notion of assistance than his
agent had suggested, though he evidently shrank from assistance to his
people that brought any authority in competition with his own plans.
Pole in fact proposed that some assistance should be given to enable the

twenty-kilometre road from Port Ellen to Bridgend, begun in the previous year, to be completed. This road was to replace the existing link between the two points which was over 25 kilometres long, of which almost half were 'on the seashore and not passable in storms' (a reference to the Big Strand along Laggan Bay). Sir Edward Pine Coffin was apparently unconvinced; he thought that Walter Frederick was 'very imperfectly informed of the real extent of the destitution . . . This seems to be a case in which it is difficult to interfere, but which it would be at the same time dangerous to consider as provided for'.[24] Sir John McNeill later also percipiently noted that he had been aware all along that Campbell of Islay was 'quite confident of the sufficiency of his own means and measures to supply the necessaries of life to all his people . . . Mr Campbell is a man of kind heart and generous nature, and if he fails, it will be from want of available means or of efficient management'.[25]

Campbell's own thoughts on the matter of governmental assistance are contained in a letter that he wrote to Sir George Grey in October 1846.[26] As they stand, his views are unexceptional by the standards of his peers and his predecessors. He suggested that government aid might include loans for public works if these were on a large scale, small grants for smaller works, promotion of fisheries, assistance for emigration, the establishment of depots for food (Indian corn) in different localities and amendments to the drainage acts. Apart from the reference to emigration, there is little to indicate a realisation that the problems were beyond the capacity of a single landlord to overcome. However, a government grant of the large sum of £30,000 over three years helped with the Gruinart reclamation by draining, using tiles manufactured in the works still visible at Foreland.[27]

Debts escalate – sequestration

1848 was a year of national financial crisis. Banks closed their doors, borrowing reached 60 per cent and the bankruptcies of many 'such small game as . . . Lord Bellhaven and Campbell of Islay' were gazetted.[28] There is little evidence in any other region of Britain of a financial catastrophe on the scale which overwhelmed the West Highland landowners. They were partly responsible for their plight with over-ambitious consumption and undermanagement of their estates and they did not live within their means. Sir James Riddell had spent over £50,000 on his Ardnamurchan and Sunart estate by 1848, without the expected returns; lord MacDonald owed over £140,000, while the debts of Walter Frederick Campbell of Shawfield and Islay eventually amounted to over £800,000.[29] Some of these debts were incurred for reasons of conspicuous consumption, such

as the improvement of estate mansions, the building of town houses and
the purchasing of fine furniture. But many were inherited and others were
due to unsuccessful investments in the infrastructure of the estate and the
provision of relief for destitute tenants during bad seasons, all of which
failed to bring in income.

As with tenants, whether a landed family survived or not, when all
other resources failed, was mainly dependent on the balance between
debt and income. When the cost of servicing interest charges became
greater than annual income, debts quickly accrued. It was difficult for
landowners to economise and reduce absolute levels of expenditure because
much debt was inherited. Estates were also burdened with annuities, life-
rents and other portions for relations, especially the younger sons and
daughters. There were three aspects to attaining solvency: income had to
be increased, costs lowered and management improved, but none seemed
likely to produce the required changes in the short term.

Since the death of his grandfather in 1816, Walter Frederick Campbell
had changed the face of Islay. In April 1847, however, a visitor to Islay
left a very dismal account. In the course of a survey of possible harbour
improvements for Islay, Jura, Colonsay and the adjoining coasts, Joseph
Mitchell, Engineer to the Fishery Board Commissioners, stayed with Walter
Frederick Campbell and his family for a fortnight. He later wrote that 'the
poor laird . . . appeared despondent beyond measure. We attributed this
to the dreadful potato blight, so disastrous to the country and his people;
but he was depressed by what was to him a more serious calamity. Owing
to the general distress, the rents were not forthcoming, and the holders of
bills and bonds were not paid their interest. The banks also became
alarmed, and stopped further advances. Hence in a few months after this
the creditors seized the property of Islay, and Mr Campbell was declared
bankrupt . . . These pecuniary difficulties . . . arose mainly from previous
embarrassments on the estate, but unfortunately Mr Campbell was no
man of business'.[30]

As can be seen from the rash of meetings and paperwork over the
summer months of 1847, the financial difficulties had been mounting for
years. In 1826 Walter Frederick had returned a list of tenants heavily in
arrears to his factor with the comment 'Being as you know extremely
distressed for money myself, I must positively request you to use all legal
means to obtain payment of these enormous arrears and from the state in
which I am myself placed, although I say it with sorrow, I must insist on
summonses of removal being served on many if not all of the above
list'.[31] This unconscious echo of the Cawdor Campbells a century earlier
is one of the first indications that the growing pressure on the island's

resources was having its effect on the laird. His request to the factor was, of course, largely unproductive: the tenants were not evading payment of their rents but were simply not able to pay. The 1828 'Black Book of Islay' was another indicator of attempts to monitor the increasing problems of arrears.[32] £210,000 was raised between 1837 and 1839 from Scottish Widows Fund and Life Assurance Company and sundry bequest funds, using bonds secured heritably on different parts of Islay. Second charges were subsequently resorted to on some of these. By 1847 £300,000 was being requested from the Royal Bank of Scotland to pay off heritable debts of £125,000 on Woodhall and personal debts of £170,000, with Woodhall and almost all of Islay as security. The arrears of rent in Islay amounted to some £32,000 by the end of October 1847.[33]

Sorting out the financial chaos was to prove time-consuming. William Webster, the factor at Woodhall and overseer in Islay, was praised for his accounts of Woodhall from 1841 to 1845, but the situation in Islay was less satisfactory.[34] By the middle of 1847, almost after the horse had bolted, the distiller and farmer, John Ramsay, was advising the Campbells, and wrote to the Islay factor, George Todd Chiene, that he had been thinking about the general management of the island since Walter Frederick Campbell either personally or through those acting for him, 'desires in future to exercise a stricter rule over his own affairs'.[35] He urged the factor to update the accounts to provide Walter Frederick Campbell with a balance sheet exhibiting the actual state of the receipts and expenditure to Whitsunday 1847. Such a past 'satisfactory analysis of the whole' would allow lessons for guidance in the future to be deduced. 'From the little time you are yourself enabled to devote to your accounts, with your present clerk, I confess I have my fears . . . these fears I admit cause the disinclination on my part to interfere, in any way with Mr Campbell's affairs'. The subsequent view of the heir, John Francis Campbell, was that Chiene was 'an honest man though not fitted for the situation'.[36]

By October the debts were thought to include heritable bonds of £490,000, banks were owed £310,000, there were personal debts of £107,000, debts in Islay of £20,000 and an annuity for Lady Charlotte Campbell or Bury of £1500, although some of the estimates were probably on the high side.[37] The net rentals for Woodhall and Islay were £11,000 and £17,000 respectively, though when they were used to calculate assets, gross rentals were used. It was estimated that twenty years' purchase at £12,300 for Woodhall would yield a sum of £246,000, while 30 years' purchase for Islay at £20,000 would provide £600,000. The demands from the bank were becoming more and more urgent, as Walter Frederick Campbell's Edinburgh agent, James McInnes, pointed out in October to the Islay factor. Signing off 'yours in tribulation', he emphasised that 'the Bank of Scotland has become more & more urgent for a payment to account, which I cannot give, indeed I am as I told you quite exhausted, and look with the utmost anxiety to hear from Islay – For my sake hasten relief, surely something *may* be done – something *must* be done. The *interest* term is close at hand'.[38]

John Ramsay then tried to get more from Islay. In writing to Chiene, he pointed out that 'Mr McInnes has produced a statement showing that your remittances for the last nine years amount only to £234,000'.[39] Without mincing words, he told the factor that it was imperative that nothing was to hinder him from getting to Edinburgh 'by Friday's steamer', or sending 'the whole Books, Vouchers, accounts, receipt Books, rentals and all other letters or documents whatever that will enable us to make up or form a general estimate of the expenditure for the period above named'.

By then Walter Frederick Campbell's affairs were in the hands of his son, John Francis Campbell and John Ramsay for, 'being advised to go abroad for some time for the recovery of his health', Walter Frederick Campbell had left for France on October 21, accompanied by his wife, younger children and some of the Islay House silverware.[40] With the rents of the estates insufficient to meet the annual interests on the heritable and personal debts and other burdens, John Francis Campbell and John Ramsay asked Counsel for guidance on immediate procedures to pay interest, recover arrears, advise creditors, possibly sell parts of the estates, and on the uncertain financial arrangements for various family marriage contracts.

Within days, and after repeated consultations with John Francis Campbell, John Ramsay and James McInnes, Counsel had given his opinion 'that it would be altogether . . . prejudicial to make any unnecessary delay in meeting the Creditors; and that any schemes of tiding over the approaching term by raising money to pay, not Interests only, but some of the more pressing debts, partly at least in principal, would not be not only unadvisable but of very questionable propriety'.[41] He strongly advised 'young Islay', John Francis Campbell, not to act as his father's commissioner, but to be prepared to come forward as a creditor, as heir of Entail and under his Mother's marriage Contract. Nor did he see any advantage in John Ramsay acting as commissioner in the circumstances, acting simply as agent for Islay. His main recommendation was to execute a Trust Deed on behalf of all the creditors and to name Trustees. He added that a great deal would depend upon the forbearance and even the indulgence of creditors and recommended not postponing 'even for a day the duty of taking the creditors into Counsel'.

A meeting of creditors in Edinburgh on November 5 recommended that Walter Frederick Campbell's affairs be handed over to a Trust and that he be formally asked to agree to sequestration. Chiene was soon writing a 'private' letter to John Ramsay in Glasgow saying that Islay was in a sad state and that he was beset 'by all who think they may suffer directly or indirectly . . . the Poor people in many cases are afraid of the Bank and are drawing their deposits from the National Bond'. John Francis Campbell was in Edinburgh, still hoping that the situation was retrievable, writing to John Ramsay, also in Edinburgh, that the creditors seemed very much inclined to put a low value on Islay and wanted to sell it '*now* to anybody for anything it will fetch'. He hoped that in that case he could find a purchaser 'who will let me make what I can out of the place for £17,000 a year. What think you of my bright idea? I fear it is a castle in the air but it is a very pretty one and I shall live in it till it tumbles down'. The castle did not materialise and by November 22, his father, Walter Frederick Campbell, was dispiritedly writing from Avranches, in Normandy, to lawyers in Edinburgh. 'As I now learn by your Letter that it is the wish of my Creditors that I should be sequestrated (though it is a bitter Pang) I at once yield to their wishes and I send herewith the proper form to enable you to take out a Sequestration before the Courts. I trust that the Creditors will not use unnecessary harshness – as I have done all in my power to do justice to them'.

By the time sequestration was awarded on 2 December 1847, the debts exceeded £750,000. In keeping with the mood, Webster told of the very stormy weather being experienced in Islay: 'the loudest Peal of thunder was this morning betwixt 1 and 2 o'clock I ever heard, the houses in the neighbourhood "they say the beds on the earthen floors" shook as if they had been in a Steam boat'. Tax personnel had almost effected a sale of the cattle and crops in Islay, which Webster managed to stall until 'we may expect to hear something of a Trustee being appointed'. After 30 years with Walter Frederick Campbell as laird and after 120 years in Shawfield ownership, the Islay estate was sequestrated. From 5 January 1848 until the end of August 1853, it was administered by an Edinburgh accountant, James Brown.[42]

Many Highland estates were in trust by mid-century. They were administered by the agents of trustees for the creditors of the landowners and their responsibility was to treat the property as an asset, run it efficiently, increase rental income and, if possible, increase its solvency for quick disposal. Financial imperatives were ahead of most other considerations. It was not therefore surprising that trustees resorted to clearance. During

1848 was the year in which Walter Frederick Campbell of Shawfield and Islay was sequestrated, and administrator James Brown was appointed to act on behalf of trustees and
creditors. Potato disease, crop difficulties and rent arrears had resulted in a further reduction in multiple tenancies and tenants, now concentrated again in the 'Glen', the northern
Rinns and the Oa (Islay Estate Papers).

the interregnum in Islay, James Brown was responsible for several further
clearances, for instance in Nosebridge and other townships in 'The Glen'.

The main concern of James Brown, of course, lay not in agricultural
improvements, but in the management and disposal of the estate on the
best terms for the creditors. Times were hard although the sporting
opportunities provided by the Highlands were coming to be appreciated
by those who were growing rich on the commercial and industrial
revolutions of the nineteenth century. One talked-of purchaser for Islay
would perhaps have put Islay clearly on the map, as James Crawford, who
had taken over from McInnes, gossiped to John Ramsay that 'Prince
Albert being so fond of Highland Sports, the Queen has resolved on
purchasing *Islay*, where her husband will have all kind of Sports, fishing,
Shooting &c &c. Of course "Islay" would be appointed "Ranger of the
Island". I wish the news were true. When I mentioned them to old

McInnes today he *smiled* – which I have not seem him do for 3 months'.[43] A very different outcome would have resulted had a scheme mooted by the Tontine Association in 1850 come to fruition. It was proposed that Islay be sold off democratically in 3,000 lots each of twenty hectares to islanders and 'others engaged in town-business, who find their health giving way in consequence, and . . . the plan here proposed would be the very thing for their case'.[44] Over £700,000 was thus to be raised by the sale of Islay alone.

Early in February 1848 John Francis Campbell was still dreaming in a letter to John Ramsay, though realism was more to the fore, saying that he had had a letter from his father saying that John Ramsay had told him that Islay would then sell at £400,000. 'I think you had better not tell them such disagreeable facts. It only sets them thinking all manner of plans which have no chance of success'. He argued that '£400,000 at five per cent is £26,000, the Islay rental is £17,000 and Chiene's books shew only £15,000. What good then would *borrowed* money do? and who is to lend it? A gift of £50 or £100,000 might do but who is to give it?' He instructed John Ramsay to send any plans direct to himself 'for I can consider them calmly but my Father takes them at once as . . . concluded and writes to people in such a strain that they are provoked . . . and this may do harm'.[45] By May of 1848, on being advised that he was likely to succeed in his claims as a creditor, he was speculating on buying the personal debts and getting the reversion of Islay. 'The worst is that I hear a rumour that young Mathieson has long been on the look out for Islay and that he has a million and a half'.[46] In the autumn of 1848 he was asking John Ramsay if any scheme could be contrived 'that would yield me an income and give me the Cottage'.[47] A few months later on return from visiting his parents in France he was still showing concern but 'unless some windfall comes my way I have little chance of recovering any considerable portion of Old Islay as for a small favour I would rather remain as I am than set up there as a "Lack Laird" with all the bother and none of the advantages of my former position'. He pressed for any information John Ramsay might 'chance to pick up. Who knows what may turn up . . . If I had the funds . . . I would venture a great deal for a footing in the old place'.[48] By then 'he was pounding away every day and beginning to understand legal jargon a little as the first step towards learning law'.[49]

For sale

Meantime, Brown's difficulties on getting a good price to raise monies may account for the elaborate overstatements in his descriptions of the

Islay estate.[50] The estate was advertised for sale at £540,000 in November 1848.[51] In March the following year John Francis Campbell was still hoping for wonders: 'I must not think of buying either "farms or districts" I have all the will to do wonders in that line, but the power is sadly deficient. However who knows what may turn up? I little thought of the down come'.[52] Standing aside, he praised Brown's wisdom 'in not allowing people to starve for want of work, and in giving useful work [on the roads] to employ them, new men have new measures and I have no doubt but that much more in the way of rent can be got, than ever was got before, by simply having the determination to demand it. I fear I never would have the heart to screw folk if I had the chance but I take it, it is better for all parties to keep clean books and no large balances one way or the other'.

But his pipedreams were thwarted and in April 1849 he surmised: 'all my schemes for buying land without money are about to be fairly swamped'.[53] He had heard that 'Morrison who bought Fonthill Abbey was going down to buy Islay. He began the world as his Father-in-law's foreman and has now an enormous fortune. I am told he is both dour and a good man of business, so if he does as he intends he will probably succeed in adding to his fortune perhaps at the expense of the present inhabitants'. He added that Morrison meant to take his wife and family to Islay to live there for two months 'so you will have a chance of studying the man'. But he warned John Ramsay not to talk too much about this, 'for reports spread rapidly in Islay and *I* don't want to spread the news till I am sure that he has made up his mind – at present it seems he has only determined on looking. I take it however he won't hesitate long for by all accounts he has the means at his disposal'.

With estates at Basildon Park in Berkshire and Fonthill in Wiltshire, James Morrison was 64, had been Member of Parliament for Inverness Burghs from 1840 to 1847 and was, like Walter Frederick Campbell, a member of the original committee of the Reform Club. In the words of his descendant and biographer, Richard Gatty, he had long 'had a weakness for the west coast of Scotland'.[54] This London 'merchant prince' took some of his large family on holiday to Islay in July 1849. They 'stayed at the inn at Bridgend and in spite of bad weather spent the inside of a week seeing something of the island'. They admired the setting of Islay House, including the 350 different rose varieties in the garden. But they did not spend two months and were not yet persuaded to part with the then upset price of £540,000.

The accountant, James Brown, might have been permitted a wry smile, had he discovered that, 'while he *did* sleep in Islay House on the night of

30th March 1851', the census enumerator had omitted recording him, the indignant supervisor having personally checked the fact.[55] John Francis Campbell was still trying to do his sums, using Scottish interest rates of $2\frac{1}{2}$ and $3\frac{1}{2}$ per cent, writing to John Ramsay: 'Islay will be the grand point on which to found . . . a loan for there the land is the thing . . . at Woodhall it is the coals. Tell me then whenever you hear anything about the state of affairs in Islay & if there be any prospect of receiving rents there were I once in a position to ask for them'.[56] By September 1852, after several fruitless advertisements, the asking figure for the Islay Estate had been reduced to £440,000. Who was likely to buy it, and why? Highland estates were in great demand from social groups outside the Highlands; despite the economic and social crisis, land prices rose and the west Highland region began to attract very wealthy purchasers, not only from the Scottish Lowlands but from further afield. Larger properties did prove more difficult to sell but even they eventually found purchasers. By mid-century, the Romantic Movement and the rise of the ideas of the sublime and the picturesque which could be applied to the grandeur and scenery of the remote Highlands and Islands appealed to Britons, especially the English, of the upper and middle classes. The region rapidly developed as a major centre for the physical sports of hunting, shooting and fishing, which required space empty of people.

The precondition for this was the revolution in communications: the replacement of sailing ships by steamers and the revolution in road transport. But the exceptional availability of Highland estates also helped to satisfy other more powerful psychological drives and needs among the wealthy. It was difficult even for the most affluent members of the new merchant and industrial classes in England to buy a great deal of land in Victorian times because few large estates ever came to market. In the western Highlands, it was possible to buy up many thousands of acres of wild and beautiful country for an outlay which would have afforded them only a small country estate elsewhere. By the 1850s the pattern of landownership in the western Highlands and Islands had been revolutionised.[57] All of the Outer Hebrides had been sold out of the hands of hereditary proprietors and large parts of Skye, most of Mull and all of Raasay, Ulva, Islay, Lismore, Rum and Eigg in the Inner Hebrides had new owners. Of the islands, only Coll, Tiree, parts of Skye and Jura remained under the control of their traditional possessors. The scale of land transfer in this region was exceptional when compared to the land market elsewhere in Britain.

The Morrison purchase

James Morrison, with Scots forebears, was possibly the richest British commoner in the nineteenth century.[58] In James Brown's words, 'At last, Mr Morrison of Basildon Park, who had formerly made special inquiries, came forward, through his eldest son, and after much negotiation, it was arranged, that on his becoming bound to offer the upset price, the Estate should . . . be exposed to public sale on the 31st August [1853] at £440,000'.[59] In the meantime, enquiries with a view to purchase had been made by a wealthy coal and iron manufacturer, Mr James Baird of Gartsherrie, the arrangement with Mr Morrison being kept private, and 'on the day the Estate was knocked down to Mr Morrison, after competition with Mr Baird at £451,000'. Entry was at Martinmas 1853, with money payable at Whitsunday 1854. £451,000 was a far cry from the £12,000 that Daniel Campbell of Shawfield had paid for Islay in the 1720s. But the trustees did not have to split up the estate into separate lots to facilitate a sale and, in the event, Morrison only acquired Islay after Baird's intervention, which pushed up the price. James Brown still had difficulties selling Woodhall, the other Campbell estate in Lanarkshire, despite the fact that this mineral-rich property lay in the very centre of the booming industrial area of west-central Scotland. It was apparently the Highland estate, with its famine-stricken population and uncertain rental which proved more attractive than the lands in Lanarkshire which were richly endowed with coal and iron-ore measures and situated close to manufacturing industry.

In 1850 John Francis Campbell had asked John Ramsay if he could point out to the Islay commissioners and trustees that they were doing no good 'in screwing my father . . . he did not screw them when he might . . . this confounded Discharge has made poor Mrs Campbell fret so that she is reduced nearly to blindness . . . crying has brought on the old illness'.[60] But it was not until early in 1853 that the personal creditors agreed to his father 'being personally discharged under the Sequestration Statute from all debts contracted by him before the Sequestration of his Estates'. The list of creditors was long and varied, including banks, agents, lawyers, landowners, relatives, friends and neighbours. Walter Frederick's affairs – in the end the debts amounted to some £815,000 – were not finally wound up until late in 1858 for Islay, and even later for Woodhall.[61]

Perhaps the saddest émigrés of all, Walter Frederick Campbell and his family, continued to live in exile in France, aided by an annuity from friends.[62] Walter Frederick lived only a few years longer, dying at Avranches in Normandy in 1855. He is buried there, instead of lying beside his first wife in the sarcophagus in the round church at Bowmore. French obituaries testify to his continuing lack of realism as far as money was concerned. To the small community in which he then lived, 'Mr Campbell gave with

both hands . . . to their wants and distresses his hand was ever open'.[63]
Islay had passed to the Morrison family and the Shawfield link with the
island had been severed.

What did James Morrison get for almost half a million pounds in
1853? One description is contained in the detailed prospectus that was
prepared in 1852 to entice prospective buyers. As one reads through the
Particulars of the Barony and Estate of Islay, the whole of the island except the
'Properties of Sunderland and Ballinaby' being offered for sale, there is a
gradual escalation of its virtues.[64] 'This very extensive and valuable Estate'
becomes 'This magnificent Property' and then an estate that 'can nowhere
be excelled'. The last sentence in the prospectus reads 'On the whole, it
may be safely said, that whether as regards present or prospective
inducements, an Estate superior to Islay has seldom, if ever, been offered
for sale'.

The mansion and the sporting attractions were given precedence over
the island economy: this was scarcely flattering to the work of the Shawfield
Campbells, but it was a buyer's market. The 'Mansion House of Islay' was
described as large and commodious, a great part of it being entirely new,
'in the best style of architecture and finishing . . . and surrounded with far
spreading plantations; and the Gardens, Pleasure Grounds, Private Drives,
and Walks around and connected with it, are very extensive and varied,
and laid out with great taste and judgment, for convenience and recreation.
Considerable streams, uniting in the grounds in their course to the sea,
add much to their ornament and beauty'. This is a recognisable description
of Islay House and some of its grounds today.

Not so the other residence for the laird in the south-east of the island,
a 'Marine Residence at Ardimersay, beautifully situated amid woodland
and rock scenery, and containing, with offices, and other appurtenances,
suitable accommodation for a genteel family. This delightful retreat, the
singularly picturesque features of which are well known, affords an agreeable
variety from the principal residence of Islay House'. This area of Kildalton
certainly provides a contrast with the head of Lochindaal, but it is not
today quite so agreeable: only the outbuildings of the former *cottage ornée*
survive and the Victorian mansion of Kildalton House, built later on an
adjacent site, stands empty and derelict.

Despite the attempt to catch the eye of those interested in shooting
and fishing, the sporting opportunities of the island are summarised in a
few short sentences. All kinds of field sport, and shooting both on land
and water were to be enjoyed 'in the highest perfection. Game of every
description, four-footed and winged, is plentiful: and fishing, either in the
sea, in lakes or in streams, is always at command; and salmon, with every

variety of sea fish, is in abundance'. In the Ardimersay area in the south-east there was an extensive stock of wild fallow-deer, and the woodcock shooting was 'believed to be unrivalled in the kingdom'. The climate was described as 'mild and salubrious' and the soil and climate as 'favourable to all kinds of agricultural crops, and the pasture . . . luxuriant'.

The economy of the island was discussed under various heads. The rental, excluding the Mansion, the factor's residence at Eallabus House and the shootings and fishings, woods and plantations, was 'about £19,045', and was expected to increase progressively due to 'the Improvements in Drainage and otherwise that have been effected within these few years'. Such a gross return at less than 5 per cent on the reserve, or upset, price at £440,000 suggests that the purchaser was not expected to buy Islay for its agricultural profitability, unless he was prepared to take a very optimistic view about the scope for such progressive increases. The previous twenty years were described as a period in which 'much improvement' to agriculture had taken place and 'the capabilities of the Estate for further improvements are very great'.

Among the attractions mentioned were the distilleries, drove routes for cattle through Jura, the cattle themselves, ferries and regular steam or sailing vessels: in each case these were put in a favourable light and the difficulties in freight and ferries were of course glossed over. Apart from the distilleries, 'there are plenty of powerful Water Falls fit for all kinds of manufactories', a remark that was not merely naïvely optimistic but even rather archaic at mid-century. So, via the partly constructed High Road, the estate tile and brick works at Foreland, the harbours, ports and the villages, the account concluded with the coastal fishery and the 'great variety of minerals' on Islay. Or rather, it concluded with the cautious understatement, 'By an extended application of capital, all these natural productions might be brought to yield valuable capital returns'.

Although he never went to the island again, James Morrison took a great interest in it and was reputedly keen to improve the peat lands with shell-sand. Jointly with John Ramsay he bought and ran the steamship *Islay*. Gatty supposed, on the basis of family tradition, that James Morrison 'seems to have had some definite scheme in mind for Islay. Unfortunately there is no record of what it was'.[65]

Notes and references

[1]   *Appendix to First Report of the Select Committee appointed to inquire into the Condition of the Population . . . and into Emigration, BPP*, 1841, VI, p. 212.

[2]   Devine, *Clanship*, p. 52.

[3]   Ibid., p. 49.

4   IEP, Sundry rentals.

5   IEP, Rentals for 1835 and 1836; see also KP, List of Tenants in the Oa, 1839, TD1284.

6   Shore, *Sketches*, 1836, p. 308.

7   R. N. Salaman, *The History and Social Influence of the Potato*, (Cambridge, 1949, reprint 1970), p. 374.

8   M. MacDonell, *The Emigrant Experience*, (Toronto, 1982), pp. 36–7.

9   A. F. Hunter, *A History of Simcoe County*, (Canada, 1909), 2 volumes, II, pp. 134–58 and 232–60.

10 A. Ronaghan, *There'll always be an Islay*, (Islay, Alberta, 1977).

11 *BPP, Emigration*, VI, p. 30.

12 Devine, *Clanship*, p. 186.

13 W. P. Reeves, *The Long White Cloud*, (London, 1956), p. 189.

14 *BPP, Emigration*, VI, p. 30.

15 Ibid., p. 53.

16 Clerk of Penicuik Papers, SRO, GD18/3470.

17 IEP, *Statistics of Lands, Occupiers, Stock and Crops in Islay 1843*, (1890).

18 Anon, 'Appendix to Report on the Disease of the Potato Crop in Scotland in the year 1845', *THAS*, New Series, 1845–47, 16, p. 460.

19 [McLeod, Dr N.], *Extracts of letters to Dr [N] McLeod regarding the famine and destitution in the Highlands and Islands of Scotland*, 1847, (Glasgow, 1847), pp. 26–31. It has been estimated that one-third of the crop was lost in 1845. (Salaman, *History and Social Influence*, p. 476).

20 Devine, *Clanship*, p. 147.

21 *Correspondence . . . relating to the Measures adopted for the Relief of Distress in Scotland, BPP*, 1847, LIII, p. 37.

22 Devine, *Clanship*, pp. 146 et seq.

23 Ibid., p. 158.

24 *BPP, Distress*, LIII, p. 71.

25 Ibid., p. 187.

26 Ibid., pp. 81–3.

27 J. Brown, *Report to the Creditors and General View of the Funds Realised*, Campbell of Jura Papers, SRO, GD64, p. 1.

28 R. Blake, *Disraeli*, (London, 1966), p. 257.

29 Devine, *Clanship*, p. 68, and Brown, *Report to the Creditors*, p. 4.

30 J. Mitchell, *Reminiscences of My Life in the Highlands*, (London, 1883–4, reprint Newton Abbot, 1971), (1883), I, pp. 299–300.

31 IEP, List of tenants heavily in arrears in 1826.

32 KP, The Black Book of Islay, 1828.

33 KP, Correspondence, 22 October 1847; Brown, *Report to the Creditors*, p. 1.

34 KP, 6 September 1845.

35 KP, 23 June 1847.

36 KP, 30 May 1847.

37 KP, 22 October 1847.

38 KP, 10 October1847.

39 KP, 26 October 1847.

40 KP, List of Islay House Silver, August 1846, with List of Silver taken by Mr Campbell on 21 October 1847.

41 KP, 27 October 1847.

42 IEP, Disposition by Walter Frederick Campbell of Islay in favour of James Brown.

43 KP, Correspondence, 7 January, 1848.

44 J. Murdoch, 'A New and Ready Way of Disposing of that Interesting Island Which would pay the debt, restore the late proprietor, and give the best return to large and small capitalists', in W. MacDonald, *Descriptive and Historical Sketch of Islay*, (Glasgow, 1850), p. 30. For further writings of J. Murdoch, see also J. Hunter, (ed.), *For the People's Cause*, (Edinburgh, 1986).

45 KP, 2 February 1848.

46 KP, 9 May 1848.

47 KP, 27 October 1848.

48 KP, 17 January 1849.

49 KP, 17 January 1849.

50 IEP, Particulars of the Barony and Estate of Islay, 1852.

51 Brown, *Report to the Creditors*, p. 1.

52 KP, 10 March 1849.

53 KP, 6 April 1849.

54 J. B. Burke, *Genealogical Dictionary*; Burke *Peerage*; R. Gatty, *Portrait of a Merchant Prince: James Morrison 1789–1857*, (Northallerton, n.d. [1977]), pp. 288–90 and p. 300; W. D. Rubinstein, *Men of Property*, (London, 1981).

55 Copy of Census enumerator's book, Census of Scotland 1851, 536/13.

56 KP, Undated, probably 1851/2.

57 Devine, *Clanship*, p. 64.

58 Ibid., p. 82.

59 Brown, *Report to the Creditors*, p. 2.

60 KP, 25 February 1850.

61 Brown, *Report to the Creditors*, p. 4.

62 Attributed to Walter Frederick Campbell in his exile, and edited by his son, J. F. Campbell, are two volumes published in 1863. Written in 1848, *Life in Normandy*, (Edinburgh, 1863), consists of 'vignettes in the life of Mr Cross who . . . with a small independence, found himself the great man of the quiet little town where he lived . . . poverty in England being wealth in Normandy'. Watercolours executed by John Francis Campbell while visiting his father in Avranches, are in the National Gallery of Scotland, Edinburgh.

63 J. F. Campbell collected French obituaries of his father: Special Collections, Glasgow University Library (GUL), Mu43-c. 17.

64 IEP, *Particulars of the Barony and Estate of Islay*.

65 Gatty, *Portrait*, p. 289.

CHAPTER 11

'This very extensive and valuable estate' after 1853

The Campbells of Shawfield were gone from Islay after 120 years; for about an equal period of time after 1853 the Morrisons were to be the principal lairds in Islay. Innovation and improvement that four generations of Shawfields had initiated was not maintained at the same rate by their successors but the need and scope for such zeal was considerably reduced as the nineteenth century passed. By 1850 the essential steps had been taken that had transformed Islay into a varied economy and society that was by then almost capable of providing a good life for the majority of its inhabitants. Although the certainty of this was clouded at mid-century by the potato disease and its aftermath, what Islay needed in the future was not so much more improvement, as a period of tranquillity in which the initiatives that had been taken in the first half of the nineteenth century could come to fruition; this the Morrisons and other lairds provided. Their wealth gave more freedom of action than their increasingly impoverished predecessors and, like their counterparts throughout the Highlands and Islands, they rebuilt farmhouses and out-buildings, added cottages, schools and churches.

It was early in 1856, after a full decade of misery, that the first optimistic reports of recovery began to appear in the Highlands and Islands, but the potato was never again so important in the Highland diet. Indeed, in Islay drought caused continuing problems for the potato that year. The majority of the population of the Western Highlands and Islands became less dependent on the land for survival and entered more fully into the cash economy, selling their labour for cash wages and buying more. Prices for Highland black cattle rose and fishing and whisky distilling expanded in the 1870s and 1880s. There was a relative improvement in living standards although the majority of inhabitants of the region continued to endure an existence of poverty and insecurity. Life was still precarious and there were still bad seasons: at best, then, 'recovery' was modest.

Already by 1854 James Morrison was being advised to take things easier for his health and the management of his estates was taken over by his two elder sons, Charles and Alfred. At the time, Charles wrote a

Charles Morrison, who brought new management and invested in Islay Estate for more
than half a century until his death in 1909 (Gatty, *Portrait*).

Victorian additions included estate workers' cottages, as at Bluehouses, Bridgend, first
occupied in the 1860s.

demurring letter to Alfred: 'as I am an unmitigated Cockney it will be much better that you should be the man'.[1] But Charles was the one who took the main role as far as Islay was concerned. Of his father he wrote 'he does now wish, never to be troubled by anything being said about it . . . he does not like to be troubled at all about the place, and only looks at his investment ledger to see how much of his capital he has spent on it'.[2] Like his father an 'outstanding businessman and financier', Charles Morrison was well read and artistically appreciative. He also wrote a political economy text, *The Relations between Labour and Capital*, published in 1854.[3] Despite a taste for exotic waistcoats, he was of what used to be described as a 'retiring disposition'. He travelled extensively in America and 'turned the fortune he had inherited into an even more substantial one'.[4] A later commentator also noted that Charles Morrison lived a 'bachelor life, devoting himself to business in the city; and as he is no sportsman or agriculturalist, the administration of the estate is given over to factors'.[5]

Charles Morrison had indeed made the successful bid for Islay and not only went there from time to time, but carried on a copious and regular correspondence with his commissioner and factors until his death in 1909. The minutiae of estate business dealt with, such as harvests, sales, rents and arrears, construction and ornamentation, as well as the perennial problems of steamer provision. There was no intention of living on the island. Despite Charles Morrison's view of the soft furnishings in Islay House being 'a parcel of old, faded, unfashionable shabby . . . rubbish', there was talk of Islay House being rented to a hotelier as it 'would make one of the most attractive houses anywhere to be met with . . . with sport for a fortnight or month'.[6] Charles Morrison emphasised that 'we must make all arrangements as if we were never going to visit the island except in flying visits and at long intervals and . . . we shall in all probability always use the Inn'.[7] His father appeared to think otherwise, saying that he or his son 'should some day build a House for some of the family to have always ready for Use'.[8] While dismissing Islay House as 'inconveniently large' and the Inns as 'fit only for drovers', he wondered whether it might be possible to use 'Webster's House' [Daill], which would be 'just the thing' for a few months at a time. It was not until 1892 that Islay House was used by the Morrisons when Mrs Alfred Morrison and the next generation began to visit more frequently. Mr Hugh Morrison was assumed to be the unofficial heir to bachelor Charles Morrison and brought his new bride, Lady Mary Leveson-Gower, to Islay in the autumn of that year when there was a great bonfire celebration on the estate.[9] From then on, Hugh Morrison and his descendants regularly visited Islay.

Charles Morrison wanted to see how things went for the first year after entry. He often refers to his father in the early correspondence with John Ramsay and William Webster. In June 1854 he wrote to his new commissioner and factor, John Dickson, subsequently also factor to the duke of Buccleuch in Dumfriesshire, 'I think I had better leave you and Webster to manage the estate at least for the present'.[10] The question of buying the arrears was finally settled, James Brown 'having used every means to extract the last farthing from the tenants that he could'.[11] Approaching the first rent collection the new laird was venturing the opinion that the tenants might try 'experiments with their new landlord, to see whether he will let them get into arrears, & we must begin at once to show them that he *will not*'.[12] The euphoria was beginning to wear thin: after harvest and at rent collection time Charles Morrison was writing:

> I begin to fear I was mistaken in thinking there were not too many people on the island. If the present aspect of our collections is any specimen of what we are to expect, there are a great deal too many. Our rental must be independent of the potato or it will be a lame affair . . . the failure of the potato crop . . . was a circumstance which we could not foresee . . . it must materially modify our views as to the extent of the diminution of population which may be requisite to make the rental a clear one, or the population manageable *when a bad time comes again* . . . While I wished to avoid anything like wholesale clearance I never intended to keep men who did not try . . . it is my father's money & my father's land which I have to deal with – we must keep down the outlay [to assuage] his desire for immediate returns.[13]

In a letter to John Ramsay there is a tantalising reference to an enclosed 'Memorandum on the management of the population in Islay', but it has not surfaced.[14] In any event, as envisaged as early as 1849, one of the first results of the Morrison purchase was the sale of several parts of the island. Although the sale of the Kildalton, Dunlossit and other areas represented a substantial transfer of land, the Morrison family continued to own the main parts of the island, whether measured in terms of acreage, agricultural value, or population. The era of Charles Morrison added further plantations, Victorian farm buildings, cottages and lodges to the Islay landscape. It was proposed at first to spend several thousand pounds a year on such improvements for a return of over 5 per cent, and a thousand pounds annually on philanthropic affairs, including the poor and knitting schemes.[15]

But by the spring of 1856 Charles Morrison was writing to John

Dickson that he had 'at least hoped to be able to pay the £7,000 interest on the mortgage of £176,000 from a nominal estate income of £16,000', but he was appalled to discover not only 'the illusory character of income of Islay' but an 'actual loss of revenue on account'.[16] Again he wondered what the state of the Islay cash account would be 'when a *bad time* for farmers comes, since it is so unfavourable after a good time'. By that time he was 'very glad' he had made a sale of part of the estate to John Ramsay.

James Morrison died in 1857, 'the richest commoner in the South', leaving several million pounds as well as estate in the United States of America, and having settled landed estates on all of his sons. There is a much more business-like approach to the monitoring of expenditure and revenue on the Islay estate, with proto-spreadsheets being sent regularly to Charles Morrison, unlike the chaotic state of affairs a decade earlier. After the fascination of reading through half a century of the correspondence between Charles Morrison and John Dickson in the archives of Islay Estate, it was a considerable shock to this author to read that John Dickson was to attend the funeral in May 1909 of the nonagenarian Charles Morrison.[17] This was followed shortly after by a telegram on November 23 announcing John Dickson's own demise.[18]

After Charles Morrison's death in 1909, the estate passed to his nephew, Hugh, Alfred's son. By Hugh's marriage to Lady Mary Leveson-Gower in 1892 the Shawfield connection with Islay had been renewed, for she was the granddaughter of Walter Frederick Campbell.[19] In 1910 a two-storey mock-Georgian wing, set back from the main Georgian tower, was added to Islay House's frontage. By 1921 it was proposed that some parts of the estate be sold, with preference to sitting tenants, but little came of it. A decade later, John Granville Morrison succeeded to the Islay estate and to other family possessions, including the Fonthill estate in Wiltshire. Sitting as Member of Parliament for Salisbury in Wiltshire from 1942 to 1964 and later becoming Lord Lieutenant of that county, he was for a number of years Chairman of the 1922 Committee of Conservative backbenchers. Created Baron Margadale of Islay in 1964, he took his title from a favourite sporting area in the remote north-eastern part of Islay. As elsewhere, the economics and management of sporting and agricultural estates have undergone many changes with many more external influences shaping them than even in the last of the Shawfield days. But the Islay Estate of today is still very much a recognisable, if areally reduced, successor to the agricultural and sporting estate purchased in 1854, although Islay House was sold in 1985.

The other estates

Within a very few years, John Ramsay (1814–1892), merchant in Glasgow with lowland whisky distilling connections, tenant of Cornabus and Ballivicar and distiller in Islay, relieved the Morrisons of the parish of Kildalton and Oa in three separate purchases. The first of these, consisting mainly of the lands north-east of Port Ellen, was effected in 1855.[20] The sale included all the land within the parish of Kildalton from, in the south, the lighthouse in Port Ellen bay to the northern boundary of Proaig on the Sound of Islay. The offer also contained a promise that, in addition to the purchase price of £70,765, John Ramsay would pay a further sum of £500 towards the fund 'required to finish the road now being made between Port Ellen and Bridgend in Islay'. After James Morrison's death, John Ramsay, now of Kildalton, offered Charles Morrison £9,500 for part of the parish of the Oa, near Port Ellen in 1858.[21]

Charles Morrison understandably wanted to dispose of the rest of the south-eastern part of his estate, particularly the Oa. Sir Smith Child, MP, of Stallington Hall in Stone, Staffordshire, a banker and husband of Miss Campbell of Jura, was also interested and he and John Ramsay were corresponding on the matter. Smith Child did not go ahead and buy the Oa, though he did become an Islay landowner shortly after. By 1861 John Ramsay, for another £45,000, had added to his lands the rest of the over-populated Oa peninsula and other holdings as far north as Laggan and Island.[22] He clearly recognised the main problem of too many tenants on the land, particularly in the Oa. Ramsay's view of the Oa expressed to Smith Child had been that 'if people were removed and some improvements made on the better part of the land, it could be made a good sheep grazing. My views, however, regarding such removals are so much in unison with your own that I could not like to meddle with any improvement which involved the removal of any tenants'.[23]

Sir John McNeill was the third son of the laird of Colonsay, who trained in medicine and served in the East Indies before being appointed the first chairman of the Board of Supervision of the Scottish Poor Law, a post which he held for over two decades after 1845. It was McNeill's *Report* of 1851 to the Board which finally discredited charitable relief as the solution to Highland destitution, as opposed to emigration. This led to the passage of the Emigration Advances Act which provided loans at low rates of interest to proprietors who wished to assist the emigration of the destitute population of their estates. Both McNeill and Sir Charles Trevelyan then became deeply involved in the formation and administration of the Island and Highland Emigration Society.

After James Morrison bought Islay in 1853 for £451,000, three major and two smaller estates resulted: a much-reduced Islay Estate, and those of Lossit, Kildalton, Sunderland and Ballinaby, which had never been in Shawfield ownership (Islay Estate Papers).

Some suspected that the eagerness of lairds and officials to support emigration derived ultimately from the fact that the costs of assisted passages were in the long run much lower than either famine relief or extension of the Scottish Poor Law. Reduction in numbers or clearance of small tenants and cottars and assisted emigration schemes all became integrated into coherent programmes of action of several Hebridean estates. After 1848 the volume of summonses of removal granted to landlords in west Highland sheriff courts dramatically increased. In a sense, the famine in some areas brutally solved the social problem of too many people on the land, which had long confronted estate landowners, thus accelerating emigration.

Elsewhere in the Highlands and Islands the new richer landlords had financed emigration schemes on a massive scale and whole areas were rapidly depopulated. Even Sir Edward Pine Coffin was concerned about the intensity of clearance, very concentrated in time and space after mid-

Revolutionary agrarian changes included some clearance of tenants to make way for single farms, sometimes physically reorganised. More formal reorganisation took place in other holdings, particularly for village and muir lotments (Islay Estate Papers).

century. Many were destitute and for the first time the poorest made up the bulk of the migrants. Increasingly, the incentives for the new landlords to promote assisted emigration became stronger. In Islay, one solution for John Ramsay lay in financial assistance for emigration from the Oa to Canada. This began in 1862 with clearance of tenants from Killeyan and their assisted emigration: it is plain that John Ramsay found this distasteful. Discussing his moral dilemma with Charles Morrison, he expressed the hope that the latter would not sell more land on Islay: 'it is not many of the Highland proprietors who direct their personal attention to the moral and intellectual improvement of the people on their land and were you to sell I should dread the risk of your estate coming into the hands of one who would buy it only for sport or profit and carry out plans in utter disregard of the interests and feelings of the people'.[24] In a paper read in Edinburgh to the National Association for the Promotion of Social Science he tried to explain his feelings and actions:

The cause of periodical destitution in the Highlands, though varied by

The policies of James Brown on the sequestrated estate and of Charles Morrison and John Ramsay after the estate was broken up, are evident in this map for 1863. Since 1848, the decline of holdings with more than two tenants is particularly pronounced in the 'Glen' and the Oa (Islay Estate Papers).

many conflicting elements, has been the excessive dependence of the people upon the produce of the soil, and the lack of sufficient application and effort to procure supplies from other sources for the increase in their number: and if so the remedy as plainly appears to be the local development of industry, so as to provide a greater supply of remunerative employment: the removal of obstacles which hinder people in their efforts to help themselves — the promotion for increased facilities for intercourse with the mainland: the aid and encouragement of spontaneous migration: and chiefly and above all and with a view to attain all, the diffusion of the blessings of a sound English education.[25]

However, he then went on to persuade entire communities to emigrate to Canada as entities, cancelling arrears of rent, buying their stock and negotiating reduced steamer fares. In 1862–3 about 400 people may have emigrated abroad from Islay, while in the decade of the 1860s, net out-migration from Islay may have amounted to about one-quarter of the population.[26] John Ramsay sincerely believed that 'voluntary' emigration to Canada, as opposed to migration to other parts of Britain, was the right solution to Islay poverty and lack of opportunity. He was more than ever convinced of this when he visited the Islay people in their new homes in 1870, documenting this visit as a *Diary*.[27] He also referred to the dilemma while speaking at the annual meeting of the Islay Association in Glasgow in 1878:

> I went . . . to visit the residents from Islay who are located on the bank of Lake Simcoe, Georgian Bay, and Lake Huron . . . and what I saw there fully satisfied me that whatever people thought of the fact of people emigrating to Western Canada, I came home with the solid conviction that it was certainly the people who had occasion to be benefited by their removal from the Western Isles. I know I am subjecting myself to the criticism of those who deprecate the removal of a single soul from the Hebrides.[28]

For the islanders who did not emigrate, John Ramsay, with Charles Morrison and others, and with government assistance, tried hard to provide other means of employment in constructing new farms and houses, ornately-decorated cottages and steadings, in draining and planting, completing the 'High' road, building the 'Low' road and helping to run the island steamer connections with the mainland. Ardimersay Cottage had proved difficult to keep weatherproof and in 1870 a Scottish baronial mansion was built on ground above Ardimersay and named Kildalton House. Surrounded by plantations of exotic trees, it was to be a home for John Ramsay and his second wife Lucy, daughter of George Martin of Auchendennan on Loch Lomondside. By this time John Ramsay had become another member of the Islay contingent at the Palace of Westminster, sitting as Member of Parliament for Stirlingshire in 1868 and for Falkirk from 1874 to 1886.[29] He achieved some importance through his interest in education, being a member of many boards and commissions and also an author on the subject.[30]

After his father's death in 1892, Captain Iain Ramsay succeeded as laird of Kildalton estate; but it was gradually broken up. The area around Kildalton House was owned in the 1920s by a colourful family. Talbot Clifton was a war correspondent in South Africa in 1901, an Arctic explorer, horseman, marksman, motor-car enthusiast and an expert on orchids. His marriage to Violet Mary Beauclerk in 1907 was widely reported in society journals; she also became a well-known writer of their travels.[31] This estate has subsequently been broken up into smaller units. Much of the Oa now forms the Kinnabus Estate where considerable farm amalgamation occurred. The rest of the Oa remained longer in Ramsay possession, but is now in the hands of various owners, including several continental Europeans. The northern part of the former Kildalton estate now forms the Laggan Estate.

Although Sir Smith Child did not take on the Oa's problems in 1860, he did purchase a substantial part of the lands around Port Askaig, for £53,960.[32] The estate was known in turn as Losset, Lossit, Glen Lossit and Dunlossit. After less than a decade, however, Smith Child's son and heir died suddenly in 1868 and the estate was sold to Kirkman Finlay of the Glasgow tea-importing firm, and of Toward on the Firth of Clyde.[33] Kirkman Finlay was the eponymous grandson of the famous cotton manufacturer and merchant who had been Lord Provost of Glasgow in 1812 and MP for Glasgow from 1812 to 1818. For more than two decades after 1868 the new owner did much of the tree planting that became such a distinctive feature of Dunlossit estate. He also incorporated the existing small shooting lodge into an enlarged Dunlossit House or Castle, before selling the estate in 1890 to Donald Martin of Auchendennan, John Ramsay's brother-in-law. After a serious fire at the mansion, Martin built the present Scottish baronial Dunlossit House, which now figures so prominently in any view of Port Askaig from the Sound of Islay, over which it commands an equally impressive view to the Paps of Jura, to Colonsay and Mull.

The Dunlossit estate changed hands three times thereafter.[34] In 1911 it passed to the Bankier family and about 1918 to Nathaniel Dunlop. The latter died in 1931, but in the uncertain times of the Depression, the trustees did not sell the estate until 1939. The purchaser then was Helmut B. Schroder, a London merchant banker who died in 1969. In the mid-1960s about 1,000 hectares of the Dunlossit estate in the upper part of the Laggan valley were the first of several Forestry Commission plantings on Islay, since cleared, with the lands reverting to the estate. In successive Schroder lairdships, further plantations were establised, many improvements were made to agricultural land and farm buildings and the estate was much favoured for shooting and fishing.

Like the Islay estate in the middle of the nineteenth century, the affairs of the Sunderland estate were also in difficulties.[35] In 1846 the estate was purchased for £28,000 from the trustees of the late Walter Campbell by Alexander McEwan, a Glasgow merchant. Of this sum, Mr McEwan paid £5,000, the balance being arranged as a mortgage on the estate. The McEwans however encountered various marital and settlement difficulties, with the result that the estate passed into the management of a trustee, Mr Balderstone. By 1861 the latter had to initiate the breakup of the Rinns into several smaller estates. The Cladville area came into the hands of the Baker family, while Coul formed a separate small estate which remained in the McLaughlin family until the 1970s. The Sunderland part of the Rinns reverted to the main landowners of the island, the Morrisons, until it in turn was divided and sold in the 1970s. The southern portion around Ellister has since been further divided into individual owner-occupied farms, the Forestry Commission acquiring Ballimony. The northern portion, based on Foreland House, was the last piece to be sold and while reduced in size is still called the Foreland Estate. Part of Ballinaby was managed by the Department of Agriculture and Fisheries for Scotland, but is now in several private hands.

Evolving landscape

Although in the Islay, Kildalton, Dunlossit and other separate estates, the enthusiasm or conservatism of different lairds has been evident in the rate and character of landscape change, the main pattern of change was the filling-in of detail. By about 1870 the present agricultural landscape and settlement pattern of Islay had largely been established and the population was about 10,000.[36] This detail was determined in part by the laird, but to an increasing extent it reflected wider concerns of national policy and conditions in agriculture and the economy as a whole.

Islay continued to remain a Hebridean exception, especially in those activities that were based on the land resource. For this reason, some of the main events in the history of the Highlands and Islands during the last century have been of less importance on Islay than elsewhere. In 1884, for example, the Royal Commission of Enquiry into Crofting Conditions found relatively few land problems to investigate in Islay.[37] There is only one lotted township, Claddich, in Islay. Much the same was true of the so-called 'Deer Forest Commission', appointed in 1892 'to inquire whether any land . . . now occupied for the purposes of a deer forest, grouse moor or other sporting purposes, or for grazing, not in the occupation of crofters or small tenants, is capable of being cultivated to profit or otherwise advantageously occupied by crofters or other small tenants'.[38] The Commission took an optimistically short-sighted view of 'profitable cultivation' and none of their recommendations was implemented in Islay.

After the First World War, the well-intentioned, but dubious, resettlement schemes for returning servicemen had some impact on Islay, though again such schemes were much more common elsewhere. Additions were made to the village lands of Port Wemyss and Port Charlotte (in Wester Ellister and Lorgbaw respectively); the two former farms of Cladville and Ballimony in the Rinns were also converted into small holdings. This did little to counter the gradual decline in the numbers on the land: the trend towards assimilation and amalgamation continued. Most of the settlement schemes initiated after the First World War subsequently re-amalgamated into larger single units.

Clearances and depopulation

At the time when Islay was purchased by the Morrisons, its population had already fallen from the peak of almost 15,000 recorded in 1831 to about 11,000.[39] Characteristic of the whole of the next hundred years was a gradual decline in the number of tenants. The interior valleys of the eastern hills and the peninsula of the Oa – the two main areas which had undergone the least visible changes in the period about 1830 – suffered the greatest population changes after the middle of the century, with reduction in numbers of tenants and clearances. Migration to the villages, to the Lowlands and assisted emigration abroad took place, especially from the Oa. Elsewhere on the island the numbers of tenants continued to decline more gradually.

The decline in numbers was accompanied by a gradual change in the rural-village balance, in age composition, gender ratios, and changing patterns of employment. In the twentieth century the widespread reduction in agricultural employment and the opportunities in the major urban centres of the Lowlands and beyond, have caused this population decline to continue on Islay, as in many other places. From a population of 12,334 in 1851, the island's population numbers declined to around 3,500 by 1991.[40] The part of the island with the largest population has always been the central parish of Killarow and Kilmeny. This was the area where improvements came first, on the relatively large area of tillable land in the island around the laird's mansion at the head of Loch Indaal. This region today includes Bowmore, the major service centre of the island, the two distillery villages of Bunnahabhain and Caol Ila and three other villages at Bridgend, Ballygrant and Kiells. The presence of these centres and their sources of employment is one reason why this parish has had a slower rate of population decline than the others.

The Rinns parish of Kilchoman was the second most populous in the early nineteenth century, reaching 4,822 at the 1831 census.[41] At that time most of the population lived on farms or in joint townships. As the decades passed, an increasing proportion was recorded in the three villages of Port Charlotte, Port Wemyss and Portnahaven. In Port Charlotte the main employment was in agriculture, fishing and distilling; in the others, the emphasis was mainly on fishing. After some clearances of joint farms and more gradual reductions in the number of tenants and others dependent

Considerable thinning out of the population clusters had taken place by 1891, and several new distillery villages had been established. The legacy of deserted buildings was referred to by Fairhurst as the 'ruins of swollen clusters' (Compiled from copies of census enumerators' schedules for 1891, New Register House, Edinburgh).

on the land, and as line fishing became less successful, the population in the Kilchoman peninsula began to decline after the 1830s. However, herring fishing increased in importance and for much of the second half of the nineteenth century there were around 200 boats engaged in fishing from Islay, each manned by perhaps a man and a boy.[42] In the 1880s a curing station at Tayovullin on Loch Gruinart was established, still visible today. A distillery was established at Bruichladdich in 1881, and the population of Kilchoman parish rose again for the next decade or so. The First World War interrupted the trade with the herring markets of Germany and Eastern Europe and by 1921 only fifty boats were registered in Islay. The later 1920s and the 1930s witnessed the virtual disappearance of the herring shoals. The closure of the distillery in Port Charlotte coincided in 1930 with the almost complete disappearance of fishing and the rate of population decline in Kilchoman became severe, with an unbalanced age structure.

In Kildalton parish in the south-east, the population was never particularly numerous, since most of the land was originally in large grazing tacks and no eighteenth-century villages were established on the model of Bowmore. But in the Oa peninsula, the interior valleys and basins supported a very high population in the first half of the nineteenth century, even though there was only a restricted amount of agricultural land. This increase in the Oa, together with nineteenth-century expansion of Port Ellen and in the smaller distillery villages in Kildalton, accounts for the increase in population of Kildalton and Oa parish which continued until after the census of 1841. Subsequently the decrease in numbers of people in the Oa and of the farmworkers in Kildalton, was only partially offset by continued growth in the industrial villages which contained five whisky distilleries in all. External influences on population change during the nineteenth century included the California gold rush, emigration to Australia and to South Africa and the Boer War, together with the labour market required for the central lowlands of Scotland and the importance of Britain as a maritime nation.[43]

Apart from the published census data, the copies of individual census enumerators' returns are available for research for the six Scottish censuses from 1841 to 1891.[44] From these returns can be traced the movements of individual people from one agricultural holding to another or from agricultural holdings into industrial villages. They also throw more light on changing densities and distributions of population and settlement and changing age and occupational structures. As a result of the major land reorganisation extending from the 1820s to the last quarter of the nineteenth century, much of the clustered settlement on Islay gradually disappeared. It was replaced by a pattern of single dispersed farmhouses and service or industrial villages. In 1841 rural settlement was still predominantly in a clustered form, but by 1891, apart from a few of the original clusters in the northern Rinns and the Oa, which were still occupied, the rural settlement pattern was predominantly the dispersed one that it is at the present day. The area of settlement had retreated, especially in the interior valleys of the south-eastern hills and in the Oa. This retreat has continued and the evidence is easily visible in the clustered ruins at isolated spots in the Oa, the Glen and in the northern Rinns.

The ruins that one sees today are often all that is left of 'swollen clusters deserted almost immediately after a period of vigorous but unhealthy growth'.[45] Some of those that were abandoned, such as those at Braid, now part of Kilchiaran, indicate a loose, unplanned grouping. Others

The ruins and former cultivation ridges of the township of Lurabus on the southern slopes of the Oa peninsula testify to the emigration of many hundreds of islanders to Ontario in the 1860s (University of Cambridge).

were more regularly laid out or spaced on the ground, such as at Olistadh in the Rinns; they may have been partially reorganised some time during the agrarian revolution. Most were occupied into the second or third quarter of the nineteenth century. Some have been reconstructed, as at Carnduncan. Associated with many of these settlements are signs of former cultivation, particularly clearly seen at certain times of the year when either the light conditions, or the state of the vegetation cover, or even more rarely, snow cover enable the outline of the cultivated ridges to be more easily recognised. This is especially true of the former shielings and summer pastures.

As elsewhere in Scotland and beyond, a significant factor in the overall decline in population was the gradual decrease in family and household size. Average size tended to remain higher in the rural areas than in the villages for some time, but household size everywhere declined during the nineteenth century. Changing age structures and gender ratios were also noticeable; by the end of the century and well into the next, the greatest imbalance in gender ratios and age structures was in the rural areas and in the isolated villages of Portnahaven and Port Wemyss. The Oa in particular had an excessive imbalance of old to young people and of men to women. Other areas show an almost complete reversal of the 1841 age pyramid. But the imbalance between males and females and between old and young has rarely been so extreme as in many other parts of the West Highland seaboard.

The unspecialised employment structure of the early-eighteenth century in Islay changed gradually through the nineteenth to a more specialised and more varied one. The male employment recorded in the census from 1841 to 1891 can be grouped into several main types, led by the primary occupations of agricultural tenants, farmers and crofters, farmworkers, estate workers and labourers. A second group comprises the secondary occupations of craftsmen (quarriers, millers, blacksmiths, joiners, plumbers, tailors, shoemakers and weavers), together with other non-agricultural workers such as fishers. Occupations in a third group consisted of services for the population such as merchants, professional people, clerks, excise and other government employees.

Employment of women on Islay was important in the nineteenth century, although even then only a small proportion of the total number of women of working age were actually in paid employment. These were essentially connected with the house or the land, acting as domestic or nursemaids, seamstresses, weavers, teachers, dairymaids, fieldworkers, postwomen and, occasionally, as nurses or midwives. In the twentieth century many of these occupations have become redundant so that shop or hotel work is now the main category of female employment and it is often part-time, other alternatives such as public relations and secretarial work in the distilleries and the professions provide year-round occupations.

Architectural Heritage

The majority of Islay's buildings are not outstanding. But to both islanders and visitors, the buildings, churchyards, monuments and other man-made elements provide visible and harmonious links between the past and present in Islay. Some buildings are statutorily listed as of architectural or historical interest, such as Islay House or the round church in Bowmore.[46] Others, particularly in the villages, are being reconstructed or rehabilitated. In addition, ruined settlements abound in the island surrounded by signs of their former cultivation. All form part of the settled ecumene. Because many of the buildings are in the vernacular or traditional style, few architects' names or plans are known. Apart from the occasional village house there

Walter Frederick Campbell's mansion was enhanced with 'policies' of plantations, gardens, a 'lake', aviaries, and Home Farm Square. Even before the Forestry Commission started planting in Islay in the 1960s, there was thus more woodland than is usual in the Hebrides. Islay House and the Home Farm Square beyond, are set in the kindly Sorn valley where it drains into Loch Indaal (Eric Thorburn).

was little development during the present century until the later 1960s, though sometimes a building's function changed.

Different stones have been quarried locally for most of the island's buildings; few building materials were brought in from the mainland until about the time of the Second World War. Bricks, concrete, timber-frame and prefabricated techniques are now all used in new buildings, particularly since changes in the ferry system in the late 1960s made awkward and large loads less of a problem to get to the island. Roofing slates were generally locally quarried until about the middle of this century, but now, as elsewhere, other roofing materials are normally used.

There are only a few large houses. Apart from the remains of medieval castles, chapels and graveyards, the main legacy of the Cawdor Campbells is in the earliest part of Islay House, begun in 1677 by Sir Hugh Campbell when he started his new 'Killarow House'.[47] Its window openings were later enlarged, but the original building is still recognisable. What else remained of the Campbell of Cawdor and earlier periods has mostly been overshadowed by efforts of the Shawfield Campbells and later owners. Daniel Campbell of Shawfield extended Islay House with two wings in 1737 and his grandson built the eastern staircase in 1760.[48] By this time the entire house was beginning to look very grand, with its Palladian windows and splendid Georgian interior. It was almost a hundred years before the Victorian additions designed by William Playfair were built in the early 1840s. In 1910, Detmar Blow designed the present two-storeyed mock-Georgian wing on the east of the house, for Hugh Morrison, but the back remains turreted in distinctly Victorian fashion.

The only other houses in Islay comparable in style, if not size, are Eallabus and Foreland House. Eallabus was built as a factor's residence, probably in the time of Daniel Campbell the Younger, and was gutted and restored in the 1980s as the laird's residence after Islay House was sold.[49] Foreland House was built about 1820 around the core of an earlier one, by Walter Campbell of Foreland and Sunderland when he retired from the East India Company.[50] The other big houses were those at Ballinaby, demolished in the 1950s after a fire, Cairnmore House near Port Ellen, now seasonally occupied, Kildalton House built in 1870 by John Ramsay but unoccupied for several decades past, and Dunlossit House, owned today by the Schroder family. The latter three houses were typical Victorian gothic-baronial shooting estate houses.

Tacksmen's houses that survive from the eighteenth century probably include those at Ardnave and perhaps also at Coul; others were constructed later in much the same style, with rounded staircases at the front. Large single farmhouses of varying dates of construction are at Sanaig, Kintra and Leorin for instance. Several were constructed with integral farm buildings; others had separate outhouses such as in Islay House Square, or in the more unusual semi-circular farmsteading at Kilchiaran.

Many of Islay's smaller buildings today reflect the period of intense estate activity connected with the agrarian and village plans of successive Campbells of Shawfield. Apart from the farmhouses and their outbuildings, there were the agricultural workers' cottages, tenants' cottages and estate lodges, some, for instance, with the intertwined initials WFC designed by Playfair for the East Lodge at Bridgend. Later Morrison landlords and the Ramsays of Kildalton added other farm buildings, cottages and lodges, those in the south-east being in a highly decorated style. But throughout the past two centuries change has also taken place in the occupance and character of the rural vernacular buildings. The traditional cruck-framed 'black house' cottages drawn for Thomas Pennant in the 1770s have been replaced through time by the dressed stone, separate dwelling and stock byres such as those seen on Glenegedale and Duich muirs.

Industrial buildings include many of the earlier mills associated with the rural economy of the island that are no longer used, such as the Starch Mill at Mulindry and the Meal or Whin Mill at Bridgend.[51] The Wool Mill near Bridgend was powered until 1979 by a water-wheel and produced Islay tweeds, blankets and the like. Since 1981 it has been revived as the Islay Woollen Mill and although no longer powered by

'Great' Daniel Campbell of Shawfield and Islay built the Whin or Meal Mill to grind flour from spring and summer wheat. Other mills ground barley and oats. The nearby Wauk Mill still produces woollens and a unique Islay tweed worn by Islay Estate personnel.

Archibald Cameron recorded many Islay scenes at the turn of the nineteenth century, such as the herring curing station on the west side of Loch Gruinart (Museum of Islay Life).

water, its tweed and other products are sold world-wide. It constitutes a
veritable museum, with the only slubbing billy left in the world, two of
the few remaining spinning jennies and much else besides. Remains of
kilns for burning limestone for agricultural purposes can be found
throughout the limestone belt from Bridgend to Port Askaig and elsewhere.
Other buildings, such as smithies, have by now generally been converted
to other uses. Little clear evidence remains of linen-weaving times, except
perhaps in the village of Kiells or in the retting dam for the lint mill at
Sunderland. For the late nineteenth-century fishing expansion, a few derelict
structures on the western shores of Loch Gruinart are the best evidence,
apart from the fishing villages themselves. The remains of mining activity
are more obvious; ruined buildings, remains of tip heaps and shafts are
easily recognisable in the Robolls, Mulreesh and Shenegart areas around
Ballygrant. There are many disused local stone quarries, and several slate
quarries.

It is of course with the distilleries that most of the remaining industrial
buildings of Islay are associated. Apart from the reconstruction of some
distilleries in the late 1960s and early 1970s and the gradual addition of
extra warehouses for storing the whisky as it matures, many of the buildings
connected with Islay whisky-making are recognisably old. Relics of illicit
distilling in the past are on display in the Museum of Islay Life at Port
Charlotte.

The most obvious attempts to change the face of Islay in infrastructure
and public buildings were in the village of Bowmore. Much of the core of
the present village was built in the late-eighteenth century and has remained
little modified externally. Elsewhere, construction activity in the second
quarter of the nineteenth century has left many more legacies in the
domestic architecture of the villages of Kiells, Port Charlotte, Port Wemyss
and Port Ellen. Some of the roads, piers, lighthouses, bridges, schools
and churches also date from this period. The churches and manses at
Risabus in the Oa and Portnahaven and the manse at Kilmeny were built
in 1828 to plans by Thomas Telford, as part of his work for the
Parliamentary Commissioners appointed in 1823 to build additional 'Places
of Worship' in the Highlands and Islands. How difficult it is today, standing
in the windy ruins of the church in the Oa, to imagine it in 1831 being
'always well filled; so much so, that at present 55 heads of families are
unable to procure accommodation'.[52] The chequered religious history of
Scotland is reflected in the many churches of different denominations,
except Roman Catholic, whose adherents attend mass in the Scottish
Episcopal Church at Bridgend.

In the late-eighteenth century Daniel Campbell the Younger encouraged education with his Bowmore school and schoolmaster. After that, schools multiplied and in Walter Frederick Campbell's time there were four 'parochial' schools under his patronage in Bowmore, Kilmeny, Kilchoman and Kildalton.[53] In addition there were twenty-eight other schools, two of which were supported by the Gaelic Society in Edinburgh. The teachers of the smaller single-teacher schools were 'young men . . . engaged and paid by the parents of the children under instruction, which never exceeds 2s. 6d. [12½p] per quarter. At these small schools, without salary, the instruction afforded is not all that could be wished'. Nevertheless the figures of readers and writers for this and other parishes were quite creditable. Many of the teachers had been educated outside Islay, the Bowmore schoolmaster in Penrith, for example. There is no mention in the early-nineteenth century of women teachers, but by the middle of the century they had become assistants. John Ramsay of Kildalton founded several schools, including a 'female' one, and education was one of his main interests.[54]

The landowners were eventually overtaken by local government and schooling became more centralised. Schools at Kiells, Newton, Port Charlotte, Portnahaven, Bowmore and Port Ellen catered for local primary children while all senior schoolchildren travelled to Bowmore by bus. Bowmore school, up on the hill above the village and harbour, was much extended in the 1960s and in 1974 local parents successfully petitioned for it to have sixth form status to obviate the need to send children to the mainland. It was then re-named Islay High School and subsequently extended, and there have also been several new primary school buildings.

With the breakup of the main estate and the harder times in the island during the middle of the nineteenth century there was a lull in the changing appearance of the island. But the new landowners later in the century and the county council gradually effected change by adding housing to the edges of the villages, widening roads and so on. New industrial villages were created around the distilleries at Bruichladdich and Bunnahabhain. There was renewed activity in the estates, with much tree planting, particularly in the Islay, Dunlossit and Kildalton estates, new farm cottages and estate lodges. Many of the hotels, shops, banks and other buildings of the period remain little changed externally to this day. The beginnings of substantial change in the villages really dates only from the end of the Second World War. This was initiated primarily by Argyll County Council; until the 1970s there was little private building on the island, in contrast to the several hundred houses built by the county council, and its successor, Argyll and Bute District Council. Changes in the ferry system in the later 1960s and early 1970s led to substantial improvements to ferry terminals, roads and bridges. The airport runway and passenger handling facilities at

Glenegedale have been upgraded several times.

Islay's many villages are not merely distinctive when compared with the settlement pattern of the remainder of the Hebrides, they are very different from one another. All of the Islay villages are calendar villages, amongst the most attractive anywhere in the Hebrides. For over two centuries, they have housed an increasing proportion of the island population and this trend continues. Not all of them provide expanding opportunities for employment and the tendency towards concentration of services in Bowmore and Port Ellen is fairly clear. Nevertheless, the villages and the limited facilities that they offer, have probably been an important factor in accounting for the relative stability of Islay's population in recent decades, when compared with the rapid decline in many other islands. They seem likely to play an even more significant role in the future.

Notes and references

[1] Gatty, *Portrait*, p. 30.

[2] IEP, 8 December 1853.

[3] C. Morrison, *An Essay on the Relations between Labour and Capital*, (London, 1854).

[4] C. Williams, *Basildon, Berkshire*, (Reading, n.d., [1994]), p. 132.

[5] Mitchell, *Reminiscences*, p. 300.

[6] IEP, 18 February and 24 April 1854.

[7] IEP, 3 June 1854.

[8] IEP, 6 July 1854.

[9] IEP, 15 September 1892.

[10] IEP, 30 June 1854.

[11] IEP, 24 November 1854.

[12] IEP, 28 October 1854.

[13] IEP, 17 November, 27 November and 8 December 1854.

[14] IEP, 7 December 1854.

[15] IEP, 8 December 1854 and 20 January 1856.

[16] IEP, 10 May 1856.

[17] IEP, 25 May 1909.

[18] IEP, 23 November 1909.

[19] IEP, Various biographical sources.

[20] IEP, Missives.

[21] Idem.

[22] Idem.

[23] Ramsay, *John Ramsay*, p. 34.

[24] Ibid., pp. 37–8.

[25] Ibid., pp. 38–9.

[26] Calculated from census and registration changes.

[27] Ramsay, *John Ramsay*, p. 48.

[28] *Report on the Proceedings at the Annual Meeting of the Islay Association*, (Glasgow, 1878), p. 29.

[29] Foster, *Members of Parliament*, p. 293.

[30] J. Ramsay, *A Letter to . . . the Lord Advocate of Scotland on the State of Education in the Outer Hebrides, in 1862*, (Glasgow, 1863).

[31] V. Clifton, *The Book of Talbot*, (London, 1933).

[32] IEP, Disposition by Charles Morrison, 1860.

[33] C. Brogan, (ed.), *James Finlay and Company Limited manufacturers and East India merchants, 1750-1950*, (Glasgow, 1950).

[34] Information from Dunlossit Estate.

[35] *BPP, Distress*, LIII, p. 75.

[36] *Census of Scotland, 1951.* (1953), Table 3.

[37] *Report of Her Majesty's Commissioners of Enquiry into the Condition of the Crofters and Cottars in the Highlands and Islands of Scotland, BPP*, 1884, C.3980.

[38] *Minutes of Evidence, Royal Commission (Highlands and Islands, 1892), 1895 BPP*, C.7668-1, II.

[39] *Census of Scotland 1951*, (1953), Table 3.

[40] *Census of Scotland 1991*, Small Area Statistics.

[41] *Census of Scotland 1961, Argyll County Report*, (Edinburgh, 1964), Table 4B.

[42] *Appendix C to Second Report of the Tidal Harbours Commissioners, BPP*, 1848, XXXII; *Annual Reports of the Fishery Board for Scotland.*

[43] Macdonald, *TSA*, pp. 343-4.

[44] Storrie, 'Census of Scotland'.

[45] H. Fairhurst, 'The Archaeology of Rural Settlement in Scotland', *TGAS*, New Series, 1960, 15, p. 144.

[46] Statutory List of Buildings of Architectural or Historic Interest, designated by Argyll and Bute Council and approved by Scottish Heritage and the Scottish Office. Killarow or Bowmore Church is category A (of national as well as local interest) and Islay House is category B (of more local than national interest, but also of special interest). The older parts of most of the villages in Islay have been designated 'conservation areas'.

[47] Innes, *Thanes of Cawdor*, p. xxxiii.

[48] Forman, 'Islay House', p. 38 and p. 40.

[49] *NSA, Argyleshire*, p. 651.

[50] RCAHMS, *Argyll Inventory*, *V*, p. 290.

[51] *Minutes of Evidence, Royal Commission (Highlands and Islands) 1892, BPP*, C.7668-1, II, p. 832.

[52] *Sixth Report of the Commissioners appointed for building additional Places of Worship in the Highlands and Islands of Scotland, BPP*, 1831, XI, p. 30.

[53] *Abstracts of Education Returns (Scotland) 1834, BPP*, 1837, XLVIII, Argyll, pp. 68–101.

[54] J. Ramsay, *Letter.*

CHAPTER 12

Islay and whisky

Islay and whisky come almost as smoothly off the tongue as Scotch and water. Why should this particular small island off the west coast of Scotland have become one of the principal manufacturing centres for a product with a world-wide reputation? Or, as the Islay resident might be inclined to ask, how has it happened that the island of Islay should account for such a disproportionate share of the revenues of the United Kingdom, through the excise duty on whisky? The reasons are complex and depend partly on historical accident.

One reason for Islay's interest in distilling is to be found in geography. Although Irish whiskey is much less important in world markets today than 'Scotch', it is generally believed that uisge-beatha, or *aqua vitae*, was introduced into the Highlands and Islands of Scotland from Ireland about the fifteenth century. Islay, as the Hebridean island nearest to Ireland, was well placed to benefit from this transfer of technology, especially as the necessary raw materials were readily available – barley, water of suitable quality and peat. The 'art' of making the spirit spread to the central and eastern Highlands and Islands and further afield. Distillers became larger producers especially in areas where greater supplies of grain were available. Small pot distilleries gave way to large patent stills; single malt whiskies tended to give way to blended whiskies, Scotch became a national drink rather than a Highland one and subsequently an international one.

Today, backed by skilful marketing and legislative and other controls on production, a commodity that is both attractive to world-wide tastes and also capable of almost infinite adaptation to changes in taste, Scotch is universally renowned, though the total quantity of Scotch whisky and Irish whiskey that is produced is far less than that of other whiskies. Unlike products such as 'Cheddar' cheese, which are now manufactured in many places far from their original area, true Scotch whisky is still produced solely in Scotland. Attempts have been made to imitate Scotch elsewhere, but some protection is provided by legislation, which in Britain at least prevents the operation of Scotch whisky distilleries outside the borders of Scotland. Scotch is not a homogeneous product: while *aficionados* often prefer a single malt whisky from a favourite distillery, most Scotch whisky is consumed in blended form, a single bottle containing the products of several distilleries. The possibilities of blending are infinite: there are several thousand different blends on sale throughout the world at any one time, in a diverse number of brands and bottles.

Illicit distilling

Such subtleties did not trouble those who developed the art on Islay over five centuries ago. Produced in small pot stills on farms and grain mills in many glens of the Highlands and Islands, the raw materials used were locally-grown bere barley, a four-rowed type suited to West Highland conditions, water that had flowed through peat, and peat itself, used both in the barley-malting process and as a fuel to heat the distilling apparatus. The resulting spirit varied in quantity and quality from season to season and year to year and was consumed locally for several centuries. The amount produced depended to a considerable extent on the amount of local barley available in excess of that needed as cattle food. Distilling was usually a seasonal occupation during the agriculturally inactive months of late autumn, winter and early spring, when water was plentiful in the small burns.

Throughout this evolution taxation and excise duties have been as much a part of whisky as the water, barley and peat. If barley had to be imported from Ireland or England before the Act of Union, it was dutiable. Customs and excise duties were levied through Boards of Commissioners, but in Scotland they were both still 'in farm', i.e. the duties and taxes were collected by middlemen under contract. After the Union, the Crown assumed direct responsibility for their collection throughout Scotland, except in Islay where the excise levy apparently remained 'in farm' to the laird.[1] This seems to have led to less than efficient collection of excise dues on Islay and to illicit distillation and smuggling on a far greater scale than was possible elsewhere in the islands or on the mainland.

The rapid expansion of illicit whisky manufacture and distribution after the middle of the eighteenth century was a response to market opportunity.[2] Traditionally, beer and wine had been favourite drinks in Scotland but the consumption of plain malt spirit became more popular. Urbanisation and an increasing population stimulated an expansion in demand for all food and drinks, including spirits. The government levied duties on malt, on the distilling of spirit and on the finished product. The incentive to cheat the Revenue by avoiding payment of duty became most pressing precisely at the same time as the consumption of whisky was on the increase. Illicit spirits from the Highlands and Islands, when marketed in the Lowlands, fetched a substantially higher price. The apparatus for pot-still distillation could be purchased for less than a few pounds and 'distillation was well suited to the socio-economic communalism of the Highlands where social links at local level preserved fellow feeling against the law so vital to the success of the illicit trade'.[3] The law was consequently defied on a remarkable scale.

Rises in the malt tax had always encouraged illegal production, particularly after 1786, when a system of still licensing was adopted throughout Scotland, albeit with a differential favouring the Highland zone with its higher costs. At the same time it was forbidden to transport Highland whisky across a 'Highland line' from the Sound of Jura to the Moray Firth, thereby encouraging smuggling. Licence duties rose dramatically and subsequently, stills below 40 gallons' still-content were declared illegal. Previously, every person who had a still whose contents were limited to twelve gallons by law might distil for his own use and the outlawing of small stills drove private household and family production underground. There was often no alternative supplier to the illicit distillers in remoter localities. In Campbeltown, for instance, no still licences were issued between 1797 and 1817, although there were hundreds of illicit stills in the Kintyre region.

The Church of Scotland minister who wrote the Kildalton parish survey in The Statistical Account in 1794 was not, of course, a sympathetic witness: 'This island hath the liberty of brewing whisky, without being under the necessity of paying the usual excise duty to government. We have not an excise officer in the whole island. The quantity therefore of whisky made here is very great; and the evil, that follows drinking to excess of this liquor, is very visible in this island'.[4] He described how poverty-stricken farmers sold their barley to the distillers for 17s. (85p) a boll, then had to buy barley for their stock, sometimes at 23s. (£1.15). This anomalous situation was corrected later, but illicit distilling and the associated smuggling remained serious problems on Islay and elsewhere, because of the high level of excise duty.

Subsequent legislation merely confirmed and strengthened the trend towards illegality and the vastly inflated revenue demands of the Naopleonic wars produced a marked rise in all of the taxes. During the wars, imports of French brandy and claret were threatened by rising tariff duties and interrupted trade. Because of the very high grain prices during the Napoleonic wars, distillation was forbidden in 1800–1, 1804–8, 1809–10 and then occasionally up to 1813. From 1814 stills of less than 500 gallons (later reduced to 200 gallons) were banned in the Highland area and this was to outlaw all but a tiny minority of licensed distillers in the

In the 1830s distilleries fluctuated in output by season, both in numbers and output. The total production from twelve Islay distilleries in 1833 was 170,000 gallons (*BPP*, 1835, XXX).

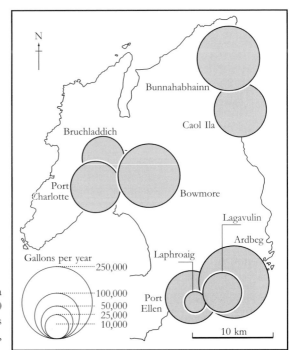

Alfred Barnard recorded a production of 1,250,000 gallons for Islay's distilleries in the 1880s (Barnard, *Whisky Distilleries*).

north. In 1816 the 'Highland line' was abolished, revenue was raised from duty on spirits rather than from annual licence fees and penalties against smaller stills were revoked but the resurgence in the fortunes of the legal sector was short-lived. In 1819 English and Scottish duties on barley were equalised and in reality this represented a tax increase and an incentive for farmers to dispose of their grain to illicit whisky-makers.

Post-war regulation

The dramatic expansion of illicit distillation after the Napoleonic wars concentrated government attention. Two major investigations in 1821 and 1822 exposed the extent to which the law was being flouted and the revenue cheated. To bring the situation under control, an Act in 1823 required legal distillers to use stills with capacities over 40 gallons; for such distilleries the excise duty was reduced from its previous high levels. By offering inducements for large-scale commercial production it was hoped that the industry could be brought under control and illicit distillation reduced or eliminated. There was one fixed rate of duty throughout Scotland and the fee to become a licensed distiller was a relatively modest £10. This substantially eroded the illicit producer's cost advantage over his licensed rival. While the decade after 1823 saw a series of violent incidents between the revenue service and groups of illicit distillers, the new policy would appear to have been spectacularly successful. The amount of duty-paid whisky almost doubled between 1823 and 1824 and the quality of the product improved markedly.[5]

In 1821 Islay accounted for ten of the 114 official distilleries listed in Scotland, although there were probably illicit ones as well, some of which would be registered after the Act was passed. By 1833 additional distilleries were registered in Islay and the official amount of whisky produced had risen from 29,731 gallons to 169,718.[6] Several of these distilleries have survived to the present day – Bowmore, Port Ellen, Laphroaig, Ardbeg and Lagavulin. Although the 1823 Act did much to bring illicit distilling under control, there were inevitably some who were unable or unwilling to meet its requirements. For much of the nineteenth century there was a continuing game of hide-and-seek between the farmer-distillers on the one hand and the excisemen on the other. Illicit distillation on a substantial scale seems to have continued longer in Islay than elsewhere in Scotland. Extant official correspondence in the Excise records from 1837 to 1849 contains many accounts of seizures of stills, malt and wash (the fermented liquid from which the spirit is distilled) from 'hovels in the muir' or from 'caves on the shores at Proaig and Ballychatrigan'.[7] Excise officers patrolling the coast in a cutter were reported to have scaled cliffs near Glenastle in the Oa to investigate distillers manufacturing in cave systems. Flight across the muir enabled the moonshiners to evade arrest, but usually at the cost of losing their stills and raw materials. One such still is in the Museum of Islay Life.

The enthusiasm with which distillers were pursued was perhaps in the long-term interest of Ilich, as well as that of the British exchequer. Lord Teignmouth noted the alcohol problem in the 1830s: 'whisky follows the Highlander from the cradle to the grave, and often accelerates his progress from one to the other . . . To try to prevent further illicit distilling, Mr Stewart Mackenzie of Lewis, the Duke of Sutherland, some of the proprietors of the Orkneys, as well as Mr Campbell of Islay, erected distilleries. This provides a more adequate, cheap and legal supply of the spirit'.[8] In his evidence to the Poor Law Inquiry in 1844 the Kildalton minister endorsed Teignmouth's views and showed much more tolerance than his predecessor half a century earlier, saying that the distilleries 'afford a great deal of employment . . . the people . . . are very temperate and industrious . . . the more distilleries they have the more temperate they become. There is not one gallon of whisky drank now for fifty that were drank when [I] came to the parish [twenty-one years before]'.[9]

Victorian Scotch
While these regulatory measures were taking effect, a fundamental technical change had taken place in whisky production. In Dublin in the early 1830s Aeneas Coffey patented the still that bears his name and this laid the basis for the production of grain whisky, a less potent product than the Highland malt whiskies. The Coffey still process used only a small proportion of malted barley to unmalted cereals and the new grain distilleries could therefore be established wherever there were plentiful supplies of barley or other cereals, even if these were distant from peat sources. The character of the water was also less important since the process itself produced whisky with fewer impurities through more efficient distillation than that of malt pot stills. During the remainder of the nineteenth century, the art of blending these grain whiskies with one or more malt whiskies gradually developed. Blending was itself a logical extension of the old process of vatting, the mixing of malts from different seasons or different distilleries. Scotsmen spread across the expanding Victorian empire and the world, creating a steadily rising demand for Scotch in overseas markets. Of the many new distilleries built in Scotland three were on Islay, at Bunnahabhain and Caol Ila on the Sound of Islay and at Bruichladdich on the Rinns. The coastal sites and their individual supplies of water were ideal for whisky production.

A detailed record of the distilleries on Islay at the height of the 1880s boom was provided by Alfred Barnard in his amply-illustrated book, The *Whisky Distilleries of the United Kingdom*.[10] The title, it should be noted, was deliberately precise. Legislation had not yet limited British whisky production to Scotland and Barnard's survey included a number of remote outposts of the industry, including one distillery beside the Regent's Canal in east London. Barnard provided distillery sketches and descriptions of the historical development, production methods, quantities, personnel and other details of each of the distilleries he visited. It is evident from the 27 pages devoted to Islay that very little in the external appearances of the distilleries or their villages changed until comparatively recently. Nine distilleries, then producing 4.5 million litres of malt whisky annually, were described for Islay: Ardbeg, Lagavulin, Laphroaig, Port Ellen, Bowmore, Lochindaal (Port Charlotte), Bruichladdich, Caol Ila and Bunnahabhain, six or seven of which produce about 12.5 million litres today. This contrasts with Campbeltown in nearby Kintyre; of 21 distilleries listed there in 1887, only two survive today.

Barnard records that 'isolated' Ardbeg was not officially established until 1815 but it had for long before been a haunt of smugglers. With access to the waters of Lochs Airighnambeist and Uigeadail for whisky making and with access to sea transport on the south-east coast, the original owners, the MacDougalls, subsequently built the main distillery buildings, pier, school and also many of the houses that are still there today. Even in Barnard's time, Ardbeg was producing one-quarter of a million gallons of whisky a year. The peat used had to be brought only about three kilometres, its chief characteristic being the absence of 'sulphur or other offensive material'. As with most Islay distilleries, the annual output of 'pure Islay Malt' was 'taken up by the . . . wine and spirit merchants in Glasgow, Liverpool and London'. Half of the spent grain or draff, left after the distilling process, was used on local farms for cattle feed, the remainder being exported to Ireland.

According to Barnard, Lagavulin began in 1742 when 'it consisted of ten small and separate smuggling bothies for the manufacture of "moonlight" [moonshine], which . . . were all subsequently absorbed into one establishment', probably in the 1830s. Some of the mystique that still pervades malt whisky production is evident in his description: 'the Lagavulin water has a hundred falls before it reaches the Distillery and . . . travels over moss and peat lands all the way down, which is said to give the pronounced flavour to the Lagavulin whisky'. At the beginning of the nineteenth century Lagavulin produced only a few thousand gallons a year and even in Barnard's time the annual output was only 75,000 gallons.

The process of condensing vapour in a coil immersed in cold water has to be conjured up for this illicit still now on display in the Museum of Islay Life.

Barnard painstakingly toured all the United Kingdom distilleries in the mid-1880s. The pot stills used today are almost identical to those of Barnard's time: peat is still used in malting, but other power is diesel or electric (Barnard, *Whisky Distilleries*, 1887).

In quality, however, 'we tasted some eight years old . . . which was exceptionally fine'. Most was used for blending, but not all: 'there are only a few of the Scotch Distillers that turn out a spirit for use as single Whiskies and that made at Lagavulin can claim to be one of the most prominent'. After a long interval in which the output all went for blending, some is again bottled as a 'single malt'. A reception centre opened in 1980, created out of the former maltings of the small Malt Mill distillery beside Lagavulin.

Almost next door to Lagavulin is Laphroaig distillery, built in 1820. According to Barnard it looked from the distance like a 'cluster of ruins, but on nearer inspection we found it to be a Distillery of a very old-fashioned type'. Personally entertained by the proprietor, Mr Johnston, Barnard agreed that the whisky made at Laphroaig was of 'exceptional character . . . and is a thick and pungent spirit of a peculiar "peat reek" flavour'. He explained that the small output of only 23,000 gallons a year then rendered it of high value in the market. He also recorded more of the mystique that surrounds the making of Scotch:

> Although the Distillery is of small dimensions, the proprietors would not attempt to disturb the present arrangements, as thereby the character of the Whisky might be entirely lost. The distilling of Whisky is greatly aided by circumstances that cannot be accounted for, and even the most experienced distillers are unable to change its character, which is largely influenced by accidents of locality, water and position. No better instance of this can be given than the case of Lagavulin and Laphroaig Distilleries, which, although situated within a short distance of one another, each produce Whisky of a distinct and varied type.[11]

Barnard's painstaking researches then took him on to Port Ellen, Bowmore and the two distilleries in the Rinns: Bruichladdich and the Lochindaal distillery at Port Charlotte. Port Ellen distillery was started as a malt mill in 1825 and is situated on the shore half a kilometre from the village of the same name. In Barnard's time the annual output was 140,000 gallons. After a break in distilling of nearly 40 years from 1930, when only the bonded warehouses were used, Port Ellen reopened and subsequently added a 30-metre-tall malting plant to the landscape. Replacing old malting floors, this supplies part of the malt requirements for many of the island's distilleries, under an agreement of 1987 called the Islay Concordat. Port Ellen pier was also transformed with a high grain storage silo.

Barnard's party 'found the coach drive from Port Ellen to Bowmore one of the most uninteresting that we had ever experienced . . . in all our wanderings we have never travelled by such a dismal and lonely road'. Their mood however revived when staying at the 'picturesque hotel' in Bridgend, 'the best and only one of any importance in Islay, possessing gardens and grounds of most enchanting loveliness'. Bowmore was founded in 1779 by a local farming family, the Simsons. Bowmore's water came by a long lade from the Laggan river and barley was shipped from north-east Scotland. The distillery, then owned by the Mutters, had its own steamship to import the grain and to export its 200,000 gallons of whisky. During the Second World War, Bowmore, like other distilleries, was closed and accommodated squadrons of Coastal Command, including 422 Squadron of the Royal Canadian Air Force. Sunderland and Catalina flying boats watched over Atlantic convoys assembling off Islay.[12] Today Bowmore still has one of the few floor maltings left in Scotland. The first single Bowmore malt was marketed in 1972 and the then owners, Stanley P. Morrison Ltd, put a special bottle on the market to celebrate the distillery's bicentenary in 1979. An attractive reception centre was created out of some of the older buildings; as well as a visitors' centre for distillery tours and hospitality, this is a much-used asset to the local community. As in many other distilleries in Islay and in the other whisky areas of Scotland, a well-stocked and well-patronised shop was subsequently added. In 1991 the Mactaggart Leisure Centre was created in a former bonded warehouse, using surplus heat from the whisky-making process to help heat the swimming pool.

Barnard described Bruichladdich, (pronounced 'brew-ich-laddy'), on the shores of Loch Indaal, as 'quite an aspiring and tastefully built village ... planted on one of the finest and most healthy spots in Islay'. The new distillery of 1881 was 'a solid handsome structure in the form of a square, and entered through an archway, over which is a fine stone-built residence for the use of partners staying on the island' (this was still in use a century later). Bruichladdich's 94,000 gallons of malt whisky left 'by the steamers which leave the quay every Tuesday'. After take-over in the 1990s Bruichladdich distillery was mothballed and ceased production. Port Charlotte or Lochindaal distillery was established earlier in the century than Bruichladdich, perhaps based on an earlier mill at Skiba or on a still at Octomore farm and taking its water from Lochs Gearach and Octomore. Its 127,000 gallons in Barnard's day went either from Bruichladdich pier, or was 'floated out to the ships, ten casks being lashed together by iron pins and a chain called "dogs" and towed out by boatmen'. In 1930 Port Charlotte distillery closed down. Some of the buildings continued to be used for maturing whisky in casks for the Scottish Malt Distillers. Part of the premises were occupied by the Islay Creamery, producing cheeses of the Dunlop type, until in 1981 new premises for the Creamery were built farther north. In the 1990s other warehouses were imaginatively converted for use as a youth hostel and field centre, lecture hall and exhibition area for the Islay Natural History Trust.

Finally Barnard arrived on the Sound of Islay, where he was suitably impressed by the setting of Caol Ila ('cull-eela'), 'standing in the wildest and most picturesque locality we have seen'. He described the site and locality romantically, and the factory technically, noting that 'comfortable dwellings have been provided for the employees, forming quite a village'. The water 'said to be the finest in Islay, comes in the form of a crystal stream from a lovely lake called Torrabus'. The annual production of just under 150,000 gallons could not satisfy the demand for this 'favourite Whisky' and the output was rationed among buyers. The distillery and the earliest of the houses for its workers are crammed together at the foot of a very steep cliff that cuts the village off from much direct sunlight, especially in winter. Houses were built higher up the slope by the company and by local government. In the 1970s demand forced the reconstruction of much of the distillery itself and it can now produce as much as the entire island's output a century ago. Caol Ila's external appearance changed strikingly: the tall chimney stack and pagoda-like malt kiln chimneys disappeared.

In Barnard's day, and until the 1960s, Bunnahabhain ('bonnahaven') was only accessible from the sea or via a rough hill road: 'This portion of the island was bare, and uninhabited, but the prosecution of the distilling industry has transformed it into a life-like and civilised colony . . . The Distillery proper is a fine pile of buildings in the form of a square, and quite enclosed . . . entering by a noble gateway'. Despite extensive remodelling outside and inside, the present-day visitor can confirm that Bunnahabhain does indeed have the appearance of an impressive walled fortress. It was built in 1881 and the distillery owners also constructed the road link to the Bridgend to Port Askaig road, ('as good as it was costly') as well as a 'commodious pier' (for £3,500), at which chartered steamers and the *Islay* called. Villas were erected for the Excise Officers, houses for the workers' families, a reading room and a school room. 50 to 70 workers were then employed in the distilling season, in contrast to a few operators today; there is now a greatly increased output and virtually year-round operation, with much automation, and some of the housing is let for self-catering accommodation.

Most of Islay's distilleries were remodelled in the 1970s, on a scale inconceivable before the transport revolution of 1968. Some changed their external appearance almost beyond recognition, as for instance, at Caol Ila, on the Sound of Islay.

Islay Malts

Malt whisky production nowadays forms only a small part of the total business of 'Scotch', a business that involves distilling, maturing, bonding, blending, bottling, cooperage, promotion, sales and other activities. Yet within the trade the Islay Malts have a separate and distinguished place in

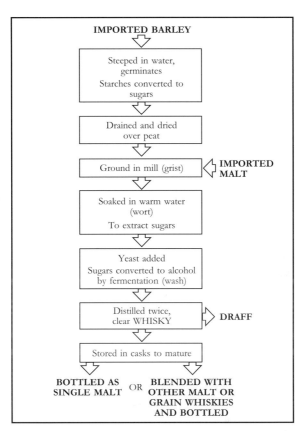

IMPORTED BARLEY

Steeped in water,
germinates

Starches converted to
sugars

Drained and dried
over peat

Ground in mill (grist) ◁ **IMPORTED MALT**

Soaked in warm water
(wort)

To extract sugars

Yeast added
Sugars converted to alcohol
by fermentation (wash)

Distilled twice,
clear WHISKY ▷ **DRAFF**

Stored in casks to mature

BOTTLED AS SINGLE MALT OR **BLENDED WITH OTHER MALT OR GRAIN WHISKIES AND BOTTLED**

The local 'bere' barley has been replaced by barley from north-east Scotland, eastern England and elsewhere; and the distilleries may be considerably automated, but the basic process of producing malt whiskies remains the same. The golden colour is achieved during maturation in former sherry casks, or by adding caramel.

the classification of Scotch whiskies. This is due to the higher degree of peatiness or 'heaviness' in their bouquet or flavour; this in turn is due to deliberately less-efficient distillation.

The visitor to Islay can normally see round a working distillery. Malt whisky production begins with the making of malt, nowadays using barley imported from elsewhere in Britain or abroad. Barley is soaked in water for two or three days until it is moist enough to allow germination to begin. After the water has been drained off, the grain is spread out on the floor of the malting shed to allow germination. It is turned over from time to time during the next week and is then transferred, as 'malt' to perforated racks above peat-fired kilns where it is dried and permeated with smoke from peat fires. This dry malt contains enzymes and starch necessary for the next process, mashing.

After the malt has been ground into a rough meal or 'grist', it is again mixed with water to form a 'mash' which is in turn heated. The enzymes help to convert the starch into various sugars such as maltose, sucrose, dextrins and other substances. The resulting sweet solution or 'wort' is subsequently run off and the process is repeated several times until the wort solution is too weak to use. The spent grain or 'draff' is then used as an important source of cattle fodder, wet or dried in pellets. Meanwhile the worts are cooled slightly and led to very large tuns or 'washbacks'. Here yeast is added and its enzymes ferment the worts to form alcohols and certain other by-products. Many of these impurities are removed in distillation, but a few traces remain to give the Islay whiskies their distinctive flavours and bouquets.

The resulting liquid, known as 'wash', is heated in a wash still, a copper vessel with a distinctive shape. It is here that the distillation process begins. Crude ethyl alcohol and its various volatile associates are separated from the remaining matter and are cooled in a pipe or 'worm', to condense into a liquid form known as 'feints' or 'low wines'. The residue is later redistilled to produce more low wines and the low wines themselves are then redistilled in smaller spirit stills. This separates the potentially potable crude whisky from the other products. A colourless liquid at this stage, it flows through a locked spirit safe into a spirit receiver. The glass-walled, but otherwise very secure, spirit safe is the official measure of production: it was introduced to Islay by John Ramsay of Kildalton and was used at Port Ellen distillery for several years before its general adoption by the Customs and Excise.[13] In the spirit receiver the whisky is mixed with water to reduce its strength before being pumped to the filling store. The raw whisky is then poured into casks or barrels that have often previously been used for sherry. The whisky must then remain in duty-free bonded warehouses for at least three years to mature. During this period the liquid volume decreases and the sherry casks help to give the characteristic light golden brown colour to the spirit.

Most of the whisky distilleries in Islay have been renovated or redeveloped. Most produce more whisky than ever before, but with a small direct labour force. The increased production has led to the construction of large new bonded warehouses near each distillery. Water supply, both as regards quantity and quality, is becoming a critical factor for some, as the distilling season is being stretched nearer a twelve month operation. Most of the whisky produced on Islay leaves the island for blending into world-renowned brand names. Few of the several thousand blended whiskies on the world market have no Islay malt in them. For a long time only Laphroaig was available as a bottled single 'malt'. Changing tastes, however, have encouraged most of the distilleries to market an increasing, though still small, proportion of their output in the same way. Islay Mist, probably better known than any of these, is not in fact a single Islay malt. It is an unusual de-luxe blend of three malt whiskies from three distilleries – Laphroaig on Islay and Glenlivet and Glen Grant on Speyside. It was specially inaugurated for the 1st Lord Margadale's coming-of-age in 1928. As with the marketing of many other products, special and expensive editions of single malts, new blends of malts such as the Islander and new brands of blends have multiplied and are able to be purchased in many mainland off-licences and supermarkets, along with imaginative descriptions of their different 'bouquets' and other attributes.

The whisky landscape

Islay, the Hebridean exception, is in no respect more distinctive than in the scale of its whisky industry. Distilleries are found in many parts of the Highlands and Islands, including the Northern Isles. There are also both malt and grain distilleries in the Lowlands. Only in the 'golden triangle' of malt whisky distilleries on Speyside is there a concentration that can match Islay's in quality of product: or, perhaps, in an annual contribution to the exchequer in excise duty equivalent to tens of thousands of pounds for every member of Islay's population.

The contribution to employment opportunities that distilling has provided directly and indirectly is still a significant element in Islay's comparative prosperity at the present time. The distilleries and their associated villages have been an equally important element in the visual landscape. They remain so today, despite changes that are not all as aesthetically pleasing as they are economically desirable. The tall and distinctive boiler-house chimney stack from the coal-firing days now only remains in a few instances; in the 1960s and 1970s many were replaced by smaller flues during conversion to oil-burning furnaces. The pagoda-like structures of the malt-drying kilns have been particularly distinctive, but some of these were threatened when malting gravitated towards the mainland in the 1960s. In 1987 the Islay Concordat was agreed whereby distilleries on Islay and Jura are supplied with malt from the Maltings at Port Ellen. The rows of distillery workers' houses are still characteristic elements of the landscape, especially in the more isolated distillery villages.

Other activities related to distilling are to be seen around the island, such as the peat cutting on the muirs, now mechanised. Containers now conceal the empty sherry casks arriving on Islay and the casks of mature, unblended whisky leave the same way, less noticeably than when they were stacked on the distillery piers, awaiting shipment by coaster or puffer.

Juggernauts negotiate the winding road to Bunnahabhain. Perhaps the most memorable contribution is not a sight but a smell: the 'peat reek' surrounding the distilleries, blending with the smell from domestic peat fires. Only in a few other areas of Scotland or Ireland can that particular blend be found.

Notes and references

1   R. O. Jarvis, communication, 1959. Youngson, *After the Forty Five*.

2   Devine, *Clanship*, p. 119.

3   Devine, *Clanship*, p. 123.

5   Sinclair, *OSA*, p. 296.

5   M. C. Storrie, 'The Scotch Whisky Industry', *TIBG*, 1962, 31, pp. 97–114; *Fifth Report of the Commissioners . . . of Excise Duties, BPP*, VII, (1823).

6   *Appendix to Seventh Report of the Commissioners of Inquiry into the Excise, BPP*, 1835, XXX, Appendix C.

7   Official Correspondence of Customs and Excise, Port Ellen District, Argyll South Collection, SRO.

8   Shore, *Sketches*, pp. 203–5.

9   *Minutes of Evidence, Poor Law Inquiry Commission for Scotland, BBP*, 1844, XXI, p. 155.

10 A. Barnard, *The Whisky Distilleries of the United Kingdom*, (London, 1887); Islay is described on pp. 87–113.

11 Ibid., p. 95.

12 Crown Film Unit, *Coastal Command*, video DD985.

13 Ramsay, *John Ramsay*, p. 18.

CHAPTER 13

The perennial grouse

Whether central in a seafaring lordship or later more peripheral, Islay has been characterised by the gradual integration of its economy and society with the wider world beyond its shores. Not all of this involved direct contact with that world: ideas and technology travelled as effectively as people. But the establishment, maintenance and improvement of links between Islay and the outside world were both a necessity for the success of the social and economic changes, especially from the eighteenth century, and also one of the most tangible measures of that success.

The drovers' route through Jura

Before the agricultural and other improvements of the eighteenth century, Islay, like other Hebridean islands, had of necessity to be largely self-reliant. Relatively few Islay residents ever left the island; what they could not obtain or make from their own resources had normally to be gone without. There were of course minor exceptions, such as tea and other luxuries. Contemporary letters recorded the difficulties of obtaining these, as seen in Chapter 5, but those who were most burdened by such afflictions were the few at the top of the social scale. The fact that they were able to commit their complaints to paper obscures the fact that literacy was almost as rare as tea.

Black cattle were sent each year from Islay to the market at Falkirk in the Lowlands, most of them ultimately finding their way to England. One route to the mainland before the late-eighteenth century was through Jura. It is nowadays normally referred to as the 'overland route', although the alignment did vary slightly from one period to another. It included two sea crossings: across the Sound of Islay and then across the Sound of Jura from Lagg to Keills in Mid Argyll. This route remained in use until early this century and one of the last drovers was Dugald MacDougall who died at Minard, Loch Fyne, in 1957.[1] The spring and summer found him out in the islands buying young cattle as 'the Islay Trysts in May and June offered the finest cattle in the West'. The Islay cattle were driven on foot from all parts of the island to Port Askaig, ferried across to Feolin in

Many views in Islay are enhanced by the backdrop of the mountainous Paps of Jura, as depicted here by Schetky. The road formed part of the 'overland route' for cattle, folk and mails.

Jura and again driven to the ferry at Lagg. There they were loaded into the ferry-boat and carried to Keills and unloaded on to the jetty. The herd made its way by Tayvallich and Bellanoch to Crinan Moss and Kilmichael and up the glen to Barmolloch. There they grazed until they were ready to be sold at the Falkirk Tryst on the second Tuesday of October.

The ferry controversy of the 1960s is evidence that many Islay residents were still inclined to look back on the period of the overland route as a golden age which might return, but there were problems associated with it that led to frequent difficulties and recriminations, especially in the early-nineteenth century. Complaints about the quality of the jetties and of the roads through Jura and on the mainland from Keills were numerous. Even the right-of-way was in question. The road to Lagg in Jura was still incomplete in 1805 and the chief proprietor, Archibald Campbell of Jura, challenged the right of Campbell of Islay to use the new road for the passage of his cattle to the ferry at Lagg, alleging that the droves were only entitled to use the old hill-track.[2] Direct, if rather unreliable and irregular, links between south-eastern Islay and the mainland had also been established and in time the overland route fell into disuse. This reflected a basic shift in technological advantage towards sea transport and away from land routes.

Sailing packets and steamers

As early as 1764 the problems and costs of maintaining a mail-carrying ferry to the mainland were preoccupying the attention of Islay's gentlemen and tacksmen and were duly recorded at their twice-yearly Stent meetings. Up to that time the financial risk involved in providing this service appears to have been borne by several of the landowners including Campbell of Shawfield, Campbell of Jura, McNeill of Colonsay, Charles Freebairn and the packet owner.[3] In 1767 the Stent provided £40 2s. 6d. towards the expense from one Hallowday (November 1) to the next. This sum was to cover both the expenses of the packet and of the Postmaster and Runners, with the provisos 'that no postage be payd for Leters from Tarbert to Ilay or from Ilay to Tarbert, And That the Baggs containing the Leters Are not to be opened at Portaskog, Or any where else in Ilay, But at Killarow'.

The man responsible for running the service, also acting as postmaster, was the merchant, David Simson. The packet was to make a return sailing every week, wind and weather permitting. Some complaints about the service were noted in 1769 and the improvements demanded then were still apparently lacking in 1771: 'the Pacquet Master & Owners must get . . . four Beds lade in the Cabine and four new Mattresses in them and . . . there [must] be locks on two of them and none but Cabine passengers admitted to them . . . there [must] be three sufficient Sailors & a Boy always in the Pacquet'. Part of the Stent subsidy for the service was withheld until the improvements were made. Even this was not effective and by October 1775 Simson was faced with an ultimatum from the committee appointed to run the packet and post:

> The present Pacquet belonging to David Simson, Mercht in Isla, & Colin Campbell, present Pacquet Master, shall be continued for the space of two months from this date, within which time the said Pacquet is to be repaired and made fitt in Masts, Sails, Rigging, & Ground Tackle, also the Cabin to be properly repaired. That while the Pacquet is repairing the Contractors shall Find a proper Boat to the satisfaction of the said Committee to ply during the absence of the other.

In the end Colin Campbell of Carnbeg was given a seven-year contract and his vessel apparently gave more satisfaction. But he did not renew his contract when it expired and the packet master, John Hill, of Port Askaig, took over responsibility. By 1794 the main complaint at the Stent meeting was that, since the packet master was residing at Tarbert and not in Islay, 'he is thereby Induced to remain at Tarbert when he coud make a good passage to Islay. It is hereby recommended . . . that his residence shall be henceforth in Islay'. The supervisory committee met every quarter, more frequently than the Stent body itself met. Over the years fares gradually crept up: the annual subsidy also increased, especially after government subsidy was withdrawn in 1812. The most persistent complaint concerned the apparent inability of the packet master to prevent steerage passengers from invading the cabin. The temptation was probably considerable: not merely was the sailing ship dependent on favourable winds but the vessels used were very small. Colin Campbell of Carnbeg had contracted to provide a vessel of at least 30 tons, but this was reduced to twenty tons for his successor.

However, a major revolution was on its way. The Stent meeting in May 1822 looked forward to the replacement of the sailing ship by a steam-driven packet. Such an innovation would bring more than merely technical advantages, for the Packet 'shall at all times be provided with food for the passengers, to Consist of Porter – Ale – Cheese – Biscuits – Teas and Sugar – and at times Cold Salt Beef'. Such luxury had to be anticipated for a while longer: the first steam-driven ferry did not arrive on the Islay service until 1825.[4] A nine-year-old wooden paddle steamer, inevitably named the *Waterloo*, she became the *Maid of Islay*. Sailing from West Loch Tarbert, she provided a connection with Clyde steamer services to the East Loch, establishing a pattern that was to endure for almost a century and a half.

Two years later a second vessel was acquired and named *Maid of Islay No. 2*. In summer *No. 2* took over what had been *No. 1*'s schedule: a Tuesday outward run to Port Askaig, and a similar run on Thursday extended to Oban, Tobermory on Mull and Portree on Skye, returning to West Loch Tarbert on Monday. Meanwhile *No. 1* provided the Clyde link from Glasgow to Greenock, Rothesay and East Loch Tarbert. In winter *No. 1* was laid up, but *No. 2* appears to have made one trip a week from Greenock to Islay, West Loch Tarbert, Oban, Tobermory, Isle Ornsay, Portree and certain other intermediate points. *No. 1* was sold in 1831, but *No. 2* continued to serve Islay as before until 1845. Her successor, between 1846 and 1849, was the *Modern Athens* and a slightly altered service was adopted. She sailed from Glasgow on Mondays for Port Ellen and then made two trips to West Loch Tarbert and back, connecting with the Clyde steamers to the East Loch, before starting her return journey to Glasgow on Fridays. The Kilchoman minister noted the 'great' improvement with satisfaction, despite the change of terminal to Port Ellen: 'a powerful steam packet plies regularly between the island and Tarbert . . . the mail is received and despatched four times weekly, twice by packet, and twice through Jura by the ferries'.[5] The overland route still seems to have been

In 1825 the paddle steamer, the *Maid of Islay*, replaced the sailing packet and William Heath's drawing suggests congestion at Port Askaig similar to the present time.

in operation. However, two routes to the mainland were steadily replacing it in importance: from Port Askaig or Port Ellen to West Loch Tarbert, with nearby connections to Loch Fyne services; or a less frequent and more circuitous route round the Mull of Kintyre to Glasgow. These two routes continued to dominate the Islay traffic scene for well over a century until the late 1960s.

Mull of Kintyre and West Loch routes

The earliest iron paddle-steamer on the Glasgow to Islay route appeared in October 1849. This was the first completely new vessel to serve the island since the sailing ships of the previous century; she was appropriately named *Islay*, later *Islay I*, and was 'powerful and fast-sailing' Her route extended beyond Islay to Oban and Skye, with occasional calls in Ireland. She ran ashore at Port Ellen in 1857, but a greater mishap occurred when she was wrecked completely in 1866. Charles Morrison, John Ramsay and T. G. Buchanan replaced her with the *Islay II*. Later taken over by David Hutcheson and Company, the precursor of David Macbrayne's company, she was stranded on Rathlin Island in 1875, and subsequently wrecked, in Red Bay, Cushendall, Antrim, in 1890.[6] The third vessel to bear the name, *Islay III*, took over the Glasgow to Islay service in 1890. She was not a new ship: as the *Princess Louise* she had already spent eighteen years shuttling between Stranraer and Larne. Serving Port Askaig, Bruichladdich and

On the Mull of Kintyre run, three successive steamers called *Islay* foundered. After surviving sundry mishaps, the *Islay III* was wrecked in 1902 on Sheep Island, not far from Port Ellen (Duckworth and Langmuir, *West Highland Steamers*).

The PS *Glencoe* was built in 1841 as the *Mary Jane*, and was introduced on the West Loch to Islay crossing in 1857. For almost half a century, while a succession of vessels on the Mull of Kintyre route was coming to grief, this iron paddle steamer served the Islay folk. She then went on to other routes until she was sold in 1931, aged 90! (Duckworth and Langmuir, *West Highland Steamers*).

Jura twice-weekly from Lancefield Quay in Glasgow, *Islay III* survived sundry mishaps. As *The Oban Times* reported in 1900:

> Quite a thrill of delight passed through the village hearts on Saturday morning when, after six weeks of absence, the *Islay* sailed into harbour under her own steam with salutes of cannon from MacArthur's Rock . . . Battered and rusty she looked certainly; but now she is safely in dock we hope to see her . . . back at an early date.[7]

But *Islay III* was also wrecked, this time on Sheep Island outside Port Ellen, in 1902.

The next ship designated to maintain the service (there were of course several short-term and seasonal replacements) was even older. Over the previous 27 years she had borne the names *La Belgique*, *Flamingo*, and *Paris*. In this last incarnation she had spent thirteen years on the Newhaven-Dieppe service but, 'though an excellent boat . . . her main fault seems to have been with respect to speed'. Perhaps to avoid the fate of her predecessors, she became not *Islay IV* but *Glendale*. The device was unsuccessful; within three years, in July 1905, she was wrecked on Deas Point, Kintyre, due to 'an error in navigation'. For the next fifteen years various ships, including the *Clydesdale II*, a single-screw vessel, maintained the service. Thereafter a succession of workhorses for David Macbrayne's company, including the *Lochdunvegan I*, *Lochbroom I*, *Lochbroom II* and finally the *Loch Ard* took over the Mull of Kintyre route. The vessels all had provision for a few passengers, but were essentially for freight. Introduction of ro-ro services from the West Loch in the late 1960s removed even the freight advantage and the last regular sailing from the Broomielaw in Galsgow to Islay round the Mull of Kintyre was in March 1970.

The route from Islay to Glasgow and the Lowlands via West Loch Tarbert was the inverse of the overland route. The latter had used the ability of the principal users, cattle, to provide their own motive power and sea crossings were reduced to a minimum. The steadily increasing flow of human beings was less manageable and they, together with mail and other urgent freight, switched to the route that maximised the advantage that steamships in the nineteenth century had over land transport beyond the railway net. For this reason the pier in the West Loch was placed so close to the head of the loch that Islay ferries were traditionally shallow in draft and were traditionally wapped on their bow rope to turn in the confined space. From there to the pier at the East Loch was only a few kilometres and then the travellers used the Clyde steamers to Glasgow or to the railhead at the Tail of the Bank.

For almost 50 years, while successive vessels on the Mull of Kintyre

The custom-built PS *Pioneer II* arrived in Islay in 1905, 'materially different from any of her predecessors, and [she] struck a distinctly modern note'. She remained on this run until 1939 when superseded by the then modern TS *Lochiel*. The *Pioneer II* ended her days as a floating laboratory, the *Harbinger*, in Portland harbour, but her name was resuscitated in 1975 for a new Caledonian MacBrayne ferry on the Islay service (Museum of Islay Life).

route came to grief, one iron paddle-steamer was the mainstay of the West Loch Tarbert service. Introduced as the *Glencoe* in 1857, she had in fact been sailing elsewhere since 1841, smaller in size and under the name of *Mary Jane*. She remained on the Islay run from 1857 until 1905, then went on to other tasks in the same fleet before being sold in 1931 at the age of 90! The *Glencoe*'s replacement in 1905 was the *Pioneer II*, newly-built for the Islay mail service. She was 'materially different from any of her predecessors and struck a distinctly modern note'. For the next 65 years, the West Loch service remained little changed, except for the replacement of the *Pioneer II* in 1939: outwards from Islay six mornings a week to connect at West Loch Tarbert with the morning sailing from the Clyde to the East Loch, this latter service also maintained almost unbroken by the MV *Loch Fyne*, then back to Islay in three hours during the afternoon. A Sunday sailing was unthinkable.

In 1939 the *Pioneer II* was succeeded by the rather squat but new twin-screw vessel, the *Lochiel* (really the *Lochiel IV*) and the service continued more or less unchanged until the end of the 1960s. During the Second World War *Pioneer II* made a brief reappearance while the *Lochiel* was transferred to the Clyde, but the *Pioneer II* was then transferred to Portland harbour where, as the *Harbinger*, she ended her days as a floating laboratory.

The 1960s were not a happy time for the *Lochiel*. The decade began disastrously when the ship struck a submerged rock at the entrance to the West Loch and sank, fortunately in shallow water and without injury or loss of life. This incident can again tactfully be described as 'an error in navigation'. The *Lochiel* was raised, somewhat remodelled and returned to the service.

Three ships, the *Glencoe*, *Pioneer II* and *Lochiel*, had served Islay from West Loch Tarbert for over a century. It was misfortune for the *Lochiel* to end her Islay service at a time of strong public debate about the reorganisation of ferry services, when the *Lochiel*'s inadequacies were very obvious. Nevertheless she and her predecessors had served the island well. Many Islay residents and visitors remember her with nostalgia, perhaps best expressed by a visitor from Bletchley. Finding her gone from her normal station, he wrote to the *Scottish Field* in July 1971 to inquire 'Where has the dear, dour, old ruin gone?'[8] The answer for the present author and family, one balmy May evening in 1980, was a nostalgic aperitif on deck before an enjoyable meal in the dining saloon of the *Lochiel*, riding high without engines and in new livery, in Bristol Harbour. She was finally broken up in 1996.

Debate, competition and reorganisation
The main problem facing the West Loch Tarbert route in the 1960s was that it was served by a conventional ship, whereas the growing number of vehicles to and from the island required something else. Cars and small vans were winched aboard and stowed in the *Lochiel*'s hold, but this was unable to cope with the demand. As an interim measure a second vessel was added to the service in summer, but this was clearly only a stop-gap solution. The initiative clearly lay with Macbrayne. The firm was nominally a company in the private sector, but in fact it depended on government assistance (especially where new capital investment was concerned) and it included Scottish Office nominees on its board of directors. Elsewhere in the Hebrides similar problems were evident and in the early 1960s Macbrayne took delivery of three large car ferries, the *Clansman*, *Hebrides* and *Columba*, serving Mull, Skye and the Outer Isles. Had a fourth vessel been ordered at the same time for the Islay service the *Lochiel*'s replacement might never have become a real issue.

By the time Macbrayne did announce an order for such a car ferry, to carry 400 passengers and 46 cars, costing £750,000, there were many on Islay and beyond who argued that this was not the best solution. One reason why these early car ferries were so large was that they were intended to encourage tourism in the Hebrides by providing sleeping accommodation

The squat TS *Lochiel* did good service for Islay until the 1960s. The decade began disastrously when she sank at the entrance to West Loch Tarbert. Despite subsequent remodelling, her winching gear for a handful of cars was not suitable for the era of the car ferry. Many, including a nostalgic English visitor, missed the 'dear, dour old ruin'.

In the late 1960s Islay became the first of the Hebrides to have competing state and private ferry companies, and the fare structure was more favourable to Ilich than to other Hebrideans. A ro-ro ferry, MV *Sound of Islay*, was introduced in April 1968 and could carry container vehicles as well as cars. The days were also numbered for the few remaining coasters or 'puffers', one of which is seen here at Port Askaig (Eric Thorburn).

in areas where hotels were few. Since hotels were reasonably plentiful on Islay at the time, why such an elaborate vessel and high fares? Why not, in fact, return to the old pattern of very short sea crossings via the overland route through Jura? An Islay Transport Users' Committee was created with the support of the Islay District Council; a Norwegian transport expert made a favourable report on the overland scheme to the Highland Transport Board in 1966.[9] The Board in turn recommended that the *Lochiel*'s service to the West Loch be abandoned in favour of the overland route. For several years the controversy raged through open meetings, closed committees, the columns of *The Oban Times* and, no doubt, also through the corridors of St Andrew's House in Edinburgh. Macbrayne, it seems clear, had not done much investigation of alternative solutions to the *Lochiel* replacement problem. A large car ferry like the others seemed the obvious answer. In fairness to Macbrayne, its social responsibility, reflected in its government subsidy, was to provide services to Gigha and Colonsay as well as to Islay and Jura; this was conveniently minimised by proponents of the overland route.

While the debate went on, experiments in new links took place. In 1966 a small company, Eilean Sea Services, began to operate a 35 ton landing craft between Port Ellen and the mainland. Its first main contract was to bring in construction materials and equipment for the rebuilding of the Port Ellen distillery. The service by the *Isle of Gigha* appeared to be thriving when the vessel suddenly capsized four miles off the Islay coast, with the loss of two lives and the lorries she was carrying. This incident seemed to many to indicate that small simple ferries, on the overland or any other route, were not the answer and once again the controversy appeared to be on the brink of resolution in favour of Macbrayne's new vessel. In 1968, however, with a minimum of advance publicity, Western Ferries, a company that had grown out of Eilean Sea Services, began operations with a much firmer financial basis and with a new, purpose-built ferry named the *Sound of Islay*. The *Sound of Islay* created a transport revolution on Islay almost overnight. The vessel was faster than any used previously, so that two and even three round trips a day were possible between Port Askaig and the new simple terminal lower down West Loch Tarbert at Kennacraig. Loading and unloading was only a matter of drive-on, drive-off, and the fares charged were well below those of Macbrayne: in some cases little more than half the vehicle rate on the *Lochiel*. There was even a service on Sundays: the islanders enthusiastically welcomed the arrival of Sunday newspapers on the day they were published.

The most profound change, however, was brought about by the ability of the *Sound of Islay* to take vehicles and trailers of almost any size. Instead of having to import barley and export whisky by coasters or puffers (including the familiar *Pibroch* and *Moonlight*), the distilling industry reorganised on a basis of road-hauled containers and much of Islay's retail trade and agricultural supply industry did the same. The first lorry drivers from the mainland had to contend with the precipitous climb out of Port Askaig (the bends were smoothed out in 1971) and with a low but solid footbridge linking two parts of Islay Estate at Bridgend.

So successful was the *Sound of Islay* that she was replaced in 1970 by a much larger vessel built on the same principle, but with more deck space and a few more comforts, the thirteen-knot *Sound of Jura*. The *Sound of Islay* went off to a run between Campbeltown and Cushendall, while the *Isle of Gigha* reappeared as the *Sound of Gigha*, in Western Ferries' colours and with improved seaworthiness, plying across the Sound of Islay between Islay and Jura, on the short crossing between Port Askaig and Feolin. Macbrayne replaced the *Lochiel* with the Clyde car ferry *Arran*. Also so successful was the competition from Western Ferries, that for a time it seemed probable that Macbrayne would withdraw completely from the route. The planned large new ferry was built and named the *Iona*, but she did not arrive on Islay. Argyll County Council saved the cost of the new terminals on Islay and in the West Loch, as well as the cost of rebuilding the road on Jura for an overland route, which went into limbo.

Nevertheless it was evident in the early 1970s that a stable pattern of service was yet to be achieved. Macbrayne announced its intention of withdrawing completely, but then changed its mind when absorbed into the Scottish Transport Group. The latter made a takeover bid for Western Ferries whose directors at first recommended acceptance. A capital reconstruction of Western Ferries averted bathos, but by the mid-1970s the future was still uncertain. Macbrayne-STG had converted the *Arran* to a drive-on, drive-off ferry, but only at the cost of making it difficult for the vessel to use the piers at Gigha and at Craighouse in Jura. In due course the *Arran* was succeeded by a new sixteen-knot vessel, the *Pioneer*, that served Port Ellen and eventually Gigha, but avoided Port Askaig. Western Ferries continued to use Port Askaig, with the link to Feolin on Jura, Colonsay henceforth looking northward to Oban. Western Ferries argued that, if the government subsidy were transferred from Caledonian MacBrayne, as it was now called, to Western Ferries, the firm could carry vehicles and passengers free to Islay ever after. This desirable development did not take place and the competition in speed and fares (together with rapidly-rising fuel costs after 1973) meant that the *Sound of Jura* had to be sold in 1976. The *Sound of Islay* took over until October 1981, when general and whisky recession forced suspension of service. Growing traffic was taken up by the *Pioneer*; Kennacraig was bought by Caledonian MacBrayne to save time and fuel consumption in the West Loch and the terminal was extended.

Eventually, in February 1979, the larger *Iona* at last arrived on the Islay run, after pier modifications at both Port Ellen and Port Askaig. She provided a thrice-daily return service from the mainland to Islay on summer weekdays, a twice-daily service on summer Sundays and winter weekdays and made a single round trip on winter Sundays. It would be difficult to deny that, for Islay, the present situation in regard to the ferry service has been a vast improvement on that of the mid-1960s, when a pattern that had survived almost without change for a century finally broke down. Pier alterations in the 1980s and 1990s for MV *Claymore* and MV *Isle of Arran* brought ro-ro facilities and the reinstatement of a once-weekly link in summer to Colonsay. At last journeys were usually more reliable and more comfortable and, apart from the costs, 'the perennial grouse' much less justified.

In peril on the sea

Sea travel to Islay was not always easy and safe. Most of the basic navigation aids and safety regulations were only developed from the nineteenth century. Around the coasts of Scotland in the 1820s there were only a dozen lighthouses; the first on Islay was started in 1824, on Orsay island off the southern tip of the Rinns. This was a belated response to a long-felt need: as early as 1785 a plea had been made for more lighthouses in the Kintyre and Islay sea area, since many shipwrecks had occurred on the west side of Kintyre, when seamen mistook the Mull of Oa for the Mull of Kintyre.[10] Ships were small, often overloaded, and bad weather and whisky also contributed to the frequency of shipwrecks around the coast of Islay. As ship design improved, as marine regulations were developed and as better navigational aids were provided, the number of such incidents decreased rapidly. By 1844 as many as 4,350 vessels a year were reported to be passing the Rinns lighthouse, although a few strandings and shipwrecks on Islay were still reported each year.[11] The map in Appendix B indicates the known locations of Islay mishaps, while those with unknown location are listed.

Islay has an honourable record of help to those stranded along its coastline. In 1785 James Anderson expressed his opinion that 'in no part of the world, would a man who had the misfortune to suffer shipwreck, have a better chance to meet with every possible assistance, than there, or

In 1842 John Francis Campbell of Islay sketched the rescue activities at Geodh Ghille Mhòire, west of Sanaig, of bodies and wreckage from the Irish emigrant ship, *Exmouth*. He recorded that 'the ship struck on the rocks to the right and no fragment more than six feet long could be recovered . . . the most of the ship was smashed into fragments a few inches square on the 23d of May. 113 bodies had been recovered and buried by Campbell of Ballinaby and Henry Rockside . . . only 3 out of 230 were saved' (Trustees of the National Gallery of Scotland).

The *Harald*, wrecked off the Oa in 1882, was only one of over 250 mishaps known around Islay's shores (Museum of Islay Life).

at a smaller expence'.[12] He described how a vessel loaded with linen yarn from Ireland had run aground on Islay a few years earlier. Despite the obvious value of the yarn to Islay's own domestic industry, over the next few weeks hundreds of islanders washed the salt out and dried the yarn so that only a few hanks were missing, 'to the utter astonishment of all the parties concerned'. Still remembered by some on Islay and America is the help extended when HMS *Otranto* was sunk off Islay a month before the end of the First World War.

Nowadays, protection to shipping around the coasts of Islay is provided in three main ways: the lighthouses, the lifeboat and the Coastguard services. Under several Acts of Parliament in the late-eighteenth and early-nineteenth centuries, the Commissioners of Northern Lighthouses were empowered to construct lighthouses at dangerous places along the coast of Scotland. In a country with such a long and indented coastline, the question of priorities must have been one of the biggest problems facing the Commissioners. In January 1823 they reported that they had under consideration 'nine different applications from the shipping interest for a new light at the Rhinnes of Islay, on the small island of Oversaa'.[13] The stone to build it was probably from a quarry on the south side of Orsay. In 1835 Robert Stevenson endorsed the need for similar help to navigators through the Sound of Islay.[14] Then, as now, this was 'much frequented by shipping as a sheltered channel, by which they avoid coasting along the island of Islay, exposed to the swell of the Atlantic Ocean'. It was not until 1859 that Rhuvaal light first marked the northern entrance to the Sound; two years later McArthur's Head light shone at the southern end.[15] Port Charlotte's lighthouse provided guidance in Loch Indaal after 1869; much earlier, in 1832, Walter Frederick Campbell had built the Port Ellen lighthouse as a memorial to his first wife. The operation of this light was taken over by the Commissioners in 1924. The programme of automated lighthouses in the 1990s was to end the long tradition of resident keepers, even if latterly their families were shore-based.

The Royal National Lifeboat Institution established its Islay station at Port Askaig in 1934 and, apart from a brief transfer to Port Ellen in 1947–48, it has remained there ever since. Two main boats in service were the *Charlotte Elizabeth* and, as a replacement in 1957, the *Francis Wotherspoon of Paisley*. In 1979, with substantial help from the Schroder family trust, a new self-righting lifeboat, capable of seventeen knots, arrived on station. Amidst island ceremony she was named the *Helmut Schroder of Dunlossit*, in her father's memory, by Mrs George Mallinckrodt. The eponymous 1990s replacement was a 25-knot Severn-Class boat. Since the 1930s, there have been many hundred launchings from Islay; two

This memorial headstone to a member of the family of an assistant lightkeeper at the Rinns lighthouse in 1845 uses the emblem of the Northern Lighthouses Board (Royal Commission on the Ancient and Historical Monuments of Scotland).)

crewmen were lost in January 1953 and many RNLI awards have been presented to coxswains and crewmen.[16] A Coastguard service for Search and Rescue of ships in distress has been in operation in Islay since 1928 and night watch and bad weather constant watch were maintained by regular officers, supplemented by auxiliaries, until the early 1970s.[17] With improved telecommunications, watchkeeping was then discontinued and replaced by a mobile coastguard service still relying on volunteer help. In 1980 a VHF radio station for shipping went on air using the mast at Kilchiaran and providing coverage from south of the Mull of Kintyre to north of Tiree, recalling its wartime forebears. In the 1990s coordination and expansion of all the rescue services went on apace.

The other way to the island

When internal air services in Britain passed the experimental stage in the 1930s, Islay was one of the first places to benefit, with a comparatively elegant service. Several grass landing strips were used, including one at Duich, but Glenegedale was the preferred site. With the coming of war, military flying superseded civil services, flying boats of the RAF Coastal Command used Loch Indaal, off Bowmore, and Glenegedale acquired surfaced runways.[18] A Sunderland crashed at Blackrock, with loss of life, and there are still remains of a training plane which crashed near Castlehill, whose pilot was buried in Bowmore. After the Second World War the DC-3, or Pionair as British European Airways termed it, became the standard aircraft on a weekday service from Glasgow to Campbeltown and Islay. Occasional experiments were made with different route patterns, especially in summer, when an evening service was provided on some days. The DC-3 was replaced by the turbo-prop Herald in 1962 and smaller Herons used on the Tiree, Barra and ambulance services occasionally provided additional flights to Islay.

The 1960s were almost as confusing in the air over Islay as they were on the ferry services. The main difference was that the ferry question was essentially a matter of how best to meet the needs of Islay and the nearby islands; in the air the main problem was how to integrate the Islay service economically with other BEA operations. In the mid-1960s BEA's primary concern seemed to be the standardisation of its fleet. Expensive runway strengthening and terminal extensions were made at Glenegedale and other Highland airports so that the Herald could be replaced in 1966 by the Viscount. Less than ten years later the reorganised British Airways abandoned this policy in favour of a more frequent service to Islay and similar places with a special fleet of smaller Islanders and Skyvans which, to put it mildly, required less runway than the Viscount. The Skyvans were not popular and in 1976 British Airways handed the Hebridean services over to Loganair. The latter provided a more frequent service, this time using small Islanders, Trislanders and the occasional 30-seater SD330. Loganair subsequently flew under British Midland and British Airways livery. Sadly a pilot was killed and several islanders were injured when the service plane crashed near Kilbride outside Port Ellen in 1986.

It is possible to see in these frequent changes an echo of the ferry debate: did Islay (or other islands) need a large, comparatively infrequent but comfortable aircraft, or should the emphasis be on simplicity, frequency and cheapness? Besides the regular Loganair services, Glenegedale has other traffic in private charter flights of specialist holidaymakers, distillery company flights and others. The peak in passenger numbers was in 1966 when almost 20,000 used the airport, but ten years later the figure was just half, perhaps a reflection of the improved ferry services, but also of rapidly increasing air fares.[19]

The Scottish Air Ambulance Service carried its first passenger from the island in 1934, although air travel had been used in an emergency a year earlier. One of the pioneers of the service, Captain David Barclay, had a close association with Islay and a plaque in Glenegedale's terminal

A Rolls-Royce was provided, free of charge, by Northern and Scottish Airways Ltd. to convey passengers to the airport at Renfrew, 'North Britain'. The Moths and Spartan Cruisers landed on a grass strip at Glenegedale, or sometimes at Duich (Weir, *Guide to Islay*).

building marked his retirement in 1965. Nearby is the site of one of the service's few fatal accidents, when, in September 1957, an incoming aircraft crashed into the muir killing the crew and the volunteer nursing sister. In April 1973 responsibility for providing the ambulance service was transferred from British Airways to Loganair. Patients include maternity cases (some babies being born in the air), victims of industrial and road accidents and others requiring more treatment than the local hospital at Bowmore can provide.[20]

Internal communications

Until the twentieth century, many an islander probably knew less about a village on the other side of the island than about the world beyond, gleaned from exiles' letters. Despite this, the improvement of communications within Islay is a continuing theme from the seventeenth century onwards. The overwhelming emphasis has been on roads and their associated bridges. Like other Hebridean islands, Islay had its belated share of railway mania, though no serious proposals resulted. *The Guide to Islay* published in 1900 is typical:

> There is no island on the west coast better suited for the purpose of a light railway than Islay. Such a line, running from Portnahaven to Port Ellen, would speedily develop and largely benefit the fishing, the agricultural, and the other industries of the island . . . With suitable pier accommodation at Portnahaven and Bowmore, and with an accelerated service of steamers and trains between Islay and Glasgow, the material prosperity of the island could be vastly increased. Improved travelling facilities would attract many tourists to visit the Queen of the Hebrides.[21]

It was, after all, not very far from Islay to Kintyre, where the Campbeltown and Machrihanish railway had begun operating in 1877.[22] Embanking appears to have been begun, along the line of the A846 between Port Ellen and Bowmore.[23]

Another form of internal link that has been of little significance is the ferry. Loch Indaal may appear an obvious place for such a facility and in the past Skiba and then Port Charlotte were linked with Laggan or Gartbreck in this way, but the potential traffic was probably always small. Only between Port Wemyss and Orsay Island have connections been essential, throughout the period when lighthouse families lived there.

Grouped settlements were linked by foot and cart tracks and the vestiges of these can still be found, as along the tracks on the southern side of the Oa, tracks that once served several hundred people. These tracks were used both by people and by animals, with belongings carried in creels or panniers. Even narrower were the drove 'roads' across Islay and Jura to the mainland. Traces of these can also be found, for example between Proaig and Storakaig.

Towards the end of the seventeenth century, tracks or roads of a kind that would be recognisable today became more important. Partly this was due to a gradual increase in the number of wheeled vehicles on Islay; partly also Islay was required to respond in some manner to Scottish, then British legislation on road building. Acts of the Scottish Parliament in 1669 and 1670 attempted to initiate road building and maintenance programmes based on labour for a number of days each year by all the local male population, together with a rudimentary management system to organise the work and to enforce the obligations.[24] It seems that this

Scottish legislation was only partially effective in the country as a whole; in the Hebrides it had even less effect. By 1718 so little progress had been made with highways in Scotland that the new united Parliament at Westminster found it necessary to pass an act for 'Amending and making more effectual the Laws for repairing the Highways, Bridges and Ferries in that part of Great Britain called Scotland'. One of the main functions performed by the Stent meeting on Islay was roads supervision. Some records of the way it discharged this duty have been published for the periods 1714 to 1843, but others are still in manuscript form.[25] Entries in the Stent Book record the appointment of overseers to ensure that road work was done, the dates usually three days in summer and three after harvest when 'roads be wrought' and the amount of money that would be 'stented' or levied. On Islay, as elsewhere, the practice of personal work on the roads by the inhabitants tended to decline during the eighteenth and early-nineteenth centuries, being replaced by a money payment, in effect a local road tax.

By the end of the eighteenth century, the management of the Stent meeting and the enthusiasm of the Shawfield Campbells had brought good results. The Rev John McLeish of Kilchoman claimed that 'none of the Western Isles can boast of such good roads and bridges as Islay. The inhabitants are every year called out to work on them; and any gentleman may drive for 30 miles through the isle in his carriage. To complete the line, our communication with the main shore is kept up by a packet'.[26] The Killarow minister took much the same line, noting that 'the roads in Islay are carried on to great perfection. Those already finished are excellent, particularly from the Sound of Islay to Bowmore, a distance of about 12 miles, wherein there are seven bridges, built with stone and lime'.[27] But in Kildalton the picture was rather different. Local enthusiasm was less and the Kildalton minister admitted that the situation was better elsewhere.

The road from Port Askaig to Bowmore was the only link of its kind on Islay at the beginning of the nineteenth century: there was no road between Bowmore and Kildalton, nor along the shore of Loch Indaal from Bridgend to Portnahaven. The Commissioners, appointed in 1802 for making roads and building bridges in the Highlands and Islands of Scotland, reported in June 1805 that they had received an application from Islay for financial help towards the extension of the road from Port Askaig through to Portnahaven.[28] In fact Walter Campbell of Shawfield was already at work on the project. With a contribution from the Commissioners, the work was finished by autumn 1806. The Commissioners later described the road as 'made on a moderate scale, and in a manner very inferior to our other roads, but it is sufficient for its purpose and situation'.[29] Meanwhile, links from Bowmore to Kildalton were still inadequate. For a long time the Big Strand along Laggan Bay had provided the most obvious route for those who needed to make the journey. After about 1818 this was gradually replaced by a road a little distance from the shore. The official records, especially the manuscript minute books of the Islay District Road Trustees, contain details of other improvements and the building of farm access and other roads, most of them planned by the laird or his factor.[30]

When the next *Statistical Account* was published in the 1840s, the quantity and quality of the roads and bridges in the different parishes did not preoccupy the ministers in their reports. This is not to say that the islanders were content and tenants in Glenchatadale or 'The Glen' petitioned Walter Frederick Campbell to improve their road connections with the other populous parts of the island.[31] By this time a new set of circumstances had appeared. The bad harvests and potato disease made road-making a means of providing necessary employment rather than a response to economic and cultural growth. Based on a survey of 1841–2, commissioned by Walter Frederick Campbell, a new road line from Port Ellen to Bridgend was considered at a special meeting of the Road Trustees in 1845.[32] It was as a result of this that the long and straight road now known as the High Road came into existence. Work on it continued despite the Shawfield sequestration; in July 1852 it was reported:

> The Trustee on the Estate of Islay, and the Highland Relief Committee having entered into an arrangement last Autumn for employing the industrious poor – The sum of Three hundred pounds stg. was given them for that purpose . . . this sum has been expended in forwarding the construction of the new line of road from Bridgend to Port Ellen, and nearly three miles have been formed during the season.[33]

By the time Argyll County Council assumed responsibility for the main roads in the late-nineteenth century, the present network was largely in place. It remained generally adequate for the needs of the island until the arrival of the *Sound of Islay* brought in the era of large lorries and articulated vehicles. The alterations to the Port Askaig hill and the estate bridge at Bridgend were the first of a series of improvements that became necessary with the increased size and frequency of traffic.

The mails and telecommunications

One of the main justifications for the establishment of a regular sailing packet in the second half of the eighteenth century was the need for a reliable mail service between Islay and the mainland. Postal communications

Neil Macgibbon's precursor of today's coaches waits at Bowmore's old post office in Shore Street (Museum of Islay Life).

Western Ferries' overnight transport revolution meant that roads were inadequate and bridges too narrow and low. This bridge linking sylvan parts of Islay Estate over the A846 had to be raised to enable container vehicles to deliver to the distilleries, but was subsequently removed in the 1990s.

for the islands of Jura and Islay appear to have lagged some way behind their development in other islands.[34] At a meeting in July 1744 it was agreed that 'its necessar a post office be Erected in this Country'.[35] For the rest of the eighteenth century the *Stent Book* contains occasional references indicating that a fairly continuous mail service was maintained. The main problem was that experienced elsewhere: the difficulty of collecting the dues on each letter. Before the prepaid postage of the 1840s the recipient paid the cost and if the postmaster was unable to collect, he had already performed the work involved.

The 1798 Stent meeting described the mail service. The Bowmore postmaster was recommended to dispatch a runner (presumably on horseback) to Port Askaig on each Monday from Candlemas to Lammas at 4 o'clock in the afternoon, and from Lammas to Candlemas at 2 o'clock in the afternoon, the difference taking into account the shorter winter daylight. There was some unwillingness, especially in Kildalton, to take on postal duties, because of the difficulties of collecting the fees. The Stent records of 1810 describe one attempted solution:

> In order to enable the Letter receiver to draw his postages regulary [sic], it is recommended that a List of Letters not taken up be placed upon the Kirk Door of a Sunday, and after this intimation and after holding the letters over eight days, he is . . . to return the Letters in Course to Bowmore, to the Postmaster there.[36]

Presumably the publicity was intended to be both a reminder to other addressees and a mild blacklist for the information of others. Not long after this, postal services became wholly the responsibility of the Post Office. By 1826 there were postmasters at Port Askaig, Bowmore, Lagavulin, Kilchoman and Portnahaven.[37] In the 1830s Islay was getting three posts a week by the Keills – Jura – Port Askaig route, with an additional once-weekly steamer from Glasgow carrying mail and other packages not paying postage.[38] As new villages were built, additional post offices became necessary and changes in the British postal system after the 1840 Act had their effect on the postal services to and within the island.[39] By the middle of the century David Macbrayne Ltd received its first mail-carrying contract for Islay, whose address was to remain 'via Greenock, North Britain' well into the twentieth century. The Caledonian MacBrayne company is still a mail carrier, as is the airline. Within Islay there are post buses and mail vans as well as a passenger bus service.

The telegraph reached Islay in the later-nineteenth century. The island was first connected to the mainland by submarine telegraph in 1871; telegraph offices were subsequently established in the main villages.[40]

Thus appeared the first of the overhead wires that, a century or so later, became a focus of island outcry on amenity and environmental grounds. The first telephone link to the mainland was on 19 September 1935 and a number of local exchanges was established, each providing the customary friendly and informative Hebridean service.[41] They were replaced in October 1974 by a centralised facility in Port Ellen, linking the island into the national Subscriber Trunk Dialling system. This was subsequently upgraded to digital communication, essential for the burgeoning use of telecommunications.

Apart from the very small needs of telegraph and telephone services, electricity on Islay was generated privately. The North of Scotland Hydro-Electric Board took over the RAF diesel station outside Bowmore in 1949: this has been enlarged several times and still acts as a back-up facility although the island was linked to the mainland grid in 1962 by a modern version of the overland route through Jura.[42] By the last decade of the twentieth century, the ageing system was causing power surges and interruptions, through technical faults, adverse weather conditions for overhead cables or disruptions for upgrading. A small, experimental wave station near Claddich on the southern tip of the Rinns was developed with sponsorship by Queen's University, Belfast, with output linked into the National Grid in 1991. Wind power was mooted in the later 1990s.

A close rival in controversy and complaints to the ferry service in the 1960s and 1970s was the vexed question of radio and television service to the island, especially in regard to the BBC licence fee, paid for what seemed to be inferior reception. Not surprisingly, the island was often a 'fringe' area for both radio and television reception. For many years, and despite considerable ingenuity, much of the island had to make do with television from transmitters in Ulster, although neither the BBC nor the commercial channel acknowledged such eavesdropping in its programme content (e.g. local news). After 1980, transmitters were erected which provided television and VHF programmes on a more dependable basis to most of the population of Islay. The biggest transformation, however, came with satellite communications.

Notes and references
1   E. R. Cregeen, 'Recollections of an Argyleshire Drover', *SS*, 1959, 3, p. 143.
2   Ibid., p. 160.
3   For this and next references see Ramsay, *Stent Book*, pp. 68ff.
4   Much information on shipping was obtained from C. L. D. Duckworth and G. E. Langmuir, *West Highland Steamers*, (Prescot, 1967). Other sources include Sinclair, *OSA*, *NSA*, *Argyllshire*, Lumsden, *Steam-Boat Companion* and various timetables.

5   *NSA, Argyleshire*, pp. 656–8.

6   *CC*, 18 September 1875.

7   *OT*, 17 February 1900, p. 5.

8   *SF*, June 1971, p. 80.

9   A variety of sources has been used in this section on transport changes: reports of the Highland Transport Board and of the Highlands and Islands Development Board; occasional material produced by the Islay Transport Users' Consultative Committee; A. Wilson, *The Sound of Silence* (Glasgow, n.d. [1975]), and *The Sound of the Clam*, (Glasgow, n.d. [1975]), and news reports in *The Glasgow Herald*, *The Ileach*, *The Oban Times* and *The Scotsman*.

10 Anderson, *Account*, p. 9.

11 *Report of the Commissioners of Northern Lighthouses, BPP*, 1846, XLIV, p. 400.

12 Anderson, *Account*, p. ix.

13 *BPP, Northern Lighthouses*, 1833, XXXIII, p. 65.

14 *BPP, Northern Lighthouses*, 1836, XLV, p. 308.

15 Information from Commissioners of Northern Lighthouses, Edinburgh.

16 *Annual Reports of the Royal National Lifeboat Institution* provided much of this information.

17 Communication from HM Coastguard, Islay, 1980.

18 D. J. Smith, *Action Stations 7: Military Airfields of Scotland, the North-East and Northern Ireland*, (Wellingborough, 1989), pp. 56–7 and 172–3. See Crown Film Unit, *Coastal Command*, video, DD 985.

19 *Scottish Abstract of Statistics* (*SAS*), 1979, 8, p. 170.

20 I. Hutchison, *Air Ambulance*, (Erskine, 1996).

21 MacNeill, *New Guide*, p. 22.

22 N. S. C. Macmillan, *The Campbeltown and Machrihanish Light Railway*, (Glasgow, 1970).

23 Letter from L. Collin, *OT*, 24 August 1978.

24 D. G. Moir, 'The Roads of Scotland: The Statute Labour Roads', *SGM*, 1957, 73, pp. 101–10 and pp. 167–75.

25 Ramsay, *Stent Book*; IEP, Minute Books of the Islay District Road Trustees.

26 *NSA, Argyleshire*, p. 282.

27 Ibid., p. 302.

28 *BPP, Roads and Bridges*, 1805, III, p. 278.

29 *BPP, Roads and Bridges*, 1805, III, pp. 237–8; 1814–15, III, p. 432; 1817, IX, p. 10 and 1821, X, p. 54.

30 IEP, Minute Books of the Islay District Road Trustees.

31 IEP, Petition from tenants of Glenchatadale.

32 IEP, Road Survey and Minute Books.

33 IEP, Minute Books.

34 A. R. B. Haldane, *Three Centuries of Scottish Posts*, (Edinburgh, 1971), p. 191. J. R. Henderson, *Post Offices in Scotland*, (Edinburgh, 1966). The Post Office archives, St Martins-le-Grand, London, provided background information on this section.

35 Ramsay, *Stent Book*, pp. 28–9 for this and following references.

[36] Smith, *Book of Islay*, p. 187.

[37] Post Office archives.

[38] Haldane, *Three Centuries*, p. 192.

[39] See J. A. Mackay, *Island Postal History Series No. 10: Islay, Jura and the other Argyll Islands*, (Dumfries, 1979).

[40] Post Office archives.

[41] Inaugural pamphlet, Museum of Islay Life.

[42] Isle of Islay Federation, Scottish Women's Rural Institute, *Islay: a project in local history*, (Islay, 1968), p. 30.

CHAPTER 14

Prospect

In the years since the first edition of this book was published in 1981, the tenor of much that was written remains little changed; the tone remains the same. Nevertheless, changes there have been. The economic recessions of the 1980s arrived somewhat belatedly on Islay, as in mainland Scotland. Any recession in the whisky industry hits the island particularly hard, with the south-eastern villages counting amongst some of the highest unemployment blackspots in Argyll. Agricultural adjustments, related to national, European Union and international policy changes, visibly affected island farming, landscape, farmers and their wives. Islay hit the national and international headlines with controversies over conservation and development issues, especially those related to proposed peat extraction at Duich Moss, which became oversimplified as geese and dragonflies versus jobs. Arguments ran for years over the protection of wild geese and farmers' needs for early grass for their stock. Seals and fishermen became antagonists. A prototype wave energy station was constructed with little controversy, unlike a proposed superquarry and a wind cluster. Fiscal forestry and designations of Sites of Special Scientific Interest, 'RAMSAR' sites and the Argyll Islands Environmentally Sensitive Area extended this debate. Bases were established on the island by the Nature Conservancy Council, later Scottish Natural Heritage, and the Royal Society for the Protection of Birds, and an Islay Land Use Forum was set up.[1] The perennial ferry debate diminished somewhat as MV *Iona* was replaced successively by MV *Claymore* and MV *Isle of Arran*. Not only was Islay able to attract a total of several thousand day-visitors each summer, but after a generation, it once more became possible from 1990 to spend summer Wednesdays on the neighbouring islands of Colonsay and Oronsay. A summer ferry link was also renewed in 1997 between Ballycastle in Northern Ireland and Campbeltown in Kintyre.

Although there are few formal recreational facilities, apart from the golf course, bowling greens, tennis, leisure centre, pony-trekking, putting and pitch-and-putt, there is much informal activity. Almost every evening in summer there is some form of entertainment for islanders and visitors,

perhaps a dance, ceilidh, concert, disco, gig or snooker, often involving
fund-raising for some island charity or activity. The principal island events
are the Feis Île, Islay Gaelic Mod Sheep-dog Trials, the Islay Open and
Kildalton Cross Golf Championships and the Agricultural Show, together
with fêtes, sports-days, ploughing competitions, poultry shows, sailing
regattas, angling competitions, and the occasional gymkhana. The normal
activities of the islanders in their many and various clubs, societies, schools,
church and secular organisations, carry on throughout much of the year,
except soccer, which is played in summer. In poor weather, in common
with many less-developed holiday areas there is still a lack of choice of
daytime activities for visitors, but the MacTaggart Leisure Centre, opened
in 1991, is much used by residents and visitors alike. Special-interest
holidays expanded, based on wildlife, diving and golf. The main villages
have cafés open during summer. There are still rather few goods handcrafted
on the island, despite the creation in 1980 of the Islay Arts and Crafts
Guild, but there are some specialist shops, unlike the general Hebridean
trend, where shops are usually multi-purpose. Several of the distilleries
now have visitor centres, tours and impressive sales points, as does the
Islay Woollen Mill.

There have been more visible changes. Islay High School has been
much extended, although some people mistake its quirky pagodas for an
extension to the nearby Bowmore distillery. Attractively laid-out housing
for the elderly has been provided in the villages by Kirk Care of Scotland.
Houses in the villages and the rural areas have been reconstructed or
rehabilitated, sensitively on the whole. Roads, parking, pavements and
street lighting have all been improved. The European Regional Development
Fund helped finance alterations at Port Ellen and Port Askaig piers to
accommodate larger ferries and what has become an island fishing fleet,
although the latter has had variable fortune.

Successive national training and employment initiatives complemented
the increased involvement of the Highlands and Islands Development
Board, Argyll and the Islands Enterprise Company, Strathclyde Regional
Council, Argyll and Bute District Council and Argyll and Bute Council, as
well as that of other bodies who have tried to create new employment to
replace that lost in more traditional sectors. The Islay and Jura Council of
Voluntary Service and its fortnightly newspaper, The *Ileach*, begun in
1973, provided a forum for controversy.[2] The Islay Farmers' Co-operative
extended its valuable services and the Islay and Jura Marketing Group
produced attractive publicity for the island and their products. A new
bakery, new coffee shops and restaurants were established. Demand and
quality in the tourism sector improved, without substantially endangering

the face of the island that attracts visitors in the first place. Bowmore boasted a small telecommunications service centre, while a youth hostel and a field and exhibition centre were opened at Port Charlotte. Another museum opened, this time at Finlaggan, the intensive archaeological investigations there producing exciting finds.

In the 1980s, too, the work of An Commun Gaidhealach Meur Île was supplemented by that of other organisations in the Islay, Jura and Colonsay Gaelic Partnership. The annual Feis Île takes place in early summer, though sadly, the highly successful international Rinns Festival, which attracted Breton, Irish, Manx, Welsh and other Celtic artistes, is no longer. The Islay Arts Association has brought many different kinds of professional performances to the island, often playing to packed houses for performances ranging from alternative theatre to Scottish Opera Go Round's Bohème, Macbeth, Tosca, Don Carlos, Eugene Onegin and Maria Stuarda. The Argyll Arts Forum co-ordinated the expansion of such activities. The lighthouse keepers on offshore Orsay Island probably enjoyed the gigs of Runrig and Wolfstone at Portnahaven Hall during Feis Île as much as the rest of us did.

The island, like mainland Argyll, continued to raise exceptional amounts of charitable monies, including six-figure sums to renovate the Round Church in Bowmore and to open a leisure centre, including a swimming pool, in a former whisky bonded warehouse in Bowmore in 1991. Fund-raising for long-established charities such as the Royal National Lifeboat Institution, Masonic and Royal Arch Lodges, and medical charities has been extended by others, including the Lions and the Round Table. By the 1980s women were prominent in many positions in Islay, including the member of parliament, regional councillors, head teacher, doctors, vets, church ministers, editors and hoteliers.

Perhaps the biggest change however, has been in the islanders' awareness of, and increasing knowledge of, their island. In storms, 'the mainland's been cut off' may still pass from lip to lip, cheerily or otherwise, but there is a greater understanding and realisation of Islay's role in the United Kingdom, Europe and beyond, than there appeared to be in the early 1980s. There is also more concern over the social problems and social fabric of the islands, with increased personal mobility and more incomers settling. The controversy during the summer of 1991 over the replacement of a native Gaelic-speaking assistant at the Museum of Islay Life by a recent incomer from south of the border aroused almost as many passions on and off the island as did Duich Moss. Debate on the island's future is thus likely to become more focused and more vigilant, boding well for the island community.

If there are any lessons to be learned from the last few centuries in Islay, the principal one is surely the importance of chance and the consequent folly of trying to predict the future with confidence. If, for instance, John Campbell of Cawdor had sought financial advice rather earlier than he did, or even if he had followed the advice that he did receive in 1723, it seems probable that the island could have remained longer in the hands of the Cawdor family. It is certainly most unlikely that it would have passed so easily into the possession of the Campbells of Shawfield. Yet if the Shawfield Campbells had not become the principal landlords on Islay for over a century, the landscape, the economy and even the size of the present population would probably all be very different from what they are now. The characteristic villages would almost certainly not be so numerous and they might have a much less attractive appearance. The landholding system would probably have followed a revolution more characteristic of other parts of the Highlands and Islands, with clearances for sheep and deer grazing and the establishment of crofting townships. In other words, Islay would probably be a Hebridean example rather than a Hebridean exception.

Similarly, the difficulties with the potato crop, the rent arrears and the other troubles that beset Walter Frederick Campbell in the mid-1840s were probably less those of an absentee landlord, generally believed to have created many of the Highlands and Islands problems, than by the fact that he had few external resources on which to draw in time of trouble. The turn of events that brought the Campbells to Islay was largely a matter of personalities; that which removed them was largely imposed on the persons involved. Both, however, were largely unpredictable and both had results of fundamental importance for Islay. It would be foolish to pretend that similar unpredictable events cannot occur again – chaos theory makes allowance for events such as the 1996 BSE cattle crisis. The financial incompetence of a landlord or his agents is less likely to be crucial nowadays, but, as also in the past, the more Islay's economy and society interact with a wider Scotland, a wider Britain, a wider Europe and the rest of the world, the more the island's future is shaped by external trends and events.

Islay and the Highland problem
One of the significant characteristics of Islay until the 1980s was a relative lack of concern about the future. The symptoms of collective worry about economic decline, depopulation, diminution of services and facilities and so on, that were evident in many parts of the Highlands and Islands, were not entirely absent from Islay, but were miniscule by comparison

with many other islands and remote Highland areas. This was evident in the ferry controversy; the debate was not tinged with fears that the island's links with the mainland were weakening. Instead, the argument was about the best way to strengthen these links, although it also included some intra-island rivalry. Another sign of the general lack of concern was the fact that the island was not the subject of one of those semi-official 'surveys' commissioned for, or by, other islands. Elsewhere, a general sense of malaise has often led to a request that a university or other source of supposed wisdom investigate in depth the nature of the problem and provide guidance on how it should be solved. The present author has been involved in surveys of this kind and no criticism of their objective, technique or usefulness is intended; the point is merely that they were not then felt necessary for Islay.[3] Although, human nature being what it is, it is doubtful whether more than a small minority of any population would declare themselves completely content, there appeared to exist a justifiable awareness that Islay's problems were small by comparison with those elsewhere. The present book, evidently, is not so much an 'investigation of the roots of the present discontent in Islay' so much as an explanation of why there is so much on the island to enjoy and be grateful for. A travel feature in *The Independent* newspaper in 1996 still referred to the island's 'enchantment'.[4]

This satisfaction appeared to be evident as far away as the virtual seat of Scottish government in St Andrew's House in Edinburgh and in the Highlands and Islands Development Board in Inverness. Naturally it was more muted in these places even than on Islay itself, lest the charge be made that central government was almost ignoring the island. In 1966 the Scottish Development Department in Edinburgh produced a White Paper entitled *The Scottish Economy 1965–1980: A Plan for Expansion*. Although the document has in many ways been superseded, it is to be hoped that the thinking it represents has not. The White Paper was a United Kingdom landmark in the long and continuing analysis of disparities in performance and opportunities between one region and another. Instead of taking those disparities as congenital and devising new or enlarged programmes of government assistance as palliatives, the White Paper argued that it was time to recognise that many of the problems had arisen because of attitudes towards the Highlands and Islands that were outdated and unreal:

> The Highlands and Islands are very different from any other region of the United Kingdom. Much earlier work on them takes this difference as a reason for treating the region as something *sui generis*, justifying its own set of standards and insulation from criteria applied elsewhere in

Britain. This tendency was fed both by Highland feeling itself and hardly less by outside sentiment which would preserve a distinctive Highland way of life. Undeniable benefits have been won as a result of special treatment. But it is arguable that in the long run the Highlands have lost more than they have gained.[5]

Implicitly and occasionally explicitly, the White Paper made it clear that government policy towards the Highlands and Islands was henceforth to be based on a much more realistic appraisal of the social and economic potential of different parts of the area. Since governments exist primarily to serve people, the size and distribution of the population and its age composition, are among the key factors influencing the nature of government policy. The White Paper went on to list thirteen zones in the Highlands and Islands from Lerwick-Scalloway in the Shetlands to Campbeltown in Kintyre where the social and economic prospects seemed reasonably bright. Two other areas in adjacent counties were also identified, Rothesay and Pitlochry. These fifteen areas contained nearly four-fifths of the population and nearly three-quarters of the unemployed in the Highlands and Islands and adjacent areas; they also contained higher proportions of younger people than the areas left out.

Although the White Paper did not say so explicitly, such a view of the Highlands and Islands is one that recognises the importance of what might be termed the minimum viable size of a community. Islay has problems similar in many ways to those which the Campbells of Shawfield were facing, though with different emphasis. It is perhaps even possible to argue today that an island like Islay is overpopulated by several criteria. This, however, is not a particularly helpful approach if one is arguing for a rise in the provision of many kinds of improved living standards. The more complex our modern society becomes, the more affluent is the population and the more sophisticated its needs and desires, the larger the size a community must be if it is to provide adequate facilities for its members. If they are not available, then the community risks stagnation or decline. Below a certain threshold of population (in practice often difficult to define), improved services may not be economically feasible, though they might occur for social and political reasons. Many indicators on viability can be chosen apart from demographic ones. Although few adequate studies of the question exist, it was suggested for Norfolk in the 1960s that a minimum population of 5,000 was needed to support 'a reasonable range of local facilities'.[6] Lower figures have been put forward for Scottish conditions, but even so, of the 125 islands off the Scottish coast that were inhabited in 1971, only five had over 5,000 people (Lewis/ Harris, mainland Shetland, mainland Orkney, Bute and Skye) and only a further ten had between 1,000 and 5,000. Of the remainder, 93 had less than 200 inhabitants each, including twenty lighthouse islands.[7]

What has all this to do with the future of Islay, whose normally resident population by 1991 was around 3,500? Two points seem important. The notion of minimum viable size is important, even for an island served with regular airline links and ferry services. In principle the Islay resident has access to the resources of Oban, Lochgilphead, Glasgow, London or the world; in practice, and despite the telecommunications revolution, the ability to utilise these resources is rather more limited than for those who live on the mainland. The Islay resident is also likely to have a fairly accurate perception of the facilities available and those not. In other words, the choice between the island and 'the outside' is still sharply defined, at least as long as ferry routes are not nationally regarded as mainland road extensions and ferry and fuel charges therefore remain substantial. This perception may remain latent for long periods, but it is likely to be very important when decisions have to be taken that involve such matters as education of children, job choice, particularly at school-leaving age, and the availability of health care for the elderly. Although the question is seldom posed so starkly, the future of Islay rests to a considerable extent on its capacity to support a population large enough in size to offer adequate facilities for its members. Growth tends to engender further growth: as the range of opportunities expands, so more people are inclined to remain on Islay or to come to it and they make possible still more opportunities for activities that require a larger market if they are to survive.[8] Equally obviously, decline tends to engender further decline and the problems facing a declining community can become acute within a short time.

The second point worth noting about the White Paper's view of regional development policy is the middle position that Islay occupied in the official mind. It was not one of the fifteen communities listed in the 1966 White Paper as being a potential centre of continued prosperity and growth. It could easily be assumed that the relatively static 'normally resident' population was not in decline; the island was more characteristic of the areas designated as 'holding' or 'stable' areas. In this situation Islay was the target neither for major government action to encourage development, nor for similar action to arrest decline (or, more realistically, to manage decline so as to reduce individual hardship). Though Islay's problems no doubt came before the attention of St Andrew's House and the Highlands and Islands Development Board quite regularly, the problems were tackled individually as they arose, without the need for a comprehensive strategy.[9]

If indeed this was the official view, then some parallels could be drawn with the situation of Islay during the 1840s. At that time, a series of government enquiries and initiatives sought to establish the need for help to avert famine in the Highlands and Islands and to provide some assistance to create employment. Throughout much of the decade, the official view was that the island was fortunate in having a landlord who 'has the character of being at all times disposed to . . . attending to the people's wants'.[10] This view was shared to some extent by the landlord himself: although he became increasingly anxious to receive government assistance, he was reluctant to see it accompanied by any restrictions on his own freedom of action. Eventually it became evident that the sensibilities of Walter Frederick Campbell were less important than his ability, or inability, to attend to his people's needs. In the 1960s and 1970s, as in the 1840s, there were many parts of the Highlands and Islands with more serious and more urgent problems than those that confronted Islay. Was this sufficient justification for the general feeling of complacency that tended to exist both on Islay and at the official level?

The answer seemed to be in the affirmative, although Islay's future probably deserved more careful analysis than it received. Historical parallels are always of doubtful significance and especially so in the present instance. Islay's prosperity depends far less on the personality and power of the principal landlord than it did in the 1840s. Even then, although the distress on Islay during the 1840s was very real, the sequestration and sale of the estate was primarily a personal tragedy for the Shawfield Campbells: it was perhaps less of a disaster for Islay. More positively, by the end of the twentieth century the world was very different from that of the 1840s: if severe problems were to beset the Islay community, the awareness of the outside would be immeasurably greater than it was before the electronic age and the techniques for managing such economic and social problems are, despite their imperfections, undeniably better than those of a century ago. More fundamentally still, the hazards that the Islay resident might face would probably strike the hungry islanders of the 1840s as only slightly inferior versions of paradise. Historical parallels seemed to be valid only in the fact that Islay was in a rather more fortunate position than many other areas in the Highlands and Islands and, therefore, St Andrew's House and the Highlands and Islands Development Board could afford to treat it, if not with 'benign neglect', at least with only a relatively small input of effort and finance.

Threats and opportunities

Although such an attitude was perhaps justifiable, it is perhaps reasonable to ask what threats to the fabric of Islay economy, society and landscape are conceivable in the future, and what alternative opportunities may arise to replace them. Any views expressed are inevitably personal ones and others may well argue that the emphasis is wrong, or that quite different factors will be the key ones in determining Islay's future. So much the better: what is important is that the island's future should be discussed, debated and, ultimately, focused and planned.

The economy of Islay, as anywhere else, consists of a complex relationship involving a number of fairly distinct, but interrelated, elements. Some of these are primary, in that they are at least partly related to the resources of the island, such as agriculture, sport, fishing and distilling. Others depend on the existence of a particular level of population and on the income and spending capacity of that population.

Employment in agriculture, for example, is unlikely to represent a significant basis for expansion in the future. The output of Islay's farms is dependent on the policies of the wider world and the income of the farmer is unlikely to be increased by an expansion in the number of those who work for that farmer; quite the reverse. The situation is scarcely more sanguine in relation to fishing. Islay has benefited from the growth in demand for lobsters, clams and other shellfish, a demand that seems likely to be permanent and widespread. Islay's relatively good air and sea links enable it to cater to this specialist, mainly export, market. It may well be that in a relatively short space of time what may be described as the 'hunting and gathering' phase of such shellfish collection may yield to more organised (and contentious) 'farming', though the employment generated is likely to be small, as is that for sport fishing or shooting. Apart from whisky, secondary manufacture in Islay is also small in terms both of output and of employment. Islay Woollen Mill apart, a small creamery producing 'Islay Cheese', really a Dunlop-type cheese, a fish factory, a few small crafts concerns and other ventures trading on the island's name have often turned out financially precarious. The world's capacity to absorb ever-increasing amounts of whisky may be changing and more public relations, advertising and sales people may be required, but the numbers of islanders producing it will continue to decline through automation. Only about two-fifths of the women over sixteen are 'economically active' in Islay and two-fifths of these are in part-time employment.[11] Between two and three times as many men as women have full-time work and this creates a restriction on the size of family income. More and more women, single and married, would welcome paid employment such as is available to their counterparts in mainland towns and cities.

An obvious activity, where growth is to be anticipated is in meeting the service and leisure demands of the future; in this Islay is but a microcosm of much of the United Kingdom. Though many would challenge the thesis and its implications, it seems at least probable that these demands will cause changes to the economy and society of Islay that could be as profound as those achieved by the Shawfield Campbells and others in the eighteenth and nineteenth centuries. Islay does have natural advantages that could lead to an expansion of existing leisure interests, to include ventures such as film-making, providing much-needed employment.[12] Such developments could profoundly change the present character of Islay, though they need not, given careful planning, be disastrous to the economy, society or the environment. Telecommuting and combining information technology with further education and training, as in the developing University of the Highlands and Islands, could provide a fillip to employment on the island, albeit requiring a robust electricity supply.[13]

Scenarios for change

At this point it is necessary to ask the classical question *cui bono*? Who benefits? There are many who would argue that the benefits that major developments would bring to Islay would be far outweighed by the disadvantages, that the benefits would be concentrated in a few people on Islay, mainly incomers, or financiers outwith the island, and that those who have lived their whole lives on the island would encounter most of the disadvantages. It is not difficult to make a strong case for the argument that the present relative tranquillity and prosperity of Islay are precious attributes that should be protected at all costs, and that highly capitalised leisure or other developments are the greatest threats to them. Those who have already bought holiday or retirement homes on Islay are likely to be amongst the strongest supporters of this thesis, but the view is not solely a selfish one. It might well be supported by a majority of the population and it is difficult to deny that in deciding the future of the island the views of the present Ilich should be paramount.[14]

This is not the place to argue either for or against a dramatic transformation of Islay society and economy. There are clearly arguments on both sides and, without a very thorough analysis, it is impossible to know whether the benefits to Islay would exceed the disadvantages or not. There would be no unanimity of view, since different people would be affected in different ways. What can be urged here is that more thought be given to the desirability or otherwise of change, especially by those most likely to be affected, the present islanders. At least three different scenarios can be sketched that need to be analysed and compared with each other.

The first scenario is one that is based on the attempt to maintain the present lifestyle and character of Islay. Residents will be on their guard to challenge revolutionary changes, as distinct from evolutionary ones. Proposals for new developments, whether related to hydrocarbons, a superquarry, energy wind clusters, tourism or whatever, will be looked at with a jaundiced eye, until Islay is convinced that the development in question is compatible with those things that are most valued in the present situation. The notion of sustainable development is a valid one. In the Baltic island of Bornholm, for example, strict monitoring of air and ferry tickets ensures that visitors never number more than the resident population. Conversely, a watch will have to be kept out for those elements that may signal a decline in the present pattern of employment or lifestyle, which may threaten the quality of life through the decline in numbers below the level needed to sustain it.

A second and quite different scenario would recognise the value that Islay would gain from the addition of new elements to its economy in the form of well-planned but highly-capitalised ventures, probably concentrated into a few areas, and at the moment most likely to be related to the growth in demand for education or leisure. To varying degrees, the Islay population would seek to encourage such growth and the main concern would be to ensure that such developments produced a net gain, that certain unique sites and irreplaceable resources were protected and that the employment involved in such developments was shared by Islay residents as well as by those coming from outside.

Although these brief outlines appear to be opposed to each other, they have one important feature in common. They both imply the development of a conscious attitude by the people of Islay towards the possibility of major change and the existence of a strategy or plan to discourage or encourage it. A third scenario is, however, much more probable and likely to be much more dangerous. This would be based on the assumption that few major changes are probable and that if they should arise, they can be dealt with on an *ad hoc* basis. It would take the view that the changes which have happened on Islay in the past few decades have on the whole been painless and desirable and that the future can be similarly left to take care of itself.

There are several dangers in such an approach. The most important is that it does not really need to be adopted. If there is no conscious desire on the part of Islay's population to develop a view of what the essential elements of the island's future should be, the third scenario will inevitably unfold. The attitude may be justified: the relative tranquillity and steadily increasing prosperity that Islay has enjoyed for much of the present century may continue and as the expectations and aspirations of the population rise, the economy and society will develop to satisfy them. But this is not inevitable; continued stability or even decline in Islay may be accompanied by rising standards elsewhere, leading to emigration of those who wish to share in that prosperity, especially by young adults. The island could move relatively quickly to a situation where its population falls below that necessary to offer the services and facilities expected by most people and further out-migration would take place. Even if that did not occur, the incomers are more likely to be older and/or with few local connections. Breeding pairs of human beings are as important as breeding birds.

Or the opposite may happen. Developments may be proposed that catch Islay unprepared: the advantages may appear, or be made to appear, considerable and it is only after the transformation has been accomplished that the problems in economy, society and the environment become evident. Even without such major individual initiatives, the slow spread of small-scale activities may eventually bring on a crisis or blight that is the more difficult to solve because it cannot be traced to a single event and cannot be easily rectified. One has only to look across the North Channel to the coasts of Ireland to see the disaster that can happen in a relatively short time. Already some incongruous public and private carbuncles have appeared on the island landscape. Creeping uglification and the garden-centre suburbanisation of Islay gathers apace. 1970s bidets and 1980s kitchens have been joined by 1990s conservatories, some of dubious design, scale or siting. The timelag between mainland and island has virtually disappeared. Signposts and telecommunications masts proliferate, along with dog loos. Island society too has been changing. The proportion of those living in Islay, but born in England, was one in eight by 1991, and in one postal district was one in four.[15] In Skye and Mull the figures were one in five and three respectively. This is not intended to be judgmental on decibels, habits or aspirations, but to show the extent of change.

Some conscious collective view has to be developed for the future of the whole of the island, while there is still time to influence that future, eliminating as far as possible unhelpful intra-island rivalries. For a population of around 3,500 there are too many overlapping organisations and committees to allow an island voice to impinge where it matters in the world outside. This dispersion of effort encourages short-termism. The natural heritage is important, locally, nationally and internationally. The pace of change in the built environment is accelerating in Islay. Aspects of island society are also changing more rapidly than before. Viewed from a world perspective since the turbulent 1970s, the odds during the next decades are probably tipped more in favour of change than of stability, and of accelerating change, with the internet further reducing distance. The long-term balance between conservation and regeneration must be carefully nurtured by planning and managing sustainable development of the interrelated natural, economic, societal and cultural heritage, including the marine environment.

> When I went back to Islay they all said how much the place had changed . . . what a lot had happened since then. There was the new ferry, and cattle grids instead of gates on the Glen road, and had I seen the new houses outside Ballygrant? I wouldn't know the place. In fact, it was the same old Islay, strikingly untouched. The changes which seemed so obvious to the local people . . . would not have been noticed on the mainland . . . I would not have believed how small the changes would be. Nothing had happened to destroy the important thing, Islay's quality of seeming not so much a corner of Scotland as a country in its own right.[16]

Alastair Borthwick's reaction, recorded in 1969 after he revisited the island on which he had lived for seven years in the 1950s, is clearly very different from the emphasis on change that has been the theme of this book. Perhaps if he were to return today he would be astonished at the 30-metre high granaries which now dominate the skyline as the ferry approaches Port Ellen, and by the articulated container vehicles that roll on and off the still larger ferries several times a day. But despite much of Islay life that is more 'mainland' than before, there is clearly an element of truth in Mr Borthwick's reaction. Possibly the really distinctive feature about Islay has been the capacity of the landscape and society to absorb change without fuss and without destroying 'the important thing'. However, for the major changes in lifestyle and landscape that are ahead, which indeed have already begun to happen, the Ilich need to be ever more vigilant to remain a Hebridean exception.[17]

Notes and references

[1]   The remit of the Islay Land Use Forum is to 'promote the social and economic needs and the reasonable aspirations of the Islay people as regards the use of the land of Islay, and at the same time sustain the outstanding quality of Islay's natural resources, while recognising and accommodating the roles and obligations of the various agencies which affect the land use on the island'.

[2] The *Ileach* is available on subscription from The Islay and Jura Council of Voluntary Service, Bowmore, Isle of Islay.

[3] M. C. Storrie and C. I. Jackson, *Arran 1980–81: 2,021?*, (Edinburgh, 1967).

[4] *The Independent*, 11 May 1996.

[5] *The Scottish Economy 1965–70: A Plan for Expansion*, 1966, Cmnd. 2864, p. 52.

[6] R. J. Green and J. B. Ayton, Paper read to the Town Planning Institute's Research Conference, 'Planning for the Countryside, October 1967, Summary.

[7] *Census 1981, Preliminary Report*, 1981, Table 3.

[8] Due in part to affirmative action, the 1991 population of the Isle of Arran, for example, had almost regained its 1951 level. Islay's population would need to increase by twenty per cent to achieve the 1951 level.

[9] Instances of assistance given by the Highlands and Islands Development Board include the pier and boat-repairing facility at Portnahaven; the reopening of the Woollen Mill at Bridgend and self-catering units at Machrie Hotel.

[10] *BPP, Emigration*, 1841, VI, p. 30.

[11] *Census of Scotland 1991*, Small Area Statistics.

[12] The island's picturesque villages and harbours featured prominently in the film, *The Maggie*, in the 1950s and in the television series *Para Handy*, in the 1990s.

[13] ETSU, The Islay Energy Study, (Didcot, 1996).

[14] In the mid-1990s the Corrom Trust initiated regeneration studies in various parts of the Highlands and Islands, including Islay and Jura, using 'bottom-up' and 'SWOT' techniques of analysis.

[15] *Census of Scotland 1991*, Small Area Statistics.

[16] A. Borthwick, 'Return to Islay', *Scotland's Magazine*, April 1969, p. 21.

[17] Storrie, 'Hebridean Exception', pp. 87–108.

Appendix A

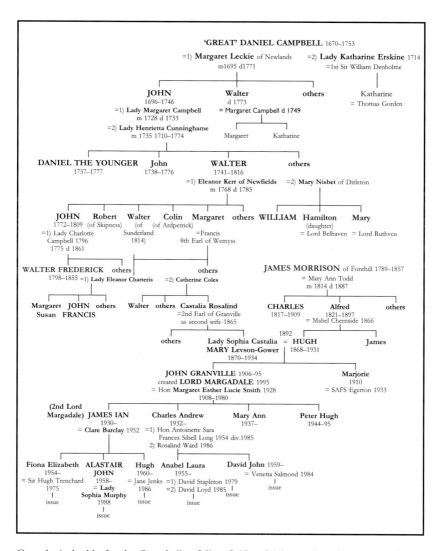

Genealogical table for the Campbells of Shawfield and Islay, and the Morrisons of Islay.

Appendix B Chronological list of strandings, founderings or wrecks around Islay's coasts, exact location unknown.

1780s Irish vessel	1881 *Progress*
American vessel	*Cwmavon*
American vessel	*Royal Arch*
1817 *Lord Wellington*	*Castle Green*
Augustus	*Fairy*
1818 *James Hamilton*	*Leonard Hollis*
1820 *Isabella Helen*	*Rob Roy*
1827 *Commerce*	*Susannah*
1833 *Gratitude*	*Isabella Wilson*
Margaret	1882 *Jane Gwynne*
Industry	*Mary Stewart*
1834 *Telegraph*	*Texa*
1835 *Kitty and Mary*	*Harold*
Julia	1883 *Nelson*
Martin	*Lady of Lake*
1842 *Undine*	1884 *Islay*
1847 *Montcalm*	*Advance*
Reform	*Hunter*
Martin	*North Star*
Ann Falcon	*Hebea*
1865 *Paramount*	*John Evans*
1867 *Falcon*	*Castle Green*
1869 *Isabella Swanson*	*Peter James*
1875 *Ella Glenesdale*	*William Hope*
1877 *Florence Muspratt*	*Louise Ann*
Providence	*Troubadour*
1880 *Nations*	*James Kenway*
Challenge	1885 *Islay*
Waree or Maree	1898 *Plover*
	1934 *St Tudal*

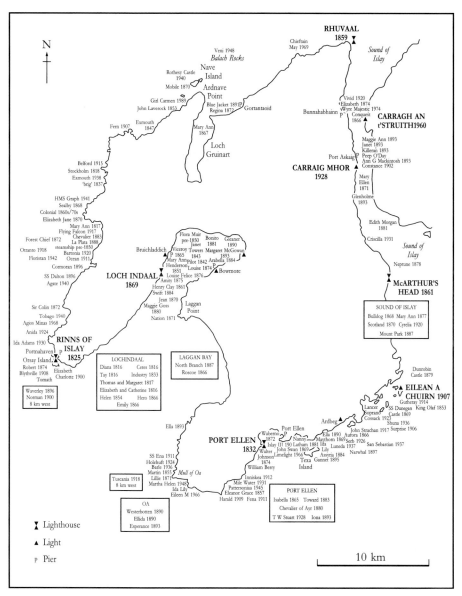

N

RHUVAAL
1859

Chieftain
May 1969

Sound of
Islay

Veni 1948
Balach Rocks

Nave
Island

Rothesy Castle
1940

Mobile 1870

Ardnave
Point

Girl Carmen 1989
John Laverock 1853

Blue Jacket 1891 P
Regina 1872

Gortantaoid

Vivid 1920
Elizabeth 1874
Wyre Majestic 1974
Conquest
1866

Bunnahabhainn P

CARRAGH AN
t'STRUITH1960

Fern 1907

Exmouth
1847

Mary Ann
1867

Loch
Gruinart

Port Askaig P

Maggie Ann 1893
Janet 1893
Killeran 1893
Peep O'Day
Ann G Mackintosh 1893
Constance 1902

Belford 1915
Stockholm 1818
Exmouth 1938
'brig' 1837

CARRAIG MHOR
1928

Mary
Ellen
1871

HMS Graph 1941
Sealby 1868
Colonial 1860s/70s
Elizabeth Jane 1870
Mary Ann 1817
Flying Falcon 1917

Glenholme
1893

Edith Morgan
1881

Forest Chief 1872
Otranto 1918
Floristan 1942

Chevalier 1883
La Plata 1888
steamship pre-1850
Bartonia 1920
Ocean 1911

Flora Muir
pre-1850
Janet
Viceroy Towers
P 1865

Bonito
1881

Gleaner
1890

Margaret McGowan
1893

Bruichladdich

Mary Ann
Pilot 1842
Henderson
1851
Louise Felice 1876
Amity 1875
Henry Clay 1861

1843

Arabella 1884

Louise 1874

Bowmore

Criscilla 1931

Sound of
Islay

SS Dalton 1896
Agate 1940

LOCH INDAAL
1869

Neptune 1878

Sir Colin 1872
Tobago 1940
Agios Minas 1968
Anida 1924
Ida Adams 1930

Jean 1870
Swift 1884
Maggie Goss
1880
Nation 1871

Laggan
Point

McARTHUR'S
HEAD 1861

RINNS OF
ISLAY
1825

Portnahaven

Orsay Island

P

SOUND OF ISLAY

Bulldog 1868 Mary Ann 1877
Scotland 1870 Cyrelia 1920
Mount Park 1887

Robert 1874
Blythville 1908
Tomath

Elizabeth
Charlotte 1900

LOCHINDAAL

Diana 1816
Tay 1816
Thomas and Margaret 1817
Elizabeth and Catherine 1816
Helen 1854
Emily 1866

Ceres 1816
Industry 1833

LAGGAN BAY

North Branch 1887
Roscoe 1866

Waverley 1896
Norman 1900
8 km west

Hero 1866

Dunrobin
Castle 1879

EILEAN A
CHUIRN 1907

Gutheray 1914
SS Dunegan King Olaf 1853
Castle 1869
Shuna 1936

Lancer
Soprano
Cossack 1923

Ella 1893

Ardbeg

John Strachan 1917 Surprise 1906

Port Ellen
Wabemo P
1872

PORT ELLEN
1832

Walter
Johnson
1874

Islay III 190 Latham 1881
John Swan 1869
Limelight 1966

Nanny
Maythorn 1869 Serb 1926
Ida Aurora 1866
Luneda 1937
Lily
Assyria 1884
Texa Gannet 1895
Island

Ella 1890

San Sebastian 1937

Narwhal 1897

SS Ena 1911
Holehuft 1924
Barle 1936
Martin 1855
Lillie 1871
Martha Helen 1948
Ida Lily
Eileen M 1966

Mull of Oa

William Berry

Inniskea 1912
Mile Water 1931
Pattersoniaa 1945
Eleanor Grace 1857
Harald 1909 Fena 1911

Tuscania 1918
8 km west

PORT ELLEN

Isabella 1865 Toward 1883
Chevalier of Ayr 1880
T W Stuart 1928 Iona 1893

OA

Westerbotten 1890
Ellida 1890
Esperance 1893

Lighthouse

Light

P Pier

10 km

Over 250 wrecks and strandings are known to have occurred around Islay's shores. About two-thirds of these are indicated here, but no exact location is known for the remainder, listed opposite. Lives lost are in three or four figures, but successive Islay lifeboats have saved many lives since the Station was first established at Port Askaig in 1934 (Compiled from information from local sources, particularly the late Gilbert Clark of Port Charlotte and James MacAulay of Port Ellen and from official sources).

Sources and Bibliography

Archives

Anderson (James) Papers, NLS, catalogued under Advocates MSS. 29.1.2.

Annexed Estates Commissioners: Daniel Campbell the Younger petitioned on several occasions for grants of money to aid his plans on the development of Islay. These requests are now in the SRO, E727/60 and E728/47.

Argyll and Bute Council, Statutory List of Buildings of Architectural or Historic Interest, designated by and approved by Scottish Heritage and the Scottish Office. Killarow or Bowmore Church is category A (of national as well as local interest) and Islay House is category B (of more local than national interest, but also of special interest). The older parts of most of the villages in Islay have been designated 'conservation areas'.

Campbell of Jura Papers, Scottish Record Office (SRO), GD64.

Campbell (Walter Frederick) obituaries, Special Collections, GUL, Mu43–c.17.

Campbell of Melfort Papers, EUL, MSS. Dk.73.151.

The Cawdor Papers are in Cawdor Castle, Nairn, and are listed in some detail in the NRA (Scotland) Survey 1400, SRO.

Census enumerators' copied schedules from 1841 to 1891 are at New Register House, Edinburgh.

Clerk of Penicuik Papers, SRO, GD18.

Customs and Excise Correspondence, Port Ellen District, Argyll South Collection, SRO, CE81.

The Islay Estate Papers are in Islay Estate Office, Bridgend, Isle of Islay, and are summarily listed in the NRA (Scotland) Survey O123. Some are deposited on loan to the City of Glasgow Archives.

The Ramsay of Kildalton Papers are deposited on loan in the City of Glasgow Archives, listed under TDF 1284.

Lloyds of London archives.

Museum of Islay Life Archives.

Museums of Glasgow.

National Gallery of Scotland.

Ordnance Survey, MS namebooks, Edinburgh.

Playfair Drawings, EUL, Special Collection, Catalogue 30.

The Post Office Archives, London.

The Royal Highland and Agricultural Society of Scotland Library.

Saltoun Papers, SRO, SB74.

The School of Scottish Studies tape archives, The University of Edinburgh.

Scottish National Portrait Gallery.

The Shawfield Papers are in the Mitchell Library, Glasgow. These mainly relate to the period before Islay was bought by Daniel Campbell of Shawfield.

University of Cambridge, Committee for Aerial Photography.

Walker (Professor John), Papers, EUL, MS. D.c.i.57.

Wrecks and Casualties, Register of Examinations, SRO, CE60.

Published Books

Adams, I. H. and Somerville, M., *Cargoes of Despair and Hope*, (Edinburgh, 1993).

Anderson, J., *An Account of the Present State of the Hebrides and Western Coasts of Scotland . . . being the Substance of a Report to The Lords of the Treasury together with the evidence before the Committee of Fisheries*, (Edinburgh, 1785).

Arrowsmith, A, *Memoir relative to the Construction of the Map of Scotland published by A. Arrowsmith in the year 1807*, (London, 1809).

Bailyn, B., *Voyages to the West*, (New York, 1986).

Balfour Paul, Sir J., *The Scots Peerage*, 9 vols, (Edinburgh, 1908).

Bannerman, J. M. W., *The Beatons,* (Edinburgh, 1986).

Barnard, A., *The Whisky Distilleries of the United Kingdom*, (London, 1887).

Bingham, C. *Beyond the Highland Line*, (London, 1991).

Blackburn, S., *Dive Islay Wrecks*, (Stoke-on-Trent, 1986).

Blake, R., *Disraeli*, (London, 1969).

Booth, C. G., *Birds in Islay*, (Islay, 1981).

Boyd, J. M. and Bowes, D. R. (eds.), *Natural Environment of the Inner Hebrides*, (Edinburgh, 1983).

Brock, W. R., *Scotus Americanus: a survey of the sources for links between Scotland and America in the eighteenth century*, (Edinburgh, 1982).

Brogan, C. (ed.), *James Finlay and Company Limited, manufacturers and East India merchants, 1750–1950*, (Glasgow, 1951).

Bumsted, J. M., *The People's Clearance*, (Edinburgh, 1982).

Burke's *Peerage, Baronetage & Knightage*, (London, 1967).

Burke, J. B., *A Genealogical and Heraldic Dictionary of the Landed Gentry of Great Britain and Ireland*, (London, 1843–9).

Bury (Campbell), Lady C. S. M., *Diary illustrative of the Times of George the Fourth*, (London, 1838–9), 4 vols.

Callander, R. M. and MacAulay, J., *The Ancient Metal Mines of the Isle of Islay*, (Sheffield, 1984).

Campbell, J. F., *Popular Tales of the West Highlands*, (Edinburgh, 1860–2), 4 vols.

Campbell, J. F. (ed.), (attr. to W. F. Campbell), *Life in Normandy*, (Edinburgh, 1863), 2 vols.

Campbell, Lady C. S. M. See Bury.

Cawdor Castle Guide, (Cawdor, n.d.).

Clan Donald Lands Trust, *Ceannas nan Gàidheal*, (Skye, 1985).

Clifton, V., *The Book of Talbot*, (London, 1933).

Cooper, D., *The Road to the Isles*, (London, 1979); *The Road to Mingulay*, (London, 1985).

Cubbage, J., *The Chronicle of Islay Golf Club and Machrie Links*, (Glasgow, 1996)

Darling, F. F., *West Highland Survey*, (Oxford, 1955).

Devine, T. M., *The Great Highland Famine*, (Edinburgh, 1988); *Clanship to Crofters' War*, (Manchester, 1994).

Dodgshon, R. A., *The Origin of British Field Systems: An Interpretation*, (London, 1980).

Donaldson, J., *Agricultural Biography*, (London, 1854).

Dorson, R. M., *The British Folklorists: A History*, (London, 1968).

Duckworth, C. L. D. and Langmuir, G. E., *West Highland Steamers*, (Prescot, 1967).

Dunbar, J. G., *The Historic Architecture of Scotland*, (London, 1966).

Elliott, R. E., *Birds of Islay*, (London, 1989).

Fleming, R. E., *Eldon Connections*, (Ontario, n.d.).

Forsyth, R., *The Beauties of Scotland*, (Edinburgh, 1805–8), 5 vols. Islay is in volume V.

Foster, J., *Members of Parliament, Scotland, including the Minor Barons, the Commissioners for the Shires, and the Commissioners for the Burghs, 1359–1882. On the basis of the Parliamentary Return 1880, with genealogical and biographical notices*, (London, 1882).

Fraser, R., *A Letter to the Right Hon. Charles Abbot, Speaker of the House of Commons, containing an inquiry into the most effectual means of improvement of the coasts and western isles of Scotland, and the extension of the Fisheries, With a letter from Dr. Anderson on the same subject*, (London, 1803).

Fullerton, A. and Baird., C. R., *Remarks on the Evils at present affecting the Highlands and Islands of Scotland; with some suggestions as to their remedies*, (Glasgow, 1838).

Gatty, R., *Portait of a Merchant Prince: James Morrison 1789–1857*, (Northallerton, n.d. [1977]).

Giblin, C. (ed.), *Irish Franciscan Mission to Scotland 1619–1646*, (Dublin, 1964).

Gillies, A., *A Hebridean in Goethe's Weimar*, (Oxford, 1969).

Gillies, H. C., *The Place Names of Argyll*, (London, 1906).

Glendinning, M., Macinnes, R., MacKechnie, A., *A History of Scottish Architecture from the Renaissance to the Present Day*, (Edinburgh, 1996).

Graham, A., *Skipness, Memories of a Highland Estate*, (Edinburgh, 1993).

Graham, R. C., *The Carved Stones of Islay*, (Glasgow, 1895).

Gray, A., *The History of Islay Place Names*, (Glasgow, 1939).

Gray, M., *The Highland Economy 1750–1850*, (London, 1957).

Haldane, A. R. B., *Three Centuries of Scottish Posts*, (Edinburgh, 1971).

Henderson, J. R., *Post Offices in Scotland*, (Edinburgh, 1966).

Historical Manuscripts Commission, *Report on the Manuscripts of Earl Bathurst*, (London, 1923), pp. 20–1.

Hunter, A. F., *A History of Simcoe County*, (Canada, 1909), 2 vols., reprint M. Hunter, (Barrie, Ontario, 1948), II Chapters 10 and 20.

Hunter, J., *The Making of the Crofting Community,* (Edinburgh, 1976); *For the People's Cause*, (Edinburgh, 1986); *Scottish Highlanders*, (Edinburgh, 1992); *A Dance Called America*, (Edinburgh, 1994).

Hutchison, I., *The Story of Loganair*, (Glasgow, 1987); Hutchison, I., *Air Ambulance*, (Erskine, 1996).

Innes, C., *The Book of the Thanes of Cawdor, A Series of Papers selected from the Charter Room at Cawdor, 1236–1742*, (Edinburgh, 1859).

Islay Archaeological Survey Group, *The Preliminary Handbook to the Archaeology of Islay*, (Keele, 1960).

Islay Association, *Report on the Proceedings at the Annual Meeting of the Islay Association*, (Glasgow, 1878).

Islay Land Use Group, *A Rural Land Use Strategy for Islay*, (Lochgilphead, 1993).

Isle of Islay Federation, Scottish Women's Rural Institutes, *Islay: a project in local history,* (Islay, 1968).

Jackson, K. H., *Campbell of Islay*, Celtica Catalogue 6, NLS, (Edinburgh, 1967).

Jupp, C., *The History of Islay from earliest times to 1848*, (Islay, 1994).

Kyd, J. G., *Scottish Population Statistics*, (Edinburgh, 1952).

Laing. A. (ed.), 'The Lord of the Isles', *Scott's Poetical Works*, (London, 1898), pp. 653ff.

Lamont, W. D., *The Early History of Islay*, (Glasgow, 1966); *Ancient and Mediaeval Sculptured Stones of Islay*, (Edinburgh, 1972).

Lenton-Halsall, P. *Nerabus: the story of a small Hebridean settlement since 1850*, (Islay, 1991).

Lewis, S., *A Topographical Dictionary of Scotland*, (London, 1846), 2 vols. and *Atlas*.

Lindsay, I. G. and Cosh, M., *Inveraray and the Dukes of Argyll*, (Edinburgh, 1973).

Lumsden, J. and Son, *The Steam-Boat Companion and Stranger's Guide to the Western Islands and Highlands of Scotland*, (Glasgow, 1825).

Lynch, M., *Scotland: A New History*, (London, 1991).

MacAlpine, N. *The Argyleshire pronouncing Gaelic Dictionary*, (Edinburgh, 1832); *A Pronouncing Gaelic Dictionary*, (Edinburgh, 1847).

MacBain, A., *Place Names, Highlands and Islands of Scotland*, (Stirling, 1922).

MacCulloch, J., *The Highlands and Western Isles of Scotland, containing descriptions of the scenery and antiquities: with an account of the political history and ancient names, and of the origin, language, agriculture . . . of the people. Founded on a series of annual journeys between . . . 1811 and 1821. In six letters to Sir Walter Scott, Bart*, (London, 1824), 4 vols.

Macdonald, C. M., *The History of Argyll up to the beginning of the Sixteenth Century*, (Glasgow, 1951).

Macdonald, C. (ed)., *The Third Statistical Account of Scotland, The County of Argyll (TSA)*, (Glasgow, 1961). Parish of Kildalton, Shanks, A. and I. D., (1955), pp. 342–9; Parish of Kilchoman, Torrie, Rev A., (1955), pp. 350–5; Parish of Kilarrow and Kilmeny, Macrae, Rev M., (1955), pp. 356–60.

Macdonald, J., *General View of the Agriculture of the Hebrides or Western Isles of Scotland: with Observations on the Means of their Improvement together with a Separate Account of the Principal Islands*, (Edinburgh, 1811).

MacDonell, M., *The Emigrant Experience*, (Toronto, 1982).

Maceacharna, D., *The Lands of the Lordship*, (Islay, 1976).

Mackay, E. (ed.), *A Description of the Western Islands of Scotland circa 1695*, with *Donald Monroe's Description of the Western Isles, 1774*, (Stirling, 1934).

Mackay, J. A., *Island Postal History Series No. 10: Islay, Jura and the other Argyll Islands*, (Dumfries, 1979); *No. 11: Scottish Islands, Supplement and Catalogue*, (Dumfries, 1980).

Mackay, J. G. (ed.), *More West Highland Tales*, I, (Edinburgh, 1940); II, (Edinburgh, 1960).

McKay, M. M. (ed.), *The Rev Dr John Walker's Report on the Hebrides of 1764 and 1771*, (Edinburgh, 1980).

Mackechnie, J. (ed.), *The Dewar Manuscripts*, (Glasgow, 1964).

McLeod, Dr. N., *Extracts of Letters to Dr [N.] McLeod regarding the famine and destitution in the Highlands and Islands of Scotland, 1847*, (Glasgow, 1847).

Macmillan, N. S. C., *The Campbeltown and Machrihanish Light Railway*, (Glasgow, 1970).

MacNeill, J. G., *The New Guide to Islay*, (Glasgow, 1900).

McNeill, P. and Nicholson, R. (eds.), *An Historical Atlas of Scotland c.400–c.1600*, (St. Andrews, 1980).

Malthus, T. R., *An Essay on The Principle of Population*, (London, 1798).

Maltman, A., Elliott, R., Muir, R. and Finches, B., *A Guide to the Geology of Islay*, (Aberystwyth, 1990).

Meyer, D., *The Highland Scots of Carolina, 1732–1776*, (N. Carolina, 1961).

Middleton, W. E. K., *Invention of the Meteorological Instruments*, (Baltimore, 1969).

Mitchell, Joseph, *Reminiscences of My Life in the Highlands*, (1883–4; reprint Newton Abbot, 1971), 2 vols.

Moir, D. G. (ed.), *The Early Maps of Scotland to 1850*, (Edinburgh, 1973).

Moir, P. and Crawford, I., *Argyll Shipwrecks*, (Wemyss Bay, 1994).

Morrison, C., *An essay on the Relations between Labour and Capital*, (London, 1854).

Munro, J. and Munro, R.W., *Acts of the Lords of the Isles 1336–1493*, (Edinburgh, 1986).

Munro, R. W., *Monroe's Western Isles of Scotland and Genealogies of the Clans 1549*, (Edinburgh, 1961).

National Library of Scotland, *Lamplighter and Story-Teller, John Francis Campbell of Islay, 1821–1885*, (Edinburgh, 1985).

National Trust, *Basildon Park, Berkshire*, (London, 1980).

Newton, N., *Islay,* (London, 1986).

Nicolaisen, W. F. H., *Scottish Place Names*, (London, 1976).

Ogilvie, M. A., *Wild Geese*, (Islay, 1978).

Ohlmeyer, J. H., *Civil War and Restoration in the Three Stuart Kingdoms: The career of Randal MacDonnell, marquis of Antrim, 1609–1683*, (Cambridge, 1993).

Osborne, B. D. and Armstrong, R., *Scottish Dates*, (Edinburgh, 1996).

Parry, M. L. and Slater, T. R. (eds)., *The Making of the Scottish Landscape*, (London, 1980).

Patten, J. M., *The Argyle Patent, Excerpted from the History of the Somonauk Presbyterian Church*, (Baltimore, 1979).

Pennant, T., *A Tour in Scotland and Voyage to the Hebrides, 1772*, (Chester, 1774).

Ramsay, F. (ed.), *John Ramsay of Kildalton. Being an Account of his life in Islay and including the Diary of his Trip to Canada in 1870*, (Toronto, 1970); *The Day Book of Daniel Campbell of Shawfield 1767 with relevant papers concerning the Estate of Islay*, (Aberdeen, 1991).

Ramsay, J., *A Letter to . . . the Lord Advocate of Scotland on the State of Education in the Outer Hebrides in 1862*, (Glasgow, 1863).

Ramsay, L. (ed.), *The Stent Book and Acts of the Balliary of Islay 1718–1843,* (Kildalton, 1890).

Reeves, W. P., *The Long White Cloud*, (London 1956).

Ritchie, G. and Ritchie, A., *Scotland: Archaeology and early history,* (London, 1981).

Ritchie, G. and Harman, M., *Exploring Scotland's Heritage: Argyll and the Western Isles,* (Edinburgh, 1985).

Ritchie, W. G. and Crofts, R., *The Beaches of Islay, Jura and Colonsay*, (Aberdeen, 1974).

Robertson, J. W., *Islay Official Guide* 2nd edition, (n.d.).

Ronaghan, A., *There'll always be an Islay*, (Islay, Alberta, 1977).

Rosa, M. W., *The Silver-Fork School*, (New York, 1936).

Royal National Lifeboat Institution, *Annual Reports.*

Rubinstein, W. D., *Men of Property*, (London, 1981).

Sadie, S. (ed.), The New G Dictionary of Opera, (London, 1992), 4 vols.

Salaman, R. N., *The History and Social Influence of the Potato*, (Cambridge, 1949).

Shaw, F. J., *The Northern and Western Islands of Scotland: their Economy and Society in the Seventeenth Century*, (Edinburgh, 1980).

Shore, C. J., (Baron Teignmouth), *Sketches of the Coasts and Islands of Scotland, and the Isle of Man*, (London, 1836), 2 vols.

Sinclair, Sir J. (ed.), *The Statistical Account of Scotland drawn up from the communications of the ministers of the different Parishes (OSA)*, (Edinburgh, 1791–9), 21 vols., (1794), XI. Kilchoman, Rev J. McLeish, pp. 276–85; Kildalton, Rev A. Robertson, pp. 286–97; Killarow and Kilmeny, Rev J. Murdoch, pp. 298–302.

Skene, W. F. (ed.), *Adomnàn: Life of Saint Columba*, (Edinburgh, 1874).

Smith, G. G. (ed.)., *The Book of Islay*, (Edinburgh, 1895).

Smith, D. J., *Action Stations 7: Military airfields of Scotland, the North-East and Northern Ireland*, (Wellingborough, 1989).

Smith, J. G., *The Old Country Houses of the Old Glasgow Gentry*, (Glasgow, 1880).

Smout, T. C., *A History of the Scottish People*, (London, 1969).

The Statistical Account of Argyleshire by the Ministers of the Respective Parishes (NSA), (Edinburgh, 1845). Kilchoman, Rev A. Cameron (1844), pp. 644–59; Kildalton, Rev A. MacTavish (1844), pp. 659–67; Killarow and Kilmeny, Rev. A. Stewart (1843), pp. 668–71.

Steer, K. A. and Bannerman, J. W. M., *Late Medieval Monumental Sculpture in the West Highlands*, (Edinburgh, 1977).

Stephen, L. (ed.), *Dictionary of National Biography*, (London, 1908).

Stevenson, D., *Highland Warrior, Alasdair MacColla and the Civil Wars*, (Edinburgh, 1994).

Stone, J., *Illustrated Maps of Scotland,* (London 1991).

Storrie, M. C. and Jackson, C. I., *Arran 1980–81: 2,021?*, (Edinburgh, 1967).

Storrie, M., *Continuity and Change: The Islay, Jura and Colonsay Agricultural Association, 1838–1988*, (Islay, 1988).

Teignmouth. See Shore.

The Third Statistical Account of Scotland, The County of Argyll: see Macdonald, C. M.

Thomson, D. S., *The Companion to Gaelic Scotland*, (Oxford, 1983).

Trevorrow, J. *Celtic Foundations*, (Islay, 1985); *Norse Invasion*, (Islay, 1987) and *Parish Churches*, (Islay, 1988).

Walker, J., *An Economical History of the Hebrides and Highlands of Scotland*, (Edinburgh,

1808), 2 vols.

Watson, W. J., *The History of Celtic Place-names of Scotland*, (Edinburgh, 1926).

Weir, L. MacN., *Guide to Islay*, (1924 edition, revised, Glasgow, 1936).

Whyte, I. D., *Scotland before the Industrial Revolution*, (London, 1995).

Williams, C. *Basildon, Berkshire*, (Reading, n.d., [1994]).

Williams, J., *The Natural History of the Mineral Kingdom*, (London, 1789).

Wilkinson, S. B., *The Geology of Islay, including Oronsay and portions of Colonsay and Jura*, (Glasgow, 1907).

Wilson, A., *The Sound of Silence*, (Glasgow, n.d.,[1975]); *The Sound of the Clam*, (Glasgow, n.d.,[1975]).

Youngson, A. J., *After the Forty Five*, (Edinburgh, 1973).

Published Articles

Alcock, L. and Alcock, E., 'Scandinavian Settlement in the Inner Hebrides: Recent Research on place-names and in the Field', *SAF*, 1980, 10, pp. 61–73.

Anderson, M. L. and Fairbairn, W. A., 'Division of Scotland into Climatic Subregions as an Aid to Silviculture', *Bulletin of the Forestry Department, University of Edinburgh*, (1955), I.

Anon., 'Appendix to Report on the Disease of the Potato Crop in Scotland in the year 1845', *THAS*, New Series, 1845–7, 15, p. 16.

Bannerman, J. W. M., 'The Lordship of the Isles', in J. M. Brown (ed.), *Scottish Society in the Fifteenth Century*, (London, 1977), pp. 209–40.

Barclay, D., 'Lauchlin Campbell of Campbell Hall and his Family', *Historical Papers of the Historical Society of Newburgh Bay and the Highlands*, 1902, 9, pp. 31–6.

Black, G. F., 'Early Islay Emigration to America', *OT*, 27 March, 2, 23 and 30 April, 1927.

Borthwick, A., ' Return to Islay', *SM*, April 1969, pp. 21–3.

Caldwell, D. H. and Ewart, G., 'Finlaggan and the Lordship of the Isles: an Archaeological Approach', *SHR*, 1993, 72, pp. 142–66.

Campbell, W. F., 'Improvement of Wasteland of a District in the Island of Islay', *TRAHS*, 1841, 13, pp. 232–5.

Celoria, F., 'Notes on the lore and customs in the district near Portnahaven Rhinns [sic] of Islay, Argyll, Scotland, *Folklore*, 1965, 76, pp. 39–47.

Childe, G., 'Notes on some duns in Islay'. *PSAS*, 1934–5, 69, pp. 81–4

Collin, L., *OT*, 24 August 1978.

Cowan, E. J., 'Clanship, kinship and Campbell acquisition of Islay', *SHR*, 1979, 58, pp. 132–57.

Cregeen, E. R., 'Recollections of an Argyleshire Drover', *SS*, 1959, 3, pp. 143–62.

Dawson, A. G., 'Lateglacial and sea-level changes and ice-limits in Islay, Jura and Scarba, Scottish Inner Hebrides', *Sc J Geol*, 1982, 18, pp. 253–65.

Dawson, J., 'The Fifth Earl of Argyle, Lordship and Political Power in Sixteenth-century Scotland', *SHR*, 1988, 67, pp. 1–27.

Delargy, J. H., 'Three Men of Islay', *SS*, 1960, 4, pp. 126–33.

Dodgshon, R. A., 'Mediaeval Settlement and Colonisation', in M. L. Parry and T.

R. Slater (eds.), *The Making of the Scottish Countryside*, (London, 1980), pp. 45–68.

Donaldson, G., 'Sources for Scottish Agrarian History before the Eighteenth Century', *AHR*, 1960, 8, pp. 82–90.

Duncan, A., 'Hector MacLean of Islay 1818–1893', *An Gaidheal*, January 1964, pp. 9–11.

Duncan, J. D., 'Notes on an Inventory of Articles which escaped the hands of the mob on the occasion of the sacking of Shawfield Mansion, 1725', *TGAS*, 1868, 1, p. xxiv and pp. 388–97.

Evans, E. E., 'The Atlantic Ends of Europe', *Adv Sci*, 1958–9, 15, pp. 54–64.

Fairhurst, H., 'The Archaeology of Rural Settlement in Scotland', *TGAS*, New Series, 1960, 15, pp. 139–58.

Forman, S., 'Islay House', *SF*, May 1960, pp. 37–40.

Grant, A., 'Scotland's "Celtic fringe" in the late Middle Ages: the MacDonald lords of the Isles and the kingdom of Scotland', in R. R. Davies (ed.), *The British Isles 1100–1500: comparisons, contrasts and connections*, (Edinburgh, 1988), pp. 118–41.

Grant, A., 'To the Medieval Foundations', *SHR*, 1994, 73, pp. 4–24.

Gray, J. M., 'Glacio-isostatic shoreline development in Scotland: an overview', *Queen Mary College Occasional Papers*, (London, 1985), 24.

Green, R. J. and Ayton, J. B., Paper read to the Town Planning Institute's Research Conference, 'Planning for the Countryside', October 1967, Summary.

The *Ileach* is available on subscription from The Islay and Jura Council of Voluntary Service, Bowmore, Isle of Islay.

Report on the Proceedings at the Annual Meeting of the Islay Association, 1878.

Jones, G. V., 'Pennant, The Observant Traveller', *SF*, June 1971.

Lamont, W. D., 'Old Land Denominations and "Old Extent" in Islay', *SS*, 1957, 1, pp. 86–106; 1958, 2, pp. 183–203; 'The Islay Charter of 1408', *PRIA*, 1960 C, pp. 163–87; 'Alexander of Islay, son of Angus Mor', *SHR*, 1981, 60, pp. 160–8.

McCann, S.B., 'The Raised Beaches of North-East Islay and Western Jura', *TIBG*, 1964, 35, pp. 1–15.

McDonald, R. A. and McLean, S. A., 'Somerled of Argyll: A New Look at Old Problems', *SHR*, 1992, 71, pp. 3–22.

Mackinnon, D., 'Education in Argyll and the Isles, 1638–1707', *SCHS*, 1936, 6, pp. 46–54.

MacQueen, J., 'Pennyland and Davoch in South-Western Scotland: a Preliminary Note', *SS*, 1979, 23, pp. 69–74; B. Megaw, 'A Note' on the above, ibid., pp. 75–7.

MacSween, M. D., 'Transhumance in North Skye', *SGM*, 1959, 75, pp. 73–88.

Moir, D. G., 'The Roads of Scotland: The Statute Labour Roads', *SGM*, 1957, 73, pp. 101–10 and 167–75.

Moisley, H. A., 'Some Hebridean Field Systems', *Gwerin*, 1960, 3, pp. 22–35; 'The Birth of a Crofting Landscape, North Uist in 1799', *SGM*, 1961, 77, pp. 89–92.

The Monthly Weather Report, 1976, Table 3.

Morton, J. K., 'The Flora of Islay and Jura (V.C. 102)', *Proceedings of the BSBI, Supplement,* 1958–60, part 3, pp. 1–59.

Murdoch, J., 'A New and Ready Way of Disposing of that Interesting Island Which would pay the debt, restore the late proprietor, and give the best return to large and small capitalists', in W. MacDonald, *Descriptive and Historical Sketches of Islay,* (Glasgow, 1850).

Ogilvie, M. A., 'Wildfowl of Islay', *PRSE,* 1983, 83B, pp. 473–89.

Piggott, S. and Piggott, C. M., 'Field work in Colonsay and Islay 1944–45', *PSAS,* 1945–6, 80, pp. 83–103.

Pryde, G. S., 'Scottish Colonisation in the Province of New York', *Proceedings of the New York State Historical Association,* 1935, 33, pp. 147–50.

Reid, J. M., 'A New Light on Old Glasgow-1: The Shawfield Papers of Daniel Campbell', *GH,* 1, 2 and 3 June 1959.

Annual Reports of the Royal National Lifeboat Institution.

Russell, Lady C., 'A Canny Scot', *Three Generations of Fascinating Women and other Sketches from Family History,* (London, 1904), pp. 154–82.

Shaw, F. J., 'Landownership in the Western Isles in the Seventeenth Century', *SHR,* 1977, 56, pp. 34–48.

Smout, T. C. and Fenton, A., 'Scottish Agriculture before the Improvers: an Exploration', *AHR,* 1965, 13, pp. 75–93.

Smout, T. C. 'The Landowner and the Planned Village in Scotland, 1730–1830, in N. T. Phillipson and R. Mitchison, *Scotland in the Age of Improvement,* (Edinburgh, 1970), pp. 73–106.

Storrie, M. C., 'Islay: A Hebridean Exception', *GR,* 1961, 51, pp. 87–108.

Storrie, M. C., 'The Census of Scotland as a source in the Historical Geography of Islay', *SGM,* 1962, 78, pp. 152–65.

Storrie, M. C., 'The Scotch Whisky Industry', *TIBG,* 1962, 31, pp. 97–114.

Storrie, M. C., 'Landholdings and Settlement Evolution in West Highland Scotland', *Geografiska Annaler,* 1965, 47, pp. 138–61.

Storrie, M. C., 'The Isle of Islay', *SF,* August 1981, pp. 11–14.

Storrie, M. C., 'Land Use and Settlement History of the southern Inner Hebrides', *PRSE,* 1983, 83B, pp. 549–66.

Stringer, K. and Grant, A., 'Scottish Foundations', in A. Grant and K. Stringer *Uniting the Kingdom. The Making of British History,* (London, 1995), pp. 85–108.

Synge, F. M. and Stephens, N., 'Late and Post-glacial Shorelines and Ice Limits in Argyll and North-East Ulster, *TIBG,* 1966, 39, pp. 101–25.

Taylor, A. B., 'Skio and Il', Pridiji Vikingafundur Third Viking Congress, Reykjavik 1956, *Arbók hins islenzka Fornleifafélags Fylgirit,* 1957, pp. 52–60.

Thomas, F. W. L., 'On Islay Place Names', *PSAS,* New Series IV, 1881–82, pp. 241–96.

British Parliamentary Papers and Official Publications
Census

Census of Great Britain, *Abstracts of the Answers and Returns: Enumeration Part III Scotland; Shire of Argyll:*

1802(1802); 1811(1812); 1821(1822); 1831(1831–4); 1841(1843); 1851(1852–4).
Census of Scotland, *Population Tables and Reports; County of Argyll* : 1861 (1862–4); 1871 (1872–4); 1881 (1881–3); 1891(1891–3).
Census of Scotland 1951, *County of Argyll Report* (1953), Table 3.
Census of Scotland 1961, *Argyll County Report*, (1964), *Supplementary Leaflet 27: Gaelic*, (1966).
Census of Scotland 1971, *Argyll County Volume*, (1973); *Usual Residence and Birthplace Tables*, (1973); *Gaelic Report*, (1975).
Census of Scotland 1981, *Preliminary Report*, (1981); *Report for Strathclyde Region*, (1983); *Gaelic Report*, (1983).
Census of Scotland 1991, Small Area Statistics, ESRC purchase.
Crown Film Unit, *Coastal Command*, video DD985.

Other Official Publications
ANCIENT MONUMENTS: RCAHMS, *Argyll: An Inventory of the Monuments, V. Islay, Jura, Colonsay and Oronsay*, (Edinburgh, 1984).
CROFTERS AND COTTARS: *Report of Her Majesty's Commissioners of Enquiry into the Condition of the Crofters and Cottars in the Highlands and Islands of Scotland, BPP*, 1884, C.3980.
DEER FORESTS: *Minutes of Evidence, Royal Commission (Highlands and Islands 1892), BPP*, (1895), C.7668.
DEVELOPMENT: *Annual Reports of the Highlands and Islands Development Board.*
The Scottish Economy 1965–70: A Plan for Expansion, BPP, 1966, Cmnd. 2864.
Robertson Research International Ltd. for the Highlands and Islands Development Board: Reconnaissance Mineral Survey of the Island of Islay, 1973.
DISTRESS: *Correspondence . . . relating to the Measures adopted for the Relief of Distress in Scotland, BPP*, 1847, LIII.
EDUCATION: *Abstracts of Education Returns (Scotland) 1834, BPP*, 1837, XLVIII, Argyll.
EMIGRATION: *Report of the Select Committee appointed to inquire into the Expediency of encouraging Emigration from the United Kingdom, BPP*, 1826, IV.
First Report of the Select Committee appointed to inquire into the Condition of the Population of the Islands and Highlands of Scotland and into the Practicability of affording the People Relief by means of Emigration, BPP, 1841, VI.
ENERGY: ETSU, *The Islay Energy Study*, (Didcot, 1996).
EXCISE: *Fifth Report of the Parliamentary Commissioners of Inquiry into the Mode of Charging Excise Duties, BPP*, 1823, VII.
Appendix to Seventh Report of the Commissioners of Inquiry into the Excise, BPP, 1835, XXX.
FISHERIES: *Annual Reports of the Fishery Board of Scotland.*
HARBOURS: *Appendix C to Second Report of the Tidal Harbours Commissioners, BPP*, 1848, XXXII.
LAND USE: Islay Land Use Group, *A Rural Land Use Strategy for Islay*, (Lochgilphead, 1993).
LIGHTHOUSES: *Reports of the Commissioners of Northern Lighthouses, BPP*, 1833

XXXIII; 1836 XLV and 1846 XLIV.

METEOROLOGY: *The Monthly Weather Report*, 1976, Table 3.

PEAT: Department of Agriculture and Fisheries for Scotland, *Scottish Peat Surveys: Western Highlands and Islands*, (Edinburgh, 1966), 5 vols. Islay is in volume 2.

POOR: *Minutes of Evidence, Poor Law Inquiry Commission for Scotland, BPP*, 1844, XXI.

Report to the Board of Supervision of the Scottish Poor Law, BPP, 1851, XXVI.

ROADS: *Reports of the Commissioners for making Roads and Building Bridges in the Highlands and Islands of Scotland, BPP*, 1805, III; 1807, III; 1810, IV and 1812–13, V.

STATISTICS: *Scottish Abstract of Statistics (SAS)*.

WORSHIP: *Sixth Report of the Commissioners appointed for building additional Places of Worship in the Highlands and Islands of Scotland, BPP*, 1831, XI.

Maps and Plans

British Geological Survey, 1: 50,000 *South Islay Sheet 19 (Scotland) Solid and Drift Geology Provisional series*, 1996; *North Islay Sheet 27*, 1995.

Gemmill, William, Ms. plans are in the Islay Estate Papers and relate mainly to the 1820s and 1830s. Photocopies are in West Register House, Scottish Record Office, Edinburgh.

Geological Survey of Scotland, *Quarter Inch Geology 13*, 1921; *One Inch Solid and Drift Sheet 98*, 1918 and *Sheet 27*, 1900.

Laughlan, Andrew, Sketch and sections of proposed road from Bridgend to Port Ellen in the Isle of Islay 1841–42, Islay Estate Papers.

MacDougall, Stephen. A few extant MS. plans are in the Islay Estate Papers. The reduced smaller-scale *Map of Islay*, 1749, lithographed in 1848, is printed in *Book of Islay*, pp. 552–3; *A Map of Taynish . . . in Argyll*, 1747. The British Library Map Room, XLIX 28; *A Map of the Island of Giga*, 1747 loc. cit., XLIX 37 1.

Ordnance Survey, *1: 50,000 Second Series, 60*, 1987; *1: 25,000 Pathfinder Series*, 1987–8; *1: 10,000 Second Edition*, 1899, revised 1981.

Ortelius, A., *Scotiae Tabula in Theatrum Orbis Terrarum*, (Antwerp, 1573).

Pont, Timothy, *Ila Insula* in J. Blaeu's *Atlas Novus*, (Amsterdam, 1654).

Index